Vanessa Kirsch, President and Founder, New Profit Inc.

"Social entrepreneurs, philanthropists, and policymakers alike will find Goldsmith's exploration of the systems that constrain innovation illuminating, and his prescriptions for transforming the way we solve problems as a nation informative and inspiring."

Geoff Mulgan, Director, The Young Foundation

"Shot through with experience and wisdom, this is essential reading for anyone wanting to understand the messy but invigorating ways in which creative individuals work both with and against big systems to change the world."

William Schambra, Director, Hudson Institute's Bradley Center for Philanthropy and Civic Renewal

"*The Power of Social Innovation* is a terrific book. Steve Goldsmith is a public figure who actually practices what he preaches in the volume, and so has a firm understanding of the promise and pitfalls of making social innovation happen through the devices of government."

The Power
of
Social Innovation

How Civic Entrepreneurs Ignite Community Networks for Good

Stephen Goldsmith

with Gigi Georges and Tim Glynn Burke

Foreword by Michael R. Bloomberg

JOSSEY-BASS
A Wiley Imprint
www.josseybass.com

Published by Jossey-Bass
A Wiley Imprint
989 Market Street, San Francisco, CA 94103-1741—www.josseybass.com

Jossey-Bass books and products are available through most bookstores. To contact Jossey-Bass directly call our Customer Care Department within the U.S. at 800-956-7739, outside the U.S. at 317-572-3986, or fax 317-572-4002.

Jossey-Bass also publishes its books in a variety of electronic formats. Some content that appears in print may not be available in electronic books.

Library of Congress Cataloging-in-Publication Data

Goldsmith, Stephen.
　　The power of social innovation: how civic entrepreneurs ignite community networks for good/Stephen Goldsmith with Gigi Georges and Tim Glynn Burke.
　　　p.　cm.
　　Includes bibliographical references and index.
　　ISBN 978-0-470-57684-7 (cloth)
　　　1. Technological innovations—Social aspects.　2. Social change.　3. Sustainable development.　4. Entrepreneurship.　I. Georges, Gigi.　II. Burke, Tim Glynn.　III. Title.
　　HM846.G65 2010
　　303.48'4—dc22

　　　　　　　　　　　　　　　　　　　　　　　　　　　　　　　　　　　　2009049563

Printed in the United States of America
FIRST EDITION
HB Printing　　　　10 9 8 7 6 5 4 3 2 1
PB Printing　　　　10 9 8 7 6 5 4 3 2 1

Contents

Acknowledgments

I would like to express gratitude to the many people who contributed to this book. Special thanks to Alberto Ibargüen and Paula Ellis at the John S. and James L. Knight Foundation who supported both the research and our Harvard Kennedy School convenings of leading civic entrepreneurs. I am indebted to Vanessa Kirsch and Kim Syman and their colleagues at New Profit Inc. for sharing their experiences and vision for promoting social entrepreneurship. Many thanks for the ongoing assistance of my own colleagues, especially Caitlin Steirman, Maureen Griffin, Christina Marchand, Kara O'Sullivan, and Emily Kaplan, and to Kennedy School students who contributed time and talent to the book: Andrea McGrath, Cheryl Scott, Scott Knox, Stephen Chan, Samantha Rubenstein, Andrew Hillis, and Janice Flynn. In addition I would like to thank the terrific staff and board members of the Corporation for National and Community Service, who every day search for ways to support the best of America's civic spirit.

The book is much better thanks to guidance from Allison Brunner and her colleagues at Jossey-Bass, and to those friends and colleagues who reviewed and commented on earlier versions, including Jeffrey Bradach, John DiIulio, Greg Dees, and Bill Eggers.

I extend immeasurable appreciation to Mark Moore and Frank Hartmann for guiding the Executive Session on Transforming Cities through Civic Entrepreneurship, and all members of the Executive Session for their generous engagement in many hours of discussion and debate. This book's best ideas were crafted and honed through those exchanges. This book would also not have been possible without the inspiring ingenuity and determination of the more than one hundred civic entrepreneurs, individual citizens, and government, nonprofit, and philanthropic officials alike, who shared their lessons and experiences with us, and many more whose stories remain untold.

My thanks to Tim Glynn Burke and Gigi Georges, who conducted many of the interviews and assisted with the writing of this book. Gigi Georges spent the past year as a Visiting Fellow at the Harvard Kennedy School's Ash Institute for Democratic Governance and Innovation. She has served as a White House Special Assistant to President William J. Clinton. Gigi holds a B.A. from Wellesley College and an M.P.A. from Princeton University's Woodrow Wilson School of International and Public Affairs.

Tim Glynn Burke, who coordinates research on social innovation at the Harvard Kennedy School's Ash Institute, is a 2006 graduate of the McCormack Graduate School of Policy Studies at the University of Massachusetts Boston and received a B.S. in public health from the University of North Carolina at Chapel Hill in 1997.

Finally, I thank my family for their love and support. Unsurprisingly, my idea of a family vacation has been going somewhere to work on the book and, surprisingly, my wife Margaret still without hesitation supports this conduct.

The Author

Stephen Goldsmith is the Daniel Paul Professor of Government and the director of the Innovations in American Government Program at Harvard University's Kennedy School of Government. Goldsmith, himself an entrepreneur, occupies the unique position of having approached these issues as a national leader across sectors—including government, for-profit corporations providing public services, and major nonprofit and philanthropic organizations.

Goldsmith served two terms as mayor of Indianapolis, America's twelfth-largest city, where he earned a reputation as one of the country's most innovative public officials. His transformative efforts to revitalize urban neighborhoods and to transfer real authority to community groups received national acclaim. Goldsmith then led reform as a special advisor to President Bush on faith-based and nonprofit initiatives and has served under both Presidents Bush and Obama as the chair of the Corporation for National and Community Service, where he has helped lead efforts to expand and strengthen the government's service agenda.

Among Stephen Goldsmith's other publications are *The Twenty-First Century City: Resurrecting Urban America* and the award winning *Governing by Network: The New Shape of the Public Sector*, both of which received wide recognition.

Foreword

The United States owes its greatness to the spirit of innovation, entrepreneurship, and civic responsibility that has always characterized the American people. Ours is a nation founded by forward-thinking pioneers dedicated to radical notions: that all men are created equal and endowed with certain unalienable rights, including the right to self-government. We have thrived because that defining spirit of freedom and experimentation has only grown stronger. America has never met a problem it couldn't fix or a challenge it couldn't meet—in no small part because we have always welcomed the best and brightest from around the world. Immigrants (from some of the founding fathers on down) have brought new ideas to their new land and helped build it into the world's strongest economy.

As Steve Goldsmith articulates so well in this book, America still has the resources, the ideas, and the collective will to put innovation to work solving the toughest problems facing our communities. But too often we are held back by the very systems that were designed to address these problems. The reality is that, in our country, meaningful change is frequently impeded by government's adherence to old ideas, precedents, and practices. And time and again a lack of transparency and accountability keeps us from being able to identify and quantify failure. Both of these problems share the same cause: a political discourse too often driven by ideological partisanship rather than innovative pragmatism.

If we are going to emerge from these challenging times stronger than ever and remain the world's leading superpower, we need to reinvigorate government with the spirit of innovation and invention that has always been America's calling card. We are going to have to improve the effectiveness and efficiency of government in dealing with age-old problems (from poverty to health care), as well as the responsiveness of government to the latest emerging challenges (from climate change to technology change). And we can do both only by tapping into the power of civic action, community service, and nonpartisan problem solving. Or, in short, by embracing the principles Goldsmith puts forth in this book.

To be successful as an entrepreneur, you have to constantly be looking at your business and asking, "How can it work better?" The same is true in government; only in government, the bottom line measures our success in improving people's lives—their health, their schools, their career prospects, their neighborhoods, and, most importantly, their safety. Are we empowering people to pursue their dreams? That's our most important task. If we're not achieving it, we have to identify what's not working and what we can do to fix it. And then we must have the guts to go for it.

In New York City, our administration has made a habit of embracing bold and controversial ideas to address long-standing problems. But equally important, we've insisted that all experimentation be subject to strict accountability measures—and we haven't been afraid to admit when an idea has *not* worked. That's so often the problem with government: once a program or an office is created, it never dies, no matter how ineffective it may be. Good intentions don't always translate into good results, and it's vitally important to recognize the difference. That's why we've been almost obsessive in collecting data. I like to say, "In God we trust. Everyone else bring data." After all, there's no way to know how to make something work better unless you first know how well it's working. This seems like a simple formula, but, as Goldsmith points out, government is too often dominated by special interests bound to the status quo, blocking the kind of bold changes we need to keep our country moving forward.

Innovation, data, accountability: We've put that mantra to work in transforming New York City's school system, which had been a case study in mismanagement. It guided us as we overhauled the city's performance management system, allowing us to focus on what matters most to city residents. It led us to rewrite the federal government's long- outdated poverty formula, which ignores subsidies, expenses, and cost-of-living differences. It prompted us to take a carbon inventory as the very first step of our plan for building an environmentally sustainable city. And it has defined our efforts in every other area of government. Throughout it all, we've tried to learn from other cities—and it's heartening to see that some of our own work has made its way into this book.

As one of the country's strongest voices for innovation in government, Steve Goldsmith brings a wealth of personal experience to the table. As mayor of Indianapolis, he was a trailblazer who helped redefine the office, cutting wasteful spending and outdated programs, putting savings to work revitalizing the city, and taking on old problems in new ways. As chair of the Corporation for National Service and a champion of civic entrepreneurship, he continues to tap into the power of people to improve our country. And as a great champion of pragmatism over partisanship, he understands that it's only by taking the best ideas from both sides of the aisle that we can achieve the best results.

Goldsmith is a firm believer in the power of everyday citizens to create change and in the important role that public-private partnerships can playing in turning dreams into reality. He recognizes that nonprofits and private entrepreneurs often enjoy a greater freedom to experiment—and that they can help government make use of the latest tools and technologies, including social networking, web-based services, and cutting-edge systems of data analysis. As we've found in New York City, these tools not only help government communicate with citizens more effectively and deliver services more efficiently, but they also help ensure accountability, reduce waste, and improve public confidence in government.

In these challenging times, some may argue that we cannot afford the risks that come with innovation. Nothing could be further from the truth. With major challenges all around us, what we can't afford is to continue upholding a failed status quo by funding programs and sustaining approaches that don't work. The silver lining in any economic crisis is that it can force government to take necessary steps that, in more comfortable times, would fall victim to the forces of inertia—but it is up to us, all of us, to seize the opportunity.

In this book, Goldsmith challenges us to do that by bringing together the voices of hundreds of leading civic entrepreneurs, government officials, business and nonprofit leaders, philanthropists, community activists, innovation experts, and everyday citizens from around the country. Each of their stories is filled with insights from the front lines of innovation. Individually, they are inspiring; collectively, they provide strong evidence in support of Goldsmith's compelling conclusions.

Goldsmith ends by painting a picture of a society in which the best ideas are free to take flight and thrive, and in which vested interests and ideological battles don't stand in the way of innovation and change. This ideal, which he calls a "fertile city," is not mere fantasy. In fact, in the first years of the 21st century, it is within our grasp. It's going to take a lot of hard work and fresh thinking to make it a reality—but that's part of our national spirit. It's a process we all can contribute to—that's democracy! And just reading this book is a big step in the right direction.

Michael R. Bloomberg
New York City
November 2009

Preface

"Entrepreneurs need to search purposefully for
the sources of innovation, the changes and their
symptoms that indicate opportunities for successful
innovation. And they need to know and to apply
the principles of successful innovation."

Peter F. Drucker

Over twenty-five years as a prosecutor, activist in child support collection, mayor of Indianapolis, and chair of America's
national service organization, the Corporation for National and
Community Service, I have been involved in local and national
efforts to find the right mix of public policies and private
approaches to help struggling families lift themselves up out of
poverty. As the first decade of the 21st century comes to a close,
I see these efforts nearing a critical juncture. The challenges we
face seem larger than ever —but so do the assets we possess to
solve them.

The sharpest illustration of these incongruities hit me in
2007, when I had the opportunity to serve as chairman of the
District of Columbia Anacostia Redevelopment Corporation.
I took the position in order to help the city bring development
and hope to one of its most hard-pressed areas but ended up
spending most of my time negotiating a new $650M baseball
stadium with Major League Baseball. The stadium, although
helpfully located in that poorly served area, did not in itself offer
opportunity for the adjoining neighborhoods, which suffered

from 27 percent unemployment, 40 percent poverty, and a high school graduation rate of only 24 percent. It would take more than an $8M pitcher in a new stadium to transform that investment into opportunity for these children.

I turned to Marguerite Kondracke, the CEO of the America's Promise Alliance, and Alma Powell, its chair, who had a long-standing interest in the area, for help in connecting this huge city investment to a broader solution for the community. The fact that they eagerly agreed to help did not surprise me, but their reasoning did. They cited a then-recent America's Promise survey showing that fewer than half of America's children believed the American Dream applied to them. This awful fact demonstrated a danger not only for these children but also for the very civic health of our cities.

I undertook this book in order to discover a framework with which communities—officials, philanthropists, civic activists, and other leaders—can turn the above challenges into opportunity. Whether in Indianapolis, where I served as mayor, or D.C., where I served as redevelopment chair, unsatisfactory social results did result from neglect. Over the past fifty years a generous American public has steadily increased its philanthropic and tax investments in a wide range of efforts that only occasionally have produced adequate social progress.

If ever there were a moment for creative civic engagement it is now. Financial insecurity, lack of educational opportunity, income disparities, and waning civic health challenge city leaders every day. With the recent economic crisis, communities are struggling with their most difficult challenges in the past half-century. The U.S. Census reports a notable increase in the number of citizens living in poverty in 2008—almost forty million Americans (13.2 percent in 2008, up from 12.5 percent in 2007).[1] High school graduation rates for students of color are as low as 33 percent in our cities, and horribly, over 60 percent of African-American males who drop out of high school at some point find themselves in prison.[2] Many children live in turbulent homes, often with a parent missing, let alone in a state of marriage. Homelessness, substance abuse, and domestic violence afflict far too many. The number of foster children, many abused or neglected, now approaches one million a year.[3] About the same number of prisoners will be released back into communities each year, and two-thirds of them will eventually be reincarcerated.

Although many individuals now labor tirelessly on meaningful efforts in education, health care, child welfare, youth development, housing, economic insecurity and poverty, and public safety, few communities have enough to show for their collective efforts. Or, as Isabel Sawhill and Ron Haskins of the Brookings Institution suggest, "The country is confronted by economic and social disparities that have proven all but impervious to public and private efforts for nearly four decades . . . We believe that the lack of more significant progress signals that the country's efforts need to be expanded and retooled."[4]

Perhaps these problems result from a legacy delivery system for social services that fails to recognize fundamental changes in both the economy and cities. According to urban scholar Jane Jacobs, cities used to build the middle class as struggling residents adopted the attitudes and learned the skills necessary to succeed.[5] With the collapse of many families, concentration of poverty and flight of manufacturing jobs, cities today simply no longer construct a ladder to the middle class.

Unfortunately, to-date, many of our "solutions" aggravate, or certainly fail to mitigate, the problem. We clearly need new methods in order to provide opportunity, hope, and civic health to hard-pressed families and neighborhoods. Although government itself sometimes stands in the way of progress, I write this book not to make a case against government participation but, rather, to argue for a new and more effective response. As a nation we approach the role of government with paralyzing polarity. Many on the right argue with good reason that government has over the past fifty years actually aggravated the problem with substantial interventions that disrupted self-help, social capital, and neighborhood support programs. They generalize that less government in and of itself will produce more vibrant neighborhoods and families. The left argues that more and bigger government will create success—as if individual values, families, community and faith organizations, and economic success were incidental.

Indeed, government dominates funding in most of these important areas with programs that address every imaginable social issue. The real question should be not *whether* government should participate in lifting up those whom "prosperity has left behind" but *how* it should participate. Scaling social innovation will require more than new venture capital; it also necessitates repurposing already appropriated government dollars. For example, recent studies show that federal government funding for schools with disadvantaged students for the most part has not led to the hoped-for improvements.[6] Yet, whether in education or other areas, the public and nonprofit providers that benefit from government programs often join with bureaucrats and politicians to resist the redirection of critical resources to programs that work.

Further, government spends taxpayer dollars on one-size-fits-all direct services or overly prescriptive procurements and grants. This causes social service providers of every stripe—nonprofit, for-profit, faith-based, or community-based—to take an artificially narrow approach. While common sense dictates that teacher performance might be connected to student health or nutrition, homelessness to mental health, and domestic violence to alcohol abuse, public spending on social services to address these problems rarely reflects even the simplest level of integration. Furthermore, multiple levels of government often touch the same family or community. No single bureaucracy has a fix on solutions to all social problems. The mayor may control job training and policing; the county executive, child welfare; an independently elected school board, education; the state, health care coverage through Medicaid; and so on. With a structure designed for a simpler time, government has become ill-equipped to handle the complex task of solving our increasingly intractable social challenges. Even more fundamentally, though, government now must deliver its assistance not through traditional rule-bound hierarchical programs but through effective civic entrepreneurs operating in dense social and community networks.

This is not a simple matter of bad government actors and good private ones. Private efforts, whether nonprofit or philanthropic, also avoid the risk of taking on the status quo and continue funding good deeds that produce unimpressive or unknown results. Business leaders serving on the boards of nonprofit human service agencies, impressed with dedicated people and good intentions, often tolerate marginal results, inadvertently masking failure. Because these service delivery systems—dominated by government funding and regulation—are often devoid of citizen choice and competition, civic entrepreneurs depend on community leadership to create the political will for true innovative solutions. Actors from across the community—nonprofit providers, individual volunteers, religious institutions, private philanthropists, and professional associations—all play a part in the design and funding of important support services. Funders operate in social networks, investing in individuals who in turn operate in their own networks.

Despite these daunting social challenges, or perhaps because of them, I am genuinely hopeful that now is our time to make things right.

Millions of citizens stand ready to deploy their goodwill and talent toward solutions that work for their communities. AmeriCorps applications in the first quarter of 2009 increased 40 percent over a year earlier. Teach For America applications rose 36 percent from 2007 to 2008, with a 28 percent larger corps starting in inner-city schools.[7] Overall, 441,000 more young adults volunteered in 2008 than in 2007.[8] Along with this appetite for service, the number of innovative, socially conscious individuals continues to increase, as does the number of social venture funds interested in their success. These entrepreneurs now take on early childhood development, literacy, homelessness, and violence with increasing success. With an impressive understanding of this trend, Washington reacted in 2009 with bipartisan support for the Kennedy/Hatch Serve America Act, supporting substantial new investments in community service and social innovation.

At the same time, collaborative electronic tools are igniting new service opportunities in previously unimagined ways. A small, inexpensive Facebook widget alone produced pledges from fifteen thousand organizations that tens of thousands of individuals would participate in service projects over the Martin Luther King and Inaugural weekends in 2009. In my work as chair of the Corporation for National and Community Service (CNCS), I see more examples than ever before of successful civic entrepreneurs who combine creativity and passion with community service to produce tangible results.

A Personal Discovery

This book reflects my own education in igniting social change through innovation and entrepreneurship—a process of personal discovery that accelerated in 2000. I had just finished my second term as mayor of Indianapolis and was serving as the chief domestic policy adviser to Governor Bush in his 2000 presidential campaign. Alan Khazei and Vanessa Kirsch called with an offer. Khazei is one of the country's top civic innovators, and he cofounded the well-regarded City Year. Kirsch had started New Profit Inc., a social venture fund. The husband-and-wife team had compiled a list of ideas about how the federal government could help grow community service and social innovation. I did not know that such an organized movement existed, but the ideas were appealing and much more creative than the standard fare I had grown used to seeing.

Fortuitously, I became chair of CNCS after the election and over the subsequent eight years helped fund and work with a broad array of exciting, committed individuals operating at the nexus of national service and social innovation. The efforts of the civic entrepreneurs whom I have met, and thousands more like them across the country, embody the adage: "You cannot do all the good the world needs, but the world needs all the good you can do." Yet I saw even the best of these innovators struggle to find room to invent and grow in systems that did not naturally accommodate bold, new interventions. Absent strong leadership, no natural process clears out the old and invites in the innovative, even in the face of lackluster results.

My CNCS experience also reinforced something I learned in Indianapolis—how much value is produced when the public and private sectors engage one another constructively. Indeed, over the past decade I have been fortunate to associate with government, for-profit, and nonprofit providers serving public purposes. Without fail, those who worked exclusively in one sector often could not appreciate the perspectives or value of the others. Further, people live and progress inside social networks. Change efforts often fail because they ignore the other providers and the family and friends who surround those in need.

With these two lessons in mind, in 2008 I asked the John S. and James L. Knight Foundation to help me assemble some of the country's top civic entrepreneurs and city government officials at Harvard University's Kennedy School of Government. About thirty practitioners and influential thinkers would eventually meet over the course of two years to explore how innovative leaders in all sectors could better collaborate in order to produce transformative social change. We started with an airing of tensions, stumbling blocks, gaps, and missteps, and in the months that followed we worked together to sort out and address these challenges. Those candid conversations underlie the principles in this book. My Harvard Kennedy School colleague Mark Moore challenged the members of our group to consider how public entities create public value, rather than perform public activities.

This book rejects the notion that innovation occurs only in one sector. It assumes that public, private, and nonprofit officials can be the problem, but that it takes more than one of them to be the solution. I have seen that terrific ideas well executed in one sector can cause changes in the others. I have written elsewhere about my policy approaches to city development, including on such issues as taxation, regulation, and privatization.[9] In this book I make the point that we urgently need more social innovation—regardless of whether the intervention or the entrepreneur comes in a liberal cast in one city and a conservative cast in another. I do not seek to place certain policy approaches or solutions above others. Rather, this book offers a framework within which engaged leaders—whether individual, government, philanthropic, or social—can supply the catalytic energy to produce civic progress in a community.

In these pages you will read powerful and inspiring stories of public officials and civic entrepreneurs. But I have set out to show that, with the right tools and skills, everyday citizens in typical communities or cities across the country can also produce extraordinary social change. Indeed, the best form of social progress will come at the community and neighborhood levels. I point out tools for community champions who invent creative interventions, advocate policy changes, or build effective organizations. My intent is to add to the growing discourse on the promise of social innovation and civic entrepreneurship in improving social service results and how these results can leverage community-wide change.

I rely on case studies from all sectors and more than one hundred in-depth interviews with civic entrepreneurs. I am indebted to the members of the Harvard Kennedy School

Executive Session and to the inspiring and creative individuals who generously shared their time, observations, experiences, and insights.

Looking Ahead

Chapters 1 and 2 offer the context and lens we use for the topic. Chapter 1 names the problem and introduces civic entrepreneurship's potential to catalyze civic progress. Chapter 2 presents cases in which the social inventor comes up with an ingredient that catalyzes the rest of the system. The catalytic ingredient can emanate from a new technology, as happened when ePals brought together 600,000 classrooms on an online learning platform, or from the network integration itself as shown by Bill Milliken, whose efforts bring critical support services into schools now serving more than 1.2 million students.

Chapter 3 addresses these issues from the demand side, showing how allowing more social service providers into a delivery system through competitive results-driven procurement can create a marketplace for innovation. In this chapter we explore the work of Chancellor Michelle Rhee of the Washington, D.C., public schools; the effects of state and federal faith-based initiatives; and the UK's decade-long efforts to build the capacity of the third sector to provide public services.

Chapter 4 begins with the assumption that good deeds do not necessarily produce great results. Every day, caring individuals in service organizations work tirelessly to help others. However, critical frontline workers in a field like homelessness are often forced to run faster and faster in place because the delivery system has not produced or scaled the type of intervention that could more broadly change lives. New York City used its authority to repurpose homeless services when the talented public official Linda Gibbs discovered that the city's funders and providers, after years of futility, "served the homeless, but they did not solve homelessness." Established organizations with creative leaders can also produce civic breakthroughs when they shift their focus from organizational activities to the sought-after outcomes. This chapter focuses on the breakthrough approaches of Michael Lomax, who leads the prestigious United Negro College Fund, and Brian Gallagher, of the United Way of America. Their stories help us see how thoughtful organizational assessments, creative energy, and fresh eyes can transform traditional players and approaches.

Chapter 5 explores the power of the individual to make social progress, highlighting various ways that citizens, whether serving or being served, cause true change. It highlights the efforts of the Bradley Foundation as it championed a controversial effort to bring school vouchers to Milwaukee, with strategies and tools that are instructive no matter where one falls in the voucher debate. This chapter also explores how building demand for social improvement through citizen activism can overcome protectionism from entrenched vendors. We look at former *Miami Herald* publisher David Lawrence, the John S. and James L. Knight Foundation, and Stand for Children to understand the innovative ways in which civic entrepreneurs are combining traditional organizing strategies with new technologies and a commitment to results. Chapter 5 also profiles Maurice Miller of the Family Independence Initiative, who demonstrates how engaging citizens inside their social networks can produce remarkable gains in transforming lives and breaking the cycle of poverty. J. B. Schramm of College Summit also focuses on individuals—in particular, raising expectations both of clients and of providers to produce dramatic gains.

Chapter 6 examines how civic entrepreneurs take on risk in a way that makes the work of other actors inside a social delivery system more effective. We extract lessons from the way Julius Walls of Greyston Bakery applies a deep knowledge of the people his organization is helping in order to take hiring risks that other employers essentially overestimate. We study how Blair Taylor takes on political risk by betting the Los Angeles Urban

League's eighty-six years of credibility and social capital on his ability to transform the Park Mesa Heights neighborhood. This chapter also looks at how the Reinvestment Fund's Fresh Food Financing Initiative applies its deep knowledge of urban communities to help drive retailing (and social good) into underserved markets. Similarly, the New York City Acquisition Fund creates social value by removing risk in new affordable housing projects, illustrating one of a number of innovative models for using financial capital to catalyze change.

The final chapter illustrates how all the pieces highlighted in the book fit together in the "fertile" city—fertile in the sense that it is ripe for civic entrepreneurship to innovate and transform the ways it addresses social problems. This chapter studies the community, mayoral, nonprofit, and school changes implemented in New York under Mayor Michael Bloomberg, with an emphasis on the work of New York Schools Chancellor Joel Klein.

To create truly vibrant cities, we need to invent new approaches. More important and more difficult, we then need to grow and execute (some say "scale") these social innovations across entire systems. Thinking of scale only in terms of broad geography or large numbers would, however, be a mistake. Social change does not mean that new, innovative providers merely replace old ones. Rather, communities need to create an environment that enables continual innovation while demanding real impact and performance.

We direct this book to leaders no matter who they are— from start-up entrepreneurs to seasoned professionals. We look to political leaders who use their authority and visibility to insist on change, and to philanthropic leaders who deploy flexible dollars and expertise to provide venture funding for change. The Annie E. Casey Foundation, willing to take more risks than the political process would allow, played this role for me during my mayoral terms. We urge corporate leaders to use their stature and business acumen while serving on nonprofit boards to demand results. And, of course, entrepreneurial nonprofit leaders can demonstrate the path of necessary reform. A particularly strong leader in one area can influence the others in a community.

Over twenty-five years, I have seen the very worst and best of communities. I have seen bad government and neglect and crime and violence and the untold harm they produce. I have worked with welfare moms abandoned by the fathers of their children as well as children reared without adequate support or education. But more recently I have seen, and done my best to support, the very best of America—the generous, civic-minded streak that is not only alive but thriving. I write this book in hope that the latter phenomenon will provide a path to the American Dream for those whose life opportunities should not be determined by the zip codes of their birth.

The Power of Social Innovation

Part I

CATALYZING SOCIAL CHANGE

1

IGNITING CIVIC PROGRESS

"I have an almost complete disregard of precedent,
and a faith in the possibility of something better.
It irritates me to be told how things have always
been done. I defy the tyranny of precedent. I go for
anything new that might improve the past."

Clara Barton

With deficits soaring and job growth problematic, now is the time to drive every possible public and philanthropic dollar to the best possible social result. Demand for government dollars will far outstrip available supply unless more Americans become productive taxpaying citizens. For economic and moral reasons, we simply cannot tolerate any longer the social conditions that leave so many citizens behind, too often trapping them as passive recipients of government help. Transformative social progress today is held back more by precedent and existing structures and processes than by resource limitations or a lack of the public's interest.

This book focuses on the lessons behind the acts of social entrepreneurs, philanthropists, business leaders, elected and appointed officials, students, and activists who make a difference in their communities. We concentrate on how these civic entrepreneurs act as catalysts that, by challenging existing assumptions and models, map the path to a better future.

Many have written on the efforts and attributes of individual "social entrepreneurs," a term popularized by the exceptional work of Bill Drayton of Ashoka. Notable contributions include *How to Change the World* by David Bornsteins; *The Power of Unreasonable People,* by John Elkington and Pamela Hartigan; and Christopher Gergen and Gregg Vanourek's *Life Entrepreneurs.* Recent books such as *Forces for Good*, by Leslie Crutchfield and Heather McLeod Grant, and *The Charismatic Organization*, by Shirley Sagawa and Deb Jospin, chronicle the features of high-performing organizations run by social entrepreneurs.[1] This book builds on those insights but looks beyond entrepreneurial individuals and organizations to entrepreneurial networks and fertile communities.

This chapter defines the concepts and identifies the reasons why social service delivery systems resist change, explains why civic entrepreneurs must be catalysts for transformative change, and concludes with cautions about engaging government.

Entrepreneurship, Innovation, and Change

Although there is little consensus on an exact definition of social entrepreneurship, I view it much as Roger Martin and the Skoll Foundation's Sally Osberg do. They define social entrepreneurs as those who identify and then challenge—with inspiration, creativity, direct action, and courage—an unjust "stable state's equilibrium."[2] These social entrepreneurs share passion, a focus on outcomes and impact that leverages other resources, a sound business model, and high expectations for not only themselves but also their clients.

Early on, many of us involved in these fields mistakenly hoped that a good organization or idea would naturally grow to scale—in the same way that commercial product innovations such as cell phones and low-cost airlines grew to transform their respective industries—without worrying too much about how. Over time I realized not only the extent of the obstacles preventing diffusion of a good idea, but that real change requires more than scaling a single organization. These discoveries led us to focus on civic entrepreneurship.

In most of the areas where social entrepreneurs are working, none exist. The individuals whom we are trying to serve do not have the money to buy needed services; thus someone else pays for them. Thus the start-up capital sufficient to prove a concept will not produce the broad growth needed for transformative change to scale.

Invariably, philanthropic and social investors rely on an exit strategy that looks to government as the sector that will eventually sustain an organization's growth. As a result, an idea's ability to grow depends on both government and the existing web of providers, funders, and politicians who have a stake in the status quo. In fact, in the areas in which social entrepreneurs operate (e.g., education, health, poverty reduction, social services, services to children and families, economic development of poor neighborhoods, low-income housing), government—its overall policies, financing, and regulation of suppliers—is the dominant force. In many of these areas, such as K–12 education, tax dollars represent most of the total spending—sometimes exceeding 90 percent.

Blaming government as the primary obstacle to progress, however, misses the mark. Comic strip character Pogo put it clearly when he said, "We have met the enemy and he is us." Existing providers and their boards, staffs, directors, and sometimes clients lobby funders—whether private or public—to increase support of their efforts regardless of results. As Mayer Zald and Roberta Ash demonstrate, organizations naturally move through stages over time: "goal transformation, a shift to organizational maintenance, and oligarchization."[3] In other words the passion that produced yesterday's transformative innovation migrates over to sustaining the organization—which in turn precipitates an effort to raise barriers to entry for potential competitors. This evolution tends to calcify the system, making it difficult to redirect a community's scarce resources to bold new interventions and players. Simply adding new innovations on a stable base of mediocrity cannot produce social transformation.

Thus, in this book we focus on a concept that overlaps social entrepreneurship: "civic entrepreneurship." Doug Henton describes civic entrepreneurship as helping communities develop and organize their economic assets and build productive, resilient relationships across the public, private, and civil sectors.

To Henton, the term "combines two important American traditions: entrepreneurship—the spirit of enterprise, and civic virtue—the spirit of community."[4] We use the term intentionally to underscore one of our major assumptions: that a leader in any sector can spark innovation, and social progress. This definition incorporates, but is not limited to, the traditional understanding of social entrepreneurship as nonprofit or for-profit endeavors with a social mission. It also includes those who enable and champion progress by providing the necessary fodder for innovation and change. To us, civic entrepreneurship represents both the spirit of change and the spirit of community.

So Many Ideas, So Little Progress

Why are we often stuck with entrenched underperforming social safety net systems of providers, government and philanthropic funders, advocates, and interest groups? Here are five reasons, which we will return to in more detail.

Irrational Capital Markets

The Center for Advancement of Social Entrepreneurship (CASE) at Duke University's Fuqua School of Business is the academic home of leading expert Greg Dees. In 2007 CASE surveyed social entrepreneurs on what they considered to be the greatest barriers preventing them from "scaling up."[5] The results showed that funders, especially foundations, make decisions on "short time horizons" attracted to the "next new thing" rather than what works. Funders, even when backing innovation, are often most likely to support a program simple in concept, easy to execute, low in political or legal hurdles, and conducive to quick results—not necessarily a recipe for complex systemic change.

We study in this book the efforts of Vanessa Kirsch and her social venture fund New Profit Inc. to change the nature of philanthropic funding. Kirsch helps her portfolio organizations understand that, since the clients for social delivery systems rarely have a choice of where to receive help, politics and bureaucracy (not efficacy) play a large part in determining who receives public funding.

We, however, assume that the growth of a social innovation requires more than private philanthropy and socially conscious investing in an organization. A civic entrepreneur seeking to remedy a particular condition in a community, such as access to behavioral health services for adolescents, will eventually need to access existing government and philanthropic dollars. Because systemwide change requires success not in a market economy but in a political economy that rewards influence, connections, and political capital, she will be unable to rely on new venture funding alone.

The civic entrepreneur inevitably discovers that incumbent interests have their protectors. We consider this to be a local social service version of the infamous military-industrial complex, or "iron triangle." It is not an insidious triangle driven by self-interest; it is the network of relationships that develop among government bureaucrats, politicians, agency heads, and funders who believe that more of the same will make a difference. This iron triangle produces barriers to entry for new actors. Indeed, many of the obstacles civic entrepreneurs face are inadvertent, caused by good people with good intentions trying, within a narrow jurisdiction, to solve problems created by matters outside their control.

Champions of a particular solution, convinced—whether correctly or not—of the value they produce, will eventually fight changes that jeopardize their funding. The political economy of social systems, not the nature of providers and other actors themselves, induces providers to seek protection over performance. As Robert Michels wrote some one hundred years ago, an oligopoly can develop when a group "dominates decision making via its control over knowledge, resources, and communication."[6] And as the amount of government influence or money an organization receives grows, even the most entrepreneurial effort runs the risk of emulating government. We are searching for conditions that will force dynamic change so that today's innovators do not inadvertently become part of tomorrow's government/nonprofit oligopoly.

Poor Metrics and Causal Confusion

With so many interlocking responses to similar issues, communities find it difficult to hold any one organization responsible for results. No one owns failure. I recently experienced one of those practice-what-you-preach moments—with discomfort. I was upbeat about President Obama's call for clear and accountable government performance until I tried to put it into action at CNCS. As chair, I enthusiastically support CNCS's goal to increase high school graduation rates through our grantees, whose AmeriCorps members can provide valuable services in a struggling school. Yet can we really hold a grantee responsible if its efforts are overwhelmed by challenges such as poor teaching or lack of school order? Obviously, impact must be measured and accountability imposed, but the *how* is difficult—and always more appropriate for the other guy. Too often public and private organizations use a lack of results as a reason to ask for even more funds. We explore measurement and accountability in Chapter 4.

Vertical Solutions for Horizontal Problems

Government's ability to collaborate has not kept pace with the growing complexity of these social service production systems. As a result, government reforms will continue to fail if they are aimed simply at improving the same old activities. We cannot solve complex horizontal problems with vertical command-and-control solutions. The speed of change toward third-party provision of all types of public services continues to outpace the ability of most public officials and agencies to manage these collaborations effectively.

In *Governing by Network*, Bill Eggers and I defined a "network" as an initiative deliberately undertaken by government to accomplish public goals, with performance metrics, responsibilities assigned to each partner, and structured information flow. But we also wrote that the ultimate goal of a network is to produce the maximum possible public value, greater than the sum of what each lone player could accomplish without collaboration.[7] Despite good intentions, many attempts to reform these social problem-solving networks (and calling them "networks" is often a stretch) result in an incrementally better solution to a problem, but not the integrated, transformative approach that true civic entrepreneurship promises.

The Curse of Professionalism

Progressive Era government reforms produced, for the most part, today's professional bureaucracies with technically proficient officials who design solutions for other people. For example, city planners in Indianapolis told community groups what their preferences for a new green space should be, and CNCS used to prescribe activities for thousands of not-for-profits, even though in both instances the "amateurs" on the front lines had a much better idea of how to solve problems. Without a market discipline, program officers, protected by legislative committees or foundation boards and convinced of their own professionalism, can become myopic. Social problems are increasingly complex and interlocking; the idea that a few smart program officers can design a solution and then issue a series of contracts governed by a set of rules misses entirely the point of civic engagement and community problem solving.

We need to open these social production systems to the community and engage it in real and substantive ways that involve a higher percentage of the community's assets and social networks in driving change. According to Drayton, "Traditional societies evolved so slowly that gradual trial-and-error expressed as customary law was all that was needed to guide them safely. As change accelerated, small elites took control of decision making. However, as society became ever more complex and as change accelerated yet again, this form of decision making could no longer cope. We now need a far more flexible, creative, quick-moving, and decentralized way of managing the planet."[8]

Not Invented Here

The nationally ambitious entrepreneur aspiring to take a tested success into a new community faces another difficult barrier. Government procurement rules or practices often give preference to local providers. More importantly, the community rightly wants to determine what it needs, under what conditions, and expects providers to respond and negotiate with it. The outside civic entrepreneur, meanwhile, might take it as a virtue not to negotiate. In fact, he has been able to sell his innovation and his organization to private funders on the basis of the results his particular model has achieved. Fidelity to the model becomes key. As Dees notes, "Some of the national social entrepreneurs feel strongly about the integrity of their approach, and they have very robust minimal critical specifications. Full-fledged, they want to have control, want a certain culture and approach, and it may rub local folks the wrong way, or they won't be comfortable with it."[9] The ensuing negotiation about the terms of the engagement carries implications and risk for both sides.

In *Governing by Network* we credited tacit knowledge—that which is not easily recognized or transferable—as the basis for many innovations. Explicit knowledge, meanwhile, naturally attracts outsiders or potential adopters, even though it might represent only 20 percent of the total knowledge needed to understand how something really works.[10] A civic entrepreneur has the tacit knowledge of her innovation, and a mayor or civic leader has tacit knowledge of the community, but both have only an explicit understanding of what the other knows. This mutual gap mistakenly increases the confidence of each that he or she is right.

As entrepreneurs come in from "the outside," issues of class, culture, and race inevitably come into play. This is especially true when those outside are predominantly white and well-educated and the communities they look to serve are low-income neighborhoods of color. Whether civic entrepreneurs are respectful enough to not offend and interested enough to engage in dialogue will determine the level of tension and, ultimately, success. Civic entrepreneurs understand that even if they try to avoid the political arena, they cannot avoid local political dynamics.

Sometimes even city hall will have the "not invented here" reaction to its own community leadership. As a motivated citizen looks to instill innovation in local delivery systems, government officials and other social service professionals will naturally ask: What is it that allows you to do that better than we do? And in either case, sanctioning someone to come in and "fix" a situation may raise questions about the authority and credibility of the mayor and civic leaders.

Teach For America has learned first-hand how to navigate such tensions as it successfully entered thirty-five communities across the country. But it discovered just how difficult overcoming them can be when Detroit's abysmal graduation rates drew the organization into that particularly challenging city. As Kevin Huffman, executive vice president of public affairs at Teach For America, remembers, "We thought, we've got to be in Detroit. When you see how dire the situation there is in terms of the gap in educational outcomes. . . . How could we not be in Detroit?"[11]

The organization's leadership successfully engaged the local philanthropic community but received "lukewarm support" from the superintendent, school board, and teacher's union. This response did not deter them, because experience had taught that Teach For America's teachers, or corps members, quickly won people over once in action. "We build a fair amount of grassroots support," Huffman says. "Principals really like us. . . . We build relationships in the political community. Parents like Teach For America corps members. Once we're in, we're usually in pretty good shape." But soon after Teach For America entered Detroit in 2002, the school district started moving its corps members to new schools, did not pay others, and would not clarify whether any would be welcomed back for the second year of their teaching commitment. Detroit is the only city from which Teach For America has withdrawn. Huffman credits a confluence of factors for this disappointing outcome:

> Very strong union, very weak superintendent, no support from the mayor or other political leaders in the city and a bureaucracy that was horribly mismanaged at the local level in the district. And all in all, the truth is we didn't have any one person or entity that was a strong political supporter who could rally other people behind us. . . . There was nobody in the system willing to expend political capital to make sure that that didn't happen.[12]

Teach For America's experience in Detroit illustrates how even the best models confront serious barriers when they attempt to grow. Sometimes the local stumbling blocks are true policy differences, but other times they are simply parochial. Either way, civic entrepreneurs must continue to work at navigating these waters, learning from past efforts as they seek to overcome obstacles to growth and systemic change. In turn, communities need to be more open to the promise of civic entrepreneurship—from both outside and within.

Civic Entrepreneurship as the Solution

In order to find how civic entrepreneurs ignite change, we studied approaches that, because of their power in either policy or delivery, caused the rest of the network to respond, forcing it to better allocate resources. We also looked for civic leadership that forced open space for change and challenging ideas. The leaders profiled in this book, rather than despair when looking at the depth of government bureaucracy and calcified social production systems, viewed the problems as opportunities to produce good. These civic entrepreneurs operate in different ways. Some convince a community that change must and can occur, like America's Promise through its attention-grabbing Grad Nation efforts. Others, like the successful College Summit program, actually produce the results themselves. Similarly, while government floundered in response to Hurricane Katrina, the heroic interventions of neighbors and faith- and community-based groups saved thousands of others. Creative, caring, and effective efforts like these demonstrate that great opportunity lies in our untapped civic potential.

The once-neglected fate of children of prisoners is one such area where civic leaders sparked change. In 2000 I participated in a small living-room discussion with presidential candidate George W. Bush and my friend John DiIulio, an insightful academic, criminal justice expert, and community activist. DiIulio unexpectedly inserted an appeal for the governor to mend a huge hole in the nation's social support net—the lack of services for children of prisoners. I thought at the time that DiIulio's plea had no chance of capturing conservative Republican attention.

Together with his colleague Wilson Goode, the former mayor of Philadelphia and a pastor, DiIulio knew that when children from disrupted families got into trouble, the government would most likely do things "to them" (jail) or "for them" (child protective services). But the entrepreneurial pair turned a problem into an opportunity. They had discovered that although many government programs touched these children—public safety, criminal justice, youth development, child welfare, and education—none really addressed the children in the way they needed to be addressed. Goode and DiIulio knew that they could succeed with earlier and better-coordinated intervention—something new and supportive. So the two secured philanthropic funding from Public Private Ventures and began building Amachi. A few years later, having proved the importance of the intervention, Amachi secured federal government resources—and high-profile promotion from President George W. Bush.

This book shows that civic entrepreneurship like that undertaken by Goode and DiIulio can drive social change. Entrepreneurial communities determined to improve the quality of life must encourage civic entrepreneurs. At the same time, aspiring civic inventors must learn how to navigate and influence their communities' existing social service production systems. In my experience, community must be the focus because that is where the human interventions occur. Without the active support of neighbors and block-by-block organizations, no outside funding will succeed. Success requires a personal touch and a deep understanding of local problems and resources. It also requires, as we will see, a familiarity with or a guide through the local political waters.

So how can all this work? Let us look at it through an example I know too well—inner-city education in Indianapolis. I engaged in a ten-year battle with the independent school board—and the even more independent school bureaucracy—to reform the city's public school system. Despite tens of millions of dollars of social programming and countless hours of professional and volunteer service, we could claim nothing but consistently awful results.

Many years later the issue popped up again with a call from the respected innovator J. B. Schramm, whom I knew from my work as chairman of CNCS. Schramm, the inventor of the College Summit program, wanted my advice in his effort to bring the program to Indianapolis. College Summit claimed it could help generate enough change to improve the city's dismal high school graduation rates (at that time less than one-third for young men of color).[13] I knew Schramm was succeeding in other cities and assumed he could change the future trajectory for many Indy students. The story of how College Summit ended up in Indianapolis provides hope not only for the city's youth, but also for thousands of Americans who aspire to make a transformative difference in their communities and in the country.

Just after Schramm graduated from divinity school in 1990, he started tutoring students at a teen center in a low-income housing project in Washington, D.C., in the hope that they would pursue higher education. Over and over, Schramm watched capable students fail to matriculate to college for lack of the institutional and family support and social networks available to most middle-class youth. Like other entrepreneurs, Schramm brought a fresh perspective to a problem others viewed and accepted as familiar. He saw individuals who had potential that could be fulfilled once barriers were removed. Schramm took a new approach to preparing his students for college. He hired a writing instructor and provided other transitional and life supports. And his protégés succeeded. From there, Schramm launched College Summit, which by 2008 had helped 35,000 high school students in ten states.[14]

Today civic entrepreneurs, armed with innovative thinking, a bottom-line sensibility, and a willingness to tackle some of the nation's most intractable social problems, are tapping into a powerful energy and sense of purpose. This growing cadre of change agents is shattering traditional policy approaches and replacing them with creative solutions and unique partnerships to produce dramatic results. Yet serious questions must be addressed. How do promising new interventions like College Summit ever flourish in a social service model dominated by top-down approaches, prescriptive government funding, and relationships that all conspire to resist or slow change?

Civic entrepreneurs have been emerging from across America's landscape: public servants and elected officials, venture capitalists and generous individual donors, faith-based providers, engaged citizens, and business leaders advocating new definitions of corporate social responsibility. Finding new ways to help people in trouble, these entrepreneurs have filled niches and changed thinking. Some of their efforts splash into the national headlines because of their appeal and success: Teach For America, Habitat for Humanity, and City Year, to name just a few. Many are local heroes, transforming communities across the country. Some, like Schramm and Wendy Kopp, the founder of Teach For America, are inventing new solutions. Other civic entrepreneurs set up the conditions for entrepreneurial success by staying active in rewriting the rules for how their communities determine priorities, make decisions, distribute funding, and monitor progress.

We include in these chapters discussions of public officials who prove that entrepreneurship can come from any sector—not just the social or private sectors. In New York City, Mayor Bloomberg and Chancellor Joel Klein boldly took on the challenge of reshaping the struggling school system, deeply integrating civic entrepreneurs into the change process. In Milwaukee, Bruce Kamradt put his knowledge and experience as a child welfare, juvenile court, and mental health administrator to work when he created an innovative and highly flexible integrated services model. Called Wraparound Milwaukee, his invention did not just coordinate but transformed the way dozens of agencies treated children with severe behavioral health issues—and their families—every year.

Clearly, the approaches and origins of civic entrepreneurship vary. For example, organizations like College Summit have grown in impact because they cross neighborhood, class, racial, and sectoral lines. Innovations in social problem solving offer more cause for hope and optimism than ever before—but only if they disrupt or transform an underperforming system for solving social problems. These important lessons led me to wonder how we can identify, nurture, and then *grow* the innovations invented or championed by the J. B. Schramms across the country in a manner which, collectively, creates enough lift for truly transformative social change.

Igniting Civic Progress

The litany of current crises mandates change not just in the way government provides services, but in the community-wide delivery systems built up around social problems. How do we nurture these civic entrepreneurs and provide them the innovative space that will leverage bold responses from the other actors in a community's social service system? To demonstrate how things could be done differently, we looked for civic entrepreneurs who emerged from the government, private, or nonprofit sectors to start or change a program, an organization, or a new policy that now produces more opportunity and progress for community residents. This search was not easy. Creative social activists discover and deliver interventions that transform individual lives—but only infrequently will their interventions also force change through the rest of a delivery system.

Even after a bold new idea proves worthwhile, replication or growth depends on how well the idea is disseminated, on how much it receives in new resources or how much it gains from new strategic partners. The civic entrepreneurs with whom we spoke struggle to take their working solutions to a scale that causes systemic change. Social progress requires that they overcome built-in barriers to transform the delivery systems in which they are operating. We explore the links between innovation, entrepreneurship, and social change. Specifically, we wanted to learn how to help civic entrepreneurs successfully catalyze broader change.

Our view of the social production system in a typical community is represented in the figure "Vortex of Social Change." Outside the circle, which represents the local community, national actors assert influence that affects local conditions and responses. These outside actors include private funders such as national foundations and large corporations; national advocacy organizations, interest groups, and professional associations; national nonprofit innovators; and federal or state funding agencies. The organizations inside the circle represent local players who can push for or impede a transformative solution. These local actors include private funders such as local philanthropists and community foundations; grassroots associations and interest groups; longtime civic institutions like the United Way, school officials and nonprofit providers; the mayor or other elected officials; and local civic entrepreneurs from all corners.

A host of forces operate on a community's social service delivery structure—few of which argue for change. The tendency to resist disruptive change does not result from a nefarious political conspiracy. Rather, it is the natural result of a system in which one closely tied group of individuals—philanthropic and government funders—makes decisions for another group—citizens in need. Yet an impassioned person with an appealing vision can act as a catalyst. The center circle in the figure on page 19 represents the civic reaction—the disruption and eventual transformation of the existing system triggered by civic entrepreneurship that produces more social good.

We do not want to suggest that these broad changes will always force existing players out of the "market." Rather, they might cause a configuration of current providers. Sarah Alvord, David Brown, and Christine Letts explored well-known social enterprises to find how they "expand and sustain their impacts and transform larger systems in which they are embedded."[15] They found that no matter the type of social intervention—local capacity building, new products or services, or movement building—social entrepreneurs achieving some level of system change worked across traditional divides. These entrepreneurs bundled services and created alliances both in the provision of assistance and in the advocacy necessary for "political leverage to have transformational impacts on both political and cultural contexts."

Vortex of Social Change

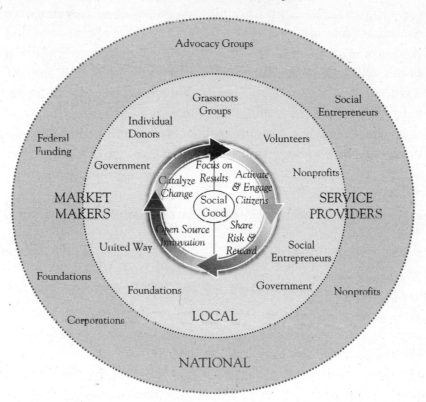

The above diagram represents the book's theory of change. The actors in the two outside circles—both service providers on the right and market makers on the left—can catalyze change among all the actors by employing one or more of the strategies depicted in the inner circle. We explore each of these strategies in subsequent chapters.

We consider market makers to be those organizations or principles that catalyze change and create the conditions for broad community solutions. They do this through programmatic and policy advocacy, funding, and rule setting that can source new providers who focus on results. Sometimes the conditions bring in new actors; other times the market makers clear the way for new arrangements of existing providers. Community leaders, grassroots organizations, and public officials promote entrepreneurship in their communities when they create environments of continuing innovation, challenge the very definition of public value, and exhibit a willingness to challenge the status quo.

Service providers engage in civic entrepreneurship as champions of a particular innovation, driving its design or identification as well as its adoption across a delivery system. The lessons that guide these champions of innovation include a mobilization of public will and political capital to demand results and change, a willingness to assume risk, and a delivery model that increases expectations of individual potential and responsibility.

We consider both market makers and service providers to be potential entrepreneurs and note that the levers of change they utilize are sometimes the same and sometimes quite different. Yet the lessons from both groups are essential to entrepreneurial communities and also to entrepreneurial organizations.

The Mandate and Caution of Engaging Government

Any process to address a community's social service production systems must keep its two dominant actors in mind—government and the individual citizen.

Government can be either a powerful ally or the primary obstacle in efforts to bring about large-scale change. On the one hand, individual entrepreneurs can certainly do much good by themselves. On the other hand, government must ultimately execute its role in ensuring the democratic values of equity and justice for all citizens. Further, the creative civic entrepreneurs who succeed by avoiding too much government entanglement eventually realize that they cannot take their innovation to any serious scale, or truly effect systemic change, without some government participation. Andrew Wolk, an early advocate for government support of social entrepreneurs, highlights the necessity of government participation in his discussion of College Summit. The organization grew impressively by 750 percent between 2000 and 2008, moving from serving 2,000 students to more than 17,000 students. "Yet, even with these results and growth," Wolk writes, "College Summit estimates they only reach about 2 percent of the one million low-income high school students in the United States."[16]

In addition, government plays such a dominant role in funding and standard setting today that broad social changes simply cannot occur without the eventual cooperation of all sectors. Government controls the area of social responses in the way it funds programs, regulates providers, sets credentials, and decides which organizations are qualified to provide services. In trying to bring innovation and change to government-dominated systems like education and public safety, one quickly finds the need to convince public officials of the value of change. No matter how noble our intentions or how dire the need, most broad change eventually involves the expenditure of tax dollars and thus the political process.

Since today's good idea could become part of tomorrow's social oligopoly, we need a process that consistently promotes innovation. Communities need to intentionally craft the structures to support this process because a truly open and competitive market does not otherwise exist. Involvement with government's command-and-control approach produces subtle dangers as well. Government funding diluted Gilded Age values such as mutual aid, character building, self-restraint, and self-help. The country moved from one in which receiving government support was considered shameful to one in which interest groups compete to maximize government assistance. It is not so much that public spending discouraged private spending, more that rule-driven, top-down government intervention affected philanthropy and civil society by reducing the communal aspect of neighbors and families taking care of one another. The nonprofit sector's important role of mediating between state and citizen will be threatened as more organizations become overly dependent on government funding.

While we argue that engagement with government is key to most social change, it also requires a fine balancing act in order to maintain the entrepreneur's integrity of voice and practice.

Beth Gazley's research on informal government-nonprofit "partnerships" found that most are not really partnerships at all—at least not in the sense that the two sides share authority and resources.[17] Government dominates the nonprofit provider. Once an entrepreneur becomes so addicted to government's deep pockets that he cannot afford to walk away, he runs the risk of losing his creative edge.

Sungsook Cho and David Gillespie studied this tension employing resource dependence theory, a useful tool for explaining the power dynamics between agencies that exchange resources.[18] Resource dependence theory assumes that people shape their organizations to attract resources; the more heavily dependent on government they become, the more likely it is that they will eventually look and act like government.

Even while starting the faith-based initiative in Indianapolis, and later assisting with the initiative at the White House, I remained concerned about inadvertent government intrusion on the mission of faith groups receiving funding. After observing government contract managers and auditors at work, I feared that faith or community organizations would begin to look and operate like government as we strove to build their capacity to comply perfectly with grant requirements. I still remember the group of highly committed pastors I met in Augusta, Georgia, after President Bush announced the faith-based initiative. Many of those present worried greatly that the risks of government partnerships might become reality. Peter Berger and Richard Neuhaus call these risks the "fatal embrace."[19] However, every day those pastors, and others, face serious challenges in feeding and housing people in crisis, and more resources mean that they can reach more of their hurting neighbors. Understanding when those resources undermine results and innovation will remain difficult, so nonprofit boards and their executives must vigilantly balance tradeoffs and opportunities.

Indiana's Les Lenkowsky studies philanthropy and has worked in various government roles including CEO of CNCS.

Despite or because of these experiences, he well articulates the caution of engaging government:

> If the nonprofit sector is now moving into an era where its role and influence will loom large and the reliance of the public on its actions will grow, the delicate balance struck between doing good through the state and doing good through private means will come under increasing stress. . . . But how to produce a healthier outcome is a challenge facing philanthropic leaders in the twenty-first century, not only to protect themselves but, at least as important, to maintain the equilibrium of public and private organizations that is so vital to the preservation of democracy.[20]

As we will see, civic entrepreneurs imaginatively engage citizens in order to maintain the personal nature of social services despite governmental grant requirements. Some public officials use their authority, credentialing procedures, and purchasing power to open up opportunities for creative nonprofit leaders to better serve people in need. We see a new role for government in social progress—one that concentrates on producing public value, not on controlling the means of producing it. In this new role, government will be much more energetic in setting up systems that ensure quality outcomes and much less dominant in accomplishing those outcomes. Part of the solution to avoiding the lure of entrenchment and supplanting by government, then, is civic renewal itself.

To produce civic renewal and social progress, any system must emphasize individual conduct and responsibility. Government, nonprofits, and for-profit companies succeed when they strengthen the talents and improve the opportunities of the person seeking help. This bias rejects ideas from both the right and the left: the idea that individuals do not deserve assistance unless they first establish certain behaviors (a view that overlooks the family, neighborhood, and school failures that reduce opportunity) and the idea that government and agencies should support the results of bad behaviors regardless. As Sawhill and Haskins have written, interventions "must be both generous enough and sufficiently tied to desirable behavior to be effective."[21]

Teaching a person to fish, done correctly, can be uplifting and supportive, not lecturing and condescending. I learned this lesson early in my public career, when I met with a small group of mothers who were receiving child support for the first time thanks to our enforcement efforts. This was before the 1996 national welfare reforms, and I wanted to see how upset they would be about the possibility that their welfare payments might stop if we succeeded in getting the dads to pay what they owed. Not one of the mothers complained. Instead they explained that they did need help with child care, transportation, or education, but they all wanted a job rather than a government check. In this vein, some of our best solutions derive from individuals themselves and from faith-based organizations that mix aid with a confidence founded on belief in a supreme being and in the potential of individual effort.

Conclusions

Growing cadres of civic entrepreneurs eager for change bring bold interventions that push the bounds of how to address public problems. They are a savvy, motivated, and results-oriented group of individuals who, through disruptive innovations, create opportunity and hope. Together with a large and growing pool of caring citizens who aspire to help others through service, they prove each day how talent and compassion can change lives and in so doing hold the key to America's future.

Civic entrepreneurship, combining as it does our communal ideals with the efficiency and technological know-how of business, represents hope for effective community change. In *The Power of Social Innovation*, we look at how energetic and passionate citizens can close the widening gap between social problems and solutions and how communities, funders, and government can indeed create an environment for social change. We intend this book to be useful to private citizens, donors, nonprofit managers, and elected officials in identifying the obstacles and assets necessary for truly transformative change in communities everywhere.

2

INNOVATION AS
CATALYTIC INGREDIENT

"To create significant and long-lasting changes,
social entrepreneurs must understand and often
alter the social system that creates and sustains the
problems in the first place."

Greg Dees

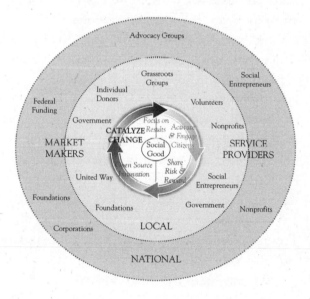

I have known Bill Milliken and his work for twenty-five years, because his start-up days took him through Indianapolis. When I recently saw him at a White House event celebrating volunteer service, he reassuringly still looked as if he would have felt more at home on an urban street corner. Milliken understands those corners and the schools nearby. After years as a youth worker on the streets of New York City, he discovered through first-hand experience that many of the existing resources available to youth were scattered in different places or buried in a maze of contradictory rules. Milliken and his co-founders of Communities in Schools (CIS) developed a coherent theory of change. They decided to integrate these resources and bring them into public school buildings. Milliken started in Atlanta, a city he understood well, using the authority of the school district to provide resources that were "more accessible, better coordinated, and also easier to measure and hold accountable."[1]

Today, CIS considers itself the largest dropout prevention network in the country, reaching more than one million youths each year in more than 3,250 schools across the country. Each local CIS affiliate brings together mentoring, health service, and other developmental and educational supports. It places more than 50,000 volunteers in schools each year, for a total of three million hours of volunteer service. CIS increases the likelihood a student will stay in school. Evaluations have shown that more than 75 percent of participating students improved attendance and academic performance, and only 3 percent dropped out.[2]

Milliken and other service integrators—especially Blair Taylor of the Los Angeles Urban League, whom we will meet in Chapter 6—well know that their task is a difficult and complex one. Picture assembling a jigsaw puzzle when some of the pieces are missing, others cannot be moved, and you don't have the photo on the outside of the box. With an effective civic discovery process to glean the right idea, and important resources like flexible financial capital, success is possible but never guaranteed. All the pieces need to fall into place.

By its very nature, government cannot easily discharge the role of integrator. It is designed to deal with a problem—drug abuse or domestic violence or homelessness—rather than a person. Equally important, even if government could somehow figure out how to best serve the person, it would most likely ignore the fact that people exist within highly influential social networks populated by other programs.

Greg Dees describes the social systems in which service providers operate as ecosystems consisting of "players" and "environmental conditions." Players are other providers; market makers such as funders, beneficiaries, and customers; and opponents and "affected or influential bystanders." The environmental conditions include politics, bureaucratic structures, regulatory decision-making processes, economics, geography and infrastructure, and culture and social fabric.[3]

Dees' list of critical components provides a very helpful way of thinking about social systems; however, we prefer the metaphor of a chemical reaction to one of an ecosystem due to the urgency of the situation. This chapter demonstrates that social change requires more than an innovative new program; it requires an entrepreneur like Milliken whose innovation catalyzes the other actors and resources of a social production system into a more valuable compound.

Throughout much of this book, we look at civic entrepreneurs as positive disruptors who leapfrog over well-intentioned tinkering at the margins in order to propel daring yet measurable progress. Professor Clay Christensen of Harvard Business School suggested that our Executive Session members apply his well-known disruptive innovation model to social problems. Recently, for example, he highlighted the need to innovate so that "we don't simply ask how we can afford health care" but, rather, make the entire system "affordable—less costly and of better quality."[4]

We like the sound of disruption. Certainly exposing obsolescence is necessary. Yet in this chapter we address how civic entrepreneurs like Milliken make substantial contributions not only by replacing the outdated with the innovative, but equally often by adding a missing ingredient that ignites drastic change in programs and other assets already operating in the community—innovation as catalytic ingredient.

We begin by considering some approaches for acquiring the insight, experience, and data necessary to unearth the missing ingredient. The process of identifying what would trigger drastic improvements inside a social delivery system like public safety or education could follow one or more of four methods: civic discovery, system discovery, personal discovery, or predictive discovery. Having identified the missing ingredient using one or more of these methods, civic entrepreneurs then invent or otherwise supply transformative interventions that fit into one of four categories: realignment of the existing players; technological or programmatic innovation; highly effective management; or new pipelines for community involvement.

Discovering the Missing Ingredient

Civic Discovery

The first approach to determining where and how to inject a solution involves a civic discovery process that identifies the talents of people in a neighborhood who are often connected through a faith or community group, or even a small business. The Indianapolis Front Porch Alliance was a mayoral initiative focused on re-creating civility, the public square, and civic engagement. To do this, we followed the work of John Kretzmann and John McKnight at Northwestern University and started with a survey of all the assets in the community to better understand how to leverage their influence and authority. Later, in my work at the Harvard Kennedy School, I was involved in applying a similar mapping tool as part of a project on "city hall and religion."[5] The city leaders we examined—Mayors Bill Purcell of Nashville and Mayor Manny Diaz of Miami—employed some variation of two key steps. First, they determined the geographic and organizational parameters, consulting with nonprofit leaders and frontline city employees to help create an accurate inventory. Second, they used the mapping as an opportunity to build rapport with local faith leaders and identify prospective allies and partners.

Bold accomplishments rarely result from a needs assessment designed to organize services, where officials identify gaps or deficiencies, set severity-based priorities, and then intervene in some way. The discovery process needs to be connected to aspirations. As Maurice Miller shows us in Chapter 5, a needs-based approach often fragments responses, leads people down the path of dependency, and gives residents neither voice nor choice. Further, Miller relies on critical assets missing from the above list—family, friends, and peers. These civic discoveries both help officials understand the social networks that influence people and neighborhoods and act to unlock civic participation and citizens' capacity to serve.

System Discovery

The second discovery method looks at systems through what economists call the "industrial organization approach." An innovator using this process looks beyond naming individual assets to explore the relationships between them. This model examines organizational behavior, governmental actions, barriers to entry, and pricing decisions.[6] In studying whether a sector is organized to succeed, this approach considers three variables, starting with structure. Is it competitive, quasi-competitive, or monopolistic? In social delivery systems, one can ask how many providers participate but, more important, whether the primary funding mechanisms allow true diversity or push them all to the same model. The second variable is the degree to which the firm's various strategies produce success and what, if any, outcome measures providers use. The third is performance.

How dynamic or steady are costs and prices? Is enough innovation happening, as evidenced by steady productivity gains? One can look at whether the system has created enough opportunity for civic innovators to challenge and improve the performance of that industry sector.[7]

The search for a community solution would take into account factors such as public policy and regulations and whether room exists to catalyze new cultural norms, build new infrastructure, or introduce new business models. These larger frames are more likely than program evaluation to locate the inflection point that can drive change in a system.

Personal Discovery

The third approach looks at individuals. Each student in a public education system, for example, has a story that could reveal the missing intervention that will best suit him or her—a mentor, for example. Entrepreneurs stimulate their imaginations through personal interactions. As we shall see, Vanessa Kirsch began her efforts with listening tours. Keith Taylor founded the online giving site ModestNeeds after being on the receiving end of just-in-time assistance from family and friends. J. B. Schramm saw the need for a cultural shift related to expectations around college while working directly with high-school-age youth at an after-school program. My own policy ideas concerning poverty were formulated as a result of hundreds of conversations over a decade with mothers receiving Aid to Families with Dependent Children (AFDC) and, later, Temporary Assistance for Needy Families (TANF).

I once asked social venture philanthropist Herb Sturz how he arrived at the innovative idea of putting homeless people to work cleaning up city neighborhoods. As in many of our civic entrepreneurs' stories, his idea originally came from personal experience, listening, and up-close observation. Sturz used to walk Manhattan's Bowery, witnessing suffering but also talking to those in need. These walks moved him to help to create the program. In Sturz's words, "I could literally see many of these individuals change as they could see the results of their work on the neighborhoods and the people in them."[8]

Personalizing services on the basis of an individual's talent can help successful innovators calibrate their models in nuanced ways that often elude government. Maurice Miller applied his community and individual knowledge to support neighborhood youths. This method allows a civic innovator to respond to the individual rather than the problem. A government program that demands the same interventions for everyone in a low-performing school in a low-income neighborhood dilutes and marginalizes results for all. By contrast, personal discovery can pinpoint the reasons that each student is dropping out.

Bill Schambra, now with the Hudson Institute's Bradley Center for Philanthropy and Civic Renewal, has provided creative thinking from the right on how this process can also lead to the identification of innovations:

> "[It is] wiser for the philanthropist to get out of that comfortable chair in the foundation office and spend most of her time quietly and discreetly poking around the neighborhood. The point is to find the unsung community leaders who have particular, concrete ideas about how the neighborhood can be improved, and who can do a great deal with a small grant at a particularly critical place and time. . . . The additional virtue of this approach is that it opens itself to the civic engagement of citizens who have otherwise often been marginalized by the larger social policy actors, and thus helps meet the pressing national need for democratic renewal."[9]

Predictive Discovery

The fourth approach for civic innovators centers on quantitative data. Civic entrepreneurs can discern solutions when, for example, they combine data from expenditures on the back end with data from client outcomes on the front end. Once these data are together in one place, decision-support systems or predictive-modeling technology will allow for the discovery of trends and correlations that lead to more-strategic decision making.

Predictive modeling systems are most common (at least in social problem solving) in the health care industry. The federal government is helping states move in the direction of this data-based discovery. In 2007 the Department of Health and Human Services provided $150 million in Medicaid Transformation Grants to encourage innovation in the modernization of states' administration of their Medicaid programs. The proposals included new methods for using information technology to reduce patient error rates; implementing electronic clinical decision-support tools; medication risk-management programs; cost savings; reducing waste, fraud, and abuse; and improving health-care access for the uninsured. State grantees' projects included Kansas's "Using Predictive Modeling Technology to Improve Preventive Healthcare in the Disabled Medicaid Population" and Illinois's "Predictive Modeling System." The Illinois plan would allow the state's Department of Healthcare and Family Services to use existing data sets from its normal auditing procedures to predict future referrals, improving the health of Medicaid clients as well as preventing fraudulent claims from providers.[10]

Many factors inhibit all four of these diagnostic processes. Sometimes the problem-solving framework distorts service delivery in a way that produces lots of activity but few results. We have seen this occur, for example, when a city focuses on operating public hospitals instead of increasing public health, or on homeless shelters instead of preventing homelessness. Other factors also limit imagination, not the least of them the "excuse culture" described by New York School Chancellor Joel Klein. Klein asserts, "From the day I got here, everybody told me we'll never fix education until we fix poverty in America. And I always say that's exactly backwards. We'll never fix poverty until we fix education."[11]

Discovering the Missing Ingredient

CIVIC DISCOVERY

Survey the institutional assets in the community—service providers, faith-based, community groups, small businesses.

1. Utilize local resources like nonprofit leaders and frontline city employees.

2. Use mapping as an opportunity to build rapport with local civic leaders.

3. Include in planning the noninstitutional assets like family and social networks.

SYSTEM DISCOVERY

Explore the relationships among actors inside the system, including barriers to entry.

1. Assess level of competition and diversity; is funding overly prescriptive and monopolistic?

2. Evaluate whether and by what measures strategies are deemed successful.

3. Determine if the system creates enough room for innovation.

PERSONAL DISCOVERY

Discover an intervention through listening, close observation, and personal experience.

1. Use this process to identify what drives individual issues and challenges.

2. Design highly nuanced responses.

3. Find innovators excluded or marginalized by the larger social policy actors.

PREDICTIVE DISCOVERY

Utilize decision-support or predictive-modeling systems to discern solutions in data.

1. Mine new and existing data sets to find trends and predict future needs.
2. Look to future data mining and analysis for more personalization.
3. Learn from examples in health care predicting referrals and reducing patient error rates.

Having identified the missing ingredient, civic entrepreneurs must then design an innovation that catalyzes improvement in the performance of the system overall. Yet choosing the right reagent is not an easy process. Social policy gravitates toward the classic mistake of acting like a large hammer looking for nails to more skillfully drive. As a prosecutor in the 1980s and a mayor in the 1990s, I remember intense debates over whether out-of-control crime should be attacked by addressing root causes like poverty or through tougher punishment. Yet New York Mayor Rudy Giuliani and Police Commissioner Bill Bratton chose a different and strikingly successful intervention to ignite change in a moribund system when they combined broken-windows theory with operational excellence in the now-popular model called CompStat. We next look at how an entrepreneur, after this discovery process, chooses the right catalysts.

Choosing the Right Catalyst

The civic entrepreneur, after this discovery process, can choose several ingredients that will make the system itself perform better. We found four categories of such ingredients: civic realignment; technological glue; filling the management gap; and new pipelines for community engagement.

Civic Realignment

While we tend to think of entrepreneurs as Bill Gates types who tinker in a garage (or at a computer), not all innovations are technical in nature. One of the great assets of a civic leader is the ability to call people together to address an issue. As mayor, I looked forward to inviting a range of individuals—community leaders, public health and government officials, clergy, and residents—to talk about a public problem I knew they cared deeply about. Those discussions always led to new relationships— people and organizations better able to discharge their missions as a result of discovering someone else's potential. Civic realignment—which drives value through a delivery system by organizing the players and their relationships differently—can indeed produce transformative value.

As we will see in the examples below, the civic realigner might take some combination of the following steps: (1) engage in an early civic or system discovery process; (2) capitalize on a crisis or other high-profile event to build broad-based support; (3) develop a coherent theory of change; (4) engage other actors, including providers, funders, and community and government leaders, to serve as partners; (5) use credibility to take on the status quo and create a culture of collaboration around shared goals; (6) look to incorporate proven models for innovation; and (7) employ data to measure success.

For twenty years, the country's urban school dropout rate has gone from bad to disgraceful. A few years ago, America's Promise Alliance leaders Marguerite Kondracke and Alma Powell joined John Bridgeland, John DiIulio, and others in igniting a national campaign against what they called the "silent epidemic." They were confident that high-profile events—attended by elected officials, business leaders, parents, teachers, scholars, and students—could trigger a serious effort within cities and states to realign resources in a way that relied on objective data and proven models and laid youth squarely in the middle of the effort.

Nowhere was the dropout issue starker than in Detroit. School offered the city's children neither rescue nor reprieve from Detroit's woes with a jailed mayor, double-digit unemployment, and the Big Three auto companies crashing at the gates of bankruptcy—not to mention a professional football team with a winless record. A public high school student in Detroit had a 25 percent chance of graduating in four years—and a 60 percent likelihood of going to prison. This record earned Detroit's school district the unwelcome distinction of ranking dead last in graduation rates of the fifty largest cities in the nation.[12]

Soon after Kondracke and Powell announced their Grad Nation campaign, United Way of Southeastern Michigan and Edsel Ford (great-grandson of Henry Ford) led Detroit civic leaders in deciding that, because they were last of the fifty big cities in performance, they needed to be first of those same cities to hold a Grad Nation summit.

By all accounts, United Way of Southeastern Michigan is a major player in Detroit, raising about $55 million a year for the community.[13] It was a logical partner with America's Promise to convene a summit and to coordinate Detroit's subsequent dropout prevention action plan. Mike Tenbusch, vice president for education preparedness at United Way of Southeastern Michigan, served as both a catalyst and a champion for United Way's leadership in this effort. Tenbusch had previously served as a Detroit school board member, worked for the city's charter school district, and been commissioned in 2007 by the local Skillman Foundation to find successful models for improving high school student achievement. According to Tenbusch, the high schools were "unsafe and just a complete waste of taxpayer money. We said, we've got to fix them immediately."[14]

Tenbusch and his new boss, United Way of Southeastern Michigan CEO Michael Brennan, launched an agenda for turning around failing high schools in the Detroit area, combining long- and short-term strategies for at-risk students. They also saw an opportunity to fold their plan into the framework of the America's Promise Grad Nation initiative. Working with America's Promise, they launched the first City Summit in April 2008, with school district leaders and intermediaries from across the country joining together to craft a solution.

Tenbusch asserts that, as is common with many civic realignment efforts, the America's Promise Dropout Prevention summit was a high-profile event that jump-started the agenda for education reform by helping convince United Way of Southeastern Michigan's somewhat risk-averse board of directors to allow them to move forward. Tenbusch used the summit to lead the board in envisioning a new role for the United Way in transforming the local school system.

United Way of Southeastern Michigan and its new partners launched the Greater Detroit Education Venture Fund to support eligible "dropout factory" high schools and partnered with proven educational intermediaries who agreed to two long-term goals: graduating 80 percent of students with an average ACT score of 18 within four years and getting 80 percent to attend college or post-secondary training.[15] As of March 2009, the fund had dedicated $4 million to launching a comprehensive turnaround effort in five schools and had closed down six more schools, some of which reopened as newly reconstituted schools.[16] Much work remains, but these efforts in Detroit illustrate the power of a community player with authority who leverages a highly public crisis or event to jump-start a new network of diverse actors. In the words of Charles Hiteshew of America's Promise Alliance, "This is an example of a civic capacity forming around the crisis of the schools that transcends the school system itself."[17]

My own experience in Washington, D.C., highlights another important ingredient for civic realignment: a high-profile champion. At the invitation of Mayors Anthony Williams and

Adrian Fenty, I had the opportunity to chair the Anacostia Waterfront Corporation, a redevelopment agency in some of the city's challenged neighborhoods. I set out to replicate Geoffrey Canada's widely celebrated and successful Harlem Children's Zone—a well-integrated and comprehensive delivery system centered on the child. I assembled leading children's advocates and foundations in an effort to import the model.

We had all the right ingredients: a coherent theory of change, a powerful idea, good partners, and impressive funding pledges. With America's Promise we engaged nationally acclaimed Bridgespan to study the feasibility, in part by interviewing a wide array of organizations in the area. The initiative had to overcome trust issues stemming from a history of outside groups making promises in the area and then disappearing. Competition among local providers proved significant. Our goal, to increase the number of youths who graduated from high school ready for college or a career, involved augmenting public support systems and connecting residents to existing services.

We lacked one ingredient—a champion like Canada. The mayor was supportive but focused on reforming the schools. The community organizations endorsed the concept (as long as one of their sister organizations was not in charge), but insisted (as did the mayor) on knowing who would do the leading. In these messy areas of civic realignment, someone with actual authority, money, focus, and personality needs to lead the way. When no galvanizing leader appeared, the effort withered, community support, funding, and a good model notwithstanding.

A successful reorganization of social services must integrate key leadership as well as service delivery. To make it work in Harlem, Canada says:

"We went out of our way to connect with high-quality partners for support. We carefully worked up-front to ensure that our expectations, and those of our partners, were clear and aligned. For example, we partnered with the Children's Health Fund to create a school-based health center. We gave the Children's Health Fund space in our headquarters, which also houses a public charter school, so it could provide our students with free medical, dental, and mental-health services. We partnered with Harlem Hospital so our families could learn to be pro-active and manage their children's asthma."[18]

One of the best-known examples of civic realignment, Harlem Children's Zone is now serving as a model for the Obama administration's Promised Neighborhood program.

Technological Glue

Civic entrepreneurs can also rely on new technologies to galvanize action. Technological entrepreneurs use the deep understanding they have gained in a discovery process to design a technology that unleashes potential within specific elements of the system. For example, often the innovation enhances the important relationship between field workers and clients. The innovator then works closely with field workers to integrate the technology into their daily routines while using feedback to refine the tools as they are utilized.

I encountered such a catalytic technology during a tour of a Houston preschool center. Pre-K teachers face some daunting days, often with little experience and few professional tools, but in this classroom they utilized mobile devices from Wireless Generation to garner regular insights into each child's cognitive, social, and emotional development. Subsequently, I met one of Wireless Generation's founders, Larry Berger, who explained the company's progress toward realizing a vision of innovative, technology-based tools, systems, and services that help teachers make better pedagogical decisions.

Because younger children do not take "bubble" tests, and teachers can learn more by watching K–3 students, these assessments are observational and frequent, producing valuable data about students' learning that informs instruction. But traditional observational assessments were challenging to give and score and buried the teacher in time-consuming paperwork.

Whereas much of the technology in education—online instruction, for example—is meant to connect learners to lessons directly without an instructor, Berger viewed teachers as "the multiplier of the inflection point" and focused the intervention on optimizing two variables important to every teacher: time and data. To get the software right, Berger and his co-founder Gunn sat in classrooms, watched teachers in action, and recorded how they spent their time. They also interviewed principals and superintendents about what data would help them do their jobs better. As Berger recalls, "We really just sat down and watched what teachers were doing and then tried to build software that would save them a ton of time in how they did it but also maybe amplify the effectiveness of it and capture data."[19] Berger combined his personal discovery with a system-level view. He and Gunn understood that the dramatically increased reporting requirements in the federal No Child Left Behind law required teachers and administrators to focus far more on paperwork.

Using mobile devices streamlined the assessment process, saving hours of teachers' time and delivering accurate, immediate results with web-based tools to help teachers interpret data and apply the findings to their instruction. Wireless Generation enhanced the efficacy of teachers by helping them combine existing data and the results of others' work with new early reading diagnostic assessments.

A third leverage point—personalized services—presents an even more significant breakthrough opportunity for large public systems. Technology accelerates the predictive discovery process, which lays the groundwork for further progress. Wireless Generation is now participating in a pilot project called "School of One" conceived by Joel Rose, the New York City schools' chief executive for human capital. School of One seeks to give teachers the capacity to personalize student learning. Schools assess students going into the program in order to identify both their differentiated needs and the best corresponding approaches. Teachers then structure daily schedules around a variety of instructional modalities, including small group instruction, peer or individual tutoring, self-paced software, online virtual tutoring, and independent learning.[20] The pilot was launched in summer 2009 in mathematics in one middle school, with hopes of gradually expanding to more middle schools through a three-year R&D period. These tools should also help identify children who need specific early interventions, which will in turn reduce special education expenditures in later years. Rose emphasizes that the technology innovation here is in fact the "learning algorithm."[21]

These inventions dramatically enhance the heretofore fragmented resources of complex systems, organizing them around the specific needs of the most important actor—the student.

Michael Fullan explains the complexity of system-level change in his thoughtful analysis of the process of education reform—the "how" versus the "what." Change across a school district, Fullan writes, must incorporate the history and frequency of current and past reform initiatives in that district, which affects attitudes toward all future change. Fullan reminds us that those frontline workers, whether teachers or others, often interpret change differently from how leaders intend it and therefore need to be engaged in developing any change. The design process must incorporate the context in which workers perform their roles. For example, in addition to the stress of the classroom at any given moment, teachers in most schools face a constant stream of multiple, overlapping demands from administrators and parents. Fullan also reminds us that it is easy to skip the deeper meaning of a change or new approach and instead focus on its superficial components—new equipment or new structures like teaming—without the necessary changes in instructional approaches. And finally, Fullan notes that "reculturing," not just restructuring, the organization is required. The effective adoption of change—especially the cultural change needed for new approaches and new assumption or beliefs—is a social process based on shared meaning and requires both support and pressure.[22]

Our search focused on technological innovations that presented catalytic potential because they unlocked personal capacity—of both the student (client) and the teacher (service worker). As Berger says, "Our whole thing was, could we build stuff that enhanced the capacity of teachers to have an impact on kids?"[23]

The huge potential of these inventions—and their universal appeal—struck me when I sat next to civic entrepreneur Martin Fisher at a dinner and listened to him explain his international program KickStart. Fisher unleashes entrepreneurship in communities by designing and selling new technologies that help people start their own businesses. His approach does not involve aid in the traditional sense. Fisher understands the important role that entrepreneurship plays in wealthy economies and believes that with help, "self-motivated private entrepreneurs" can play a similar role in developing economies.[24]

Fisher and his partner Nick Moon began their discovery with a clear understanding that their target audience—the rural poor in Kenya—were predominantly (80 percent) small-scale farmers who made just enough to survive. They also established that although land and skills were abundant in Kenya, farming that relies on seasonal rain is prey to periods of overabundance and waste followed by periods of scarcity and hunger. Irrigation would allow small-scale farmers to "spread out the production of food to meet the demand, increase incomes, and sustainably reach food and income security."[25] Fisher and Moon used these discoveries to design and then manufacture and distribute effective, affordable ($34 and $100) foot pumps for drawing water from the ground. The farmer, with his own labor, pushes on the pump he has stuck into the ground to water his crops.

KickStart's 135,000 pumps have helped latent entrepreneurs start up more than 88,000 businesses after the users grew enough crops not only to feed their families but also to become wholesalers. These enterprises lifted more than 440,000 people out of poverty in Kenya, Mali, Tanzania, and other countries.[26] KickStart, offering a one-year guarantee, underwrites the risk of the up-front capital for small-scale farmers to buy the foot pumps. Fisher and Moon anticipate that the market will eventually grow to the point where the industry will be profitable, attracting the private sector, without the need for any subsidy.

Technology in this instance unlocks value by treating individuals as latent assets rather than victims. Individual ownership, coupled with changes in production systems, allows those in poverty to enjoy a better life. Like Berger, Fisher built his inventions after spending time and sharing experiences with the people who would subsequently benefit from the technology. Demonstrating a commitment to improved performance, KickStart closely monitors its customers' progress, allowing Fisher and Moon to continually adjust their product and marketing efforts.

Filling the Management Gap

Technology makes little difference without good management, which, in fact, can be the missing ingredient that turns a mediocre social service response into a dramatically effective one. Not even a good cause, good partners, and good intentions will produce transformative results without operational excellence.

The management-oriented civic entrepreneur can pursue different paths to innovation. One path is to partner with existing providers to help improve their management. Another is to take over an existing organization and use management expertise to turn it around. In the first path, the key steps start with identifying benefits for both partners and deepening the relationship by sharing resources, knowledge, and talent.

Monitor Group's ongoing partnership with social venture fund New Profit Inc. provides an exemplar for this approach. New Profit's portfolio organizations have achieved disproportionate success in part because they benefit from the expertise and resources of Monitor's consulting firm, which helps ensure highly effective management. In 1983, Harvard Business School Professor Michael Porter, Mark Fuller, and four other entrepreneurs started Monitor, which today employs 1,500 consultants to government, corporate, nonprofit, and philanthropic organizations in more than twenty countries.[27] Monitor's receptivity to the New Profit partnership is based on what Fuller calls the "moral purpose," which he claims provides the cohesion, direction, and momentum necessary for a successful organization.[28] Further, it represents to Fuller the philosophical and social context for employees.

Monitor Group started down the path of producing social good when it became an early supporter of City Year in the late 1980s. Out of this work a relationship of trust developed between the Monitor leadership and City Year founders Khazei and Brown. In starting New Profit, Vanessa Kirsch reasoned that if nonprofits were to make progress against enormous social problems, they needed to grow their organizations. Yet through personal experience, Kirsch observed that nonprofits typically "end up developing very dysfunctional structures that can sometimes be driven by grant makers who want to be hands-off, making the relationship and the organization's path to growth a guessing game." Civic entrepreneurs need not only seed capital to grow to scale but also consulting, advice, and other professional services like those available to for-profit businesses.[29]

In 1998, Fuller and members of Monitor's leadership team decided to support New Profit in even more ways than Kirsch had initially proposed. As Kirsch recalls, the relationship developed based on mutual benefit:

"Monitor had been doing pro-bono work, but felt that it wasn't delivering the desired, measurable impact. It sought a better way to deploy its resources and truly make a difference. By combining its commitment to making a difference with its human capital strategy, Monitor built the New Profit partnership into its recruitment and development plans for employees. New Profit and its portfolio became a compelling opportunity for Monitor employees to test their leadership skills and develop their careers."[30]

Today teams of consultants from Monitor partner with New Profit portfolio managers to provide each portfolio organization with growth strategy and organizational design support, along with marketing, branding, and economic modeling. The Monitor Institute, Monitor's subsidiary focused on consulting and research for the social sector, partners with New Profit to staff and oversee the consulting teams in order to ensure high-quality outcomes for portfolio organizations. To date, Monitor's support of New Profit—valued at more than $28 million— has come in the form of three hundred Monitor consultants, including twenty-five Monitor partners involved in CEO-level coaching of portfolio organizations in 2007 alone. The Monitor/ New Profit team produced more than thirty growth plans to help civic entrepreneurs better recognize patterns, talents, and needs. As Kirsch explains it, "We have had a truly unparalleled and amazing relationship with Monitor—they provide a million dollars of pro-bono consulting for every million dollars of cash we put into organizations."

But the relationship goes deeper. A Monitor senior team member sits on the New Profit board. Monitor provides consulting services to New Profit itself, while a number of Monitor partners invest in the New Profit portfolio.[31] And in turn the Monitor Institute, which has worked on more than one hundred nonprofit-related projects around the world, benefits from New Profit's talent and experience.

Aaron Lieberman is an alumnus of the New Profit portfolio whose more recent work with Head Start illustrates the second management-as-catalyst path whereby the civic entrepreneur takes over as provider and turns around an existing organization with an infusion of management acumen that in turn affects the larger system.

Head Start promises much, but like any system, it suffers from some very low performers. In 2002 the Government Accountability Office labeled one in six Head Start programs as "deficient" and failing to meet even the most basic standards. Yet federal law gave protections to these low-performing incumbents that made it difficult for the government to terminate their grants. Typically, only 1 percent of programs ever had their grants revoked or relinquished, which was the only opportunity for new providers to compete for grants.

Lieberman, who had started the service initiative Jumpstart, which utilized work-study students to help children learn reading and literacy skills, had another idea. After years of observing Head Start operations, Lieberman started Acelero Learning, the only for-profit Head Start management company, and began offering management services to new Head Start providers when they replaced those that had lost their grants. After a few years of training and technical assistance from Acelero, these providers, serving more children with a higher quality of services, received positive federal reviews where their predecessors had struggled. Lieberman then determined that Acelero could increase its impact by directly managing Head Start centers itself. It takes a special entrepreneur to produce value in this space, as in many others that government dominates. Half of the value equation depends on high-quality services actively engaging local board members, and half depends on the ability to comply with numerous federal requirements.

As of 2009, Acelero served roughly 2,350 children and families through three local affiliates that have Head Start contracts in New Jersey and Nevada. In these programs, for the same amount of money, Acelero offers more service to more children— increasing enrollment while offering full-day services year-round. On the basis of its early results, Acelero received the Kellogg

Foundation's first direct private equity investment under its mission-driven investment strategy. Management makes Acelero different. Lieberman has managed this transformation by devolving more authority to local directors and providing them with performance data. Acelero has also raised the expectations of its staff both through a re-interview process after taking over a contract and by increasing minimum professional requirements. At the same time, it has increased teacher pay by approximately 25 percent. Aaron adds, "People rise to the challenge when it's clear what the values are and what the expectations are. We've seen an amazing number of people meet it again and again and again."[32]

New Pipelines for Community Engagement

Fuller, Kirsch, and Lieberman demonstrate that effective and inspired management can play a catalytic role. But sometimes the immediate need is to recruit and mobilize more creative and compassionate people into a delivery system. I am not an unbiased observer about the benefits of service—both to the community and to the volunteer. After almost nine years as chair of the Corporation for National and Community Service, I have personally seen the tangible benefits when one citizen helps another. While the publicly funded CNCS encourages community volunteerism, government cannot and should not be the dominant source of assistance in a community. It does not possess enough funding, legitimacy within affected populations, or compassion to produce transformative change. Instead, social progress often depends on "little platoons" of community volunteers.[33] Civic entrepreneurs can catalyze, harness, and direct the enormous (and growing) reservoir of American goodwill. These "service" entrepreneurs are capturing the broad interest in service and act as pipelines to connect service to real civic impact. In 2008, 61.8 million Americans (26.4 percent of the adult population) contributed eight billion hours of volunteer service. Despite tough economic times, the volunteering rate has held steady between 2007 and 2008, with the largest area of increase in self-organized community-based projects.[34]

Further, our research at CNCS shows that youths from disadvantaged circumstances who volunteer demonstrate more positive civic behaviors than similar youth who do not. In fact, they are nearly 50 percent more likely than the non-volunteers to say that they will probably graduate from a four-year college.[35] Aggressively expanding service to this group also appears to increase future employment and increase the percentage who earn at least an associate's degree.[36] Civic entrepreneurs who view youths as assets who can contribute and help themselves at the same time can produce remarkable outcomes. The Earth Conservation Corporation, for example, brings young people together to improve the Anacostia River. When these at-risk youths are challenged to better their environment, they also rebuild the vitality of their own lives, their communities, and their futures.

While volunteering is good in its own right, it can also have measurable impact inside the social delivery system. In the examples below, the innovator's initial discovery process involves two paths. The first identifies areas of unmet need that can be addressed by inflows of individual goodwill. Goodwill can manifest itself in a variety of ways, including volunteerism, professional pro bono expertise, and financial donations. The second identifies a community or segment of the population with untapped goodwill. Having identified places where these new inflows could catalyze major improvements, the innovator can determine how to connect these people assets to the issues at hand.

The service-oriented civic entrepreneur recognizes that, although potential volunteers or donors may express a strong interest in participating, certain barriers often prevent them from doing so. These barriers may be cultural, language-based, financial, informational, or temporal. To bridge these barriers, the entrepreneur becomes part matchmaker, part navigator and informational guide, and part manager of relationships.

In the recent marriage between NYC schools and City Year, we see three entrepreneurs engaged in a process of mutual discovery. Since its 1988 inception in Boston, City Year has spread to eighteen localities across the country and earned a national reputation. It places young people aged seventeen to twenty-four in full-time service as tutors, mentors, and role models to disadvantaged children for a year. In 2005, City Year New York Advisory Board Chair Jack Lew and Executive Director Itai Dinour saw an opportunity for their brand of innovation inside the school system. Chancellor Joel Klein had seen City Year corps members in action in their trademark red jackets, and he liked what he saw. He decided he would purchase their enthusiasm—that much eagerness and passion injected on a daily basis into a struggling school, he guessed, would ignite a broad change in attitude. Soon after, the two sides entered a five-year, $8.5 million arrangement in which five hundred City Year corps members would provide in-school mentoring and literacy work in schools in the "most under-resourced communities." In 2008, City Year was operating in eighteen elementary schools. In 2011, the final year of the current partnership, it expects to be in twenty-six.[37]

As Lew notes, in this relationship, the corps members act as positive role models as they engage students in after-school activities, tutoring, student government, or service projects. Lew maintains that these mentoring role models are "in some ways so much more important than any specific project they undertake. You're going into a community where there hasn't been that kind of a positive role model. You go into these schools and see these eight-, nine-, ten-, eleven-, twelve-year-olds hanging on to the kids in the red jackets and it's great."[38] And City Year sees its impact not only in the benefit its corps members provide to the students they serve, but also in the development of leadership skills and a long-term commitment to civic engagement in its recruits. Many of the corps members hail from disadvantaged backgrounds themselves; City Year intentionally recruits from a "diverse mix of life experiences and skill sets." The City Year relationship is a prime example of the way such partnerships can use a small amount of money and lots of enthusiasm to leverage broader cultural, leadership, and even educational change.

We can think of social change in terms of increasing the number of creative programs that change the civic landscape, whether City Year in schools or KaBOOM! in neighborhood playgrounds. But we also can think of social change in terms of the aggregate number of good deeds—from anywhere or anyone—that lift up a neighborhood. In this sense, harnessing, training, and directing millions of new volunteers will produce enormous change. Realistically, with a bit of nudging and assistance, the United States could add ten million more individuals to those now serving, who would contribute an additional 1.35 billion hours of mentoring, tutoring, case management, and other services every year.

The heightened service ethic among millennials and baby boomers would drive much of this growth and represents huge civic potential for communities. Civic Ventures is an effort aimed at harnessing the energy of the more than seventy-five million baby boomers who will retire en masse over the next decade. As John Gomperts and his partner in this initiative, Marc Freedman, point out, "Never before have so many people had so much experience—and the time to put it to good use. They constitute a potential windfall of human and social capital to nonprofit groups, a world with a surplus of goodwill and youthful ambition, and a shortage of experience and management skills."[39]

In 2003, AARP asked baby boomers about their plans for retirement. Seventy-nine percent of the respondents said they wanted to stay productive and useful and had a "growing interest" in "work that combines the seriousness and income associated with a job with the spirit and fulfillment of service."[40] Gomperts's critical role in the early years of the national service movement and AmeriCorps helped him to discover that despite this latent opportunity, nonprofits have failed to aggressively increase their outreach to and utilization of senior volunteers. Gomperts and Freedman note:

> "Many of today's volunteer opportunities for older adults were created in the 1960s and based on 'activity theory' in gerontology. Simply put, the goal was to keep the old folks busy, to get their blood flowing. As a consequence, all too many volunteer opportunities were designed without much thought to accomplishing work of any significance."[41]

Gomperts did not begin his discovery process by looking for a gap; rather, he saw an untapped supply of goodwill and has since set out to help nonprofits make their volunteer opportunities more attractive to retiring boomers. Civic Ventures's flagship initiative is Experience Corps, a national service program for older Americans. Two thousand Corps members, now in twenty-two cities across the country, volunteer their time toward social problems such as literacy.

Gomperts asserts that one must first demonstrate that an idea works and then start growing the movement. He uses a telling analogy for like-minded civic entrepreneurs: open a few Starbucks and establish loyal customers before expanding the franchise throughout the world. Gomperts points out: "[Experience Corps] isn't just a good idea, and a good way to capture the talent and idealism of people who have finished their midlife careers; it really works in helping kids learn to read." A recent study from Washington University found that students with Experience Corps tutors made better than 60 percent more progress in reading skills over a single year than non-participating students.[42]

The Serve America Act of 2009 recognized the emerging number of senior service members and altered the traditional AmeriCorps college incentive to allow a member to assign it to a child or grandchild rather than using it him- or herself. Similar changes, by government, nonprofits, and companies that allow a mix of service and paid work, must continue to achieve the potential contributions of older Americans.

More young adults and seniors are devoting time to serve and make major contributions in their communities, but what about actively engaged professionals in the middle? Aaron Hurst started the Taproot Foundation in San Francisco to develop this important opportunity. Entrepreneurship runs in Hurst's family. One of his grandfathers is Joseph Slater, who helped found the Peace Corps and was a long-time president of the Aspen Institute. As a student at the University of Michigan, Hurst spent most of his time on service learning projects, including developing a program to teach creative writing at a local prison.[43]

A 2006 report from Johns Hopkins found that barely one in three nonprofits could secure capital for its IT needs, and only one in four could find funding for staff development.[44] Seeing this gap, Hurst focused on strengthening nonprofit organizations by helping them secure pro bono professional services in marketing, information technology, human resources, and strategic planning.

The Taproot Foundation connects teams of professionals willing to share their time and expertise with nonprofit social service providers working in education and health and others working on environmental issues. The nonprofits apply for what the foundation calls "service grants," which consist of one hundred hours of free services channeled into one discrete project of about six months' duration. As of 2009, Taproot has expanded outside San Francisco to Seattle, Boston, Chicago, Los Angeles, and New York. Its professional volunteers have completed more than eight hundred projects for five hundred nonprofit clients. Collectively, these nonprofits reach eighteen thousand constituents. To achieve this impact, Taproot Foundation has recruited and organized eight thousand professionals to do 555,000 hours of service, valued by Taproot at more than $42 million.[45]

At its core, Taproot remains true to Hurst's vision of breaking down cultural barriers between the business and nonprofit sectors. Early on, Hurst confronted skepticism on both sides. Nonprofits needing the help balked at the pro bono aspect, expecting that "you get what you pay for." Others were not interested in having "arrogant" businesspeople from Silicon Valley parachuting in to tell them how to run their organizations.[46] As Hurst expected, there was a big gap between the business community and the social sector in the Bay Area. Through a measured start that included about twenty projects in year one, however, the Taproot Foundation began to build evidence that Hurst's idea worked. By screening and matching professionals to nonprofit service providers, it crosses a gap that turns out to be wider than one might expect and furnishes an important catalyst to increase the value of delivery systems.

Bridging Sectoral Divides

One example of the Taproot Foundation's impact in overcoming barriers can be seen in its work with a coalition of education nonprofits, led by the San Francisco School Volunteers, that builds support for public schools. San Francisco School Volunteers CEO Lisa Spinali leads an organization that places more than one thousand volunteers per week in schools—an impressive example of connecting community goodwill to the education system. Roughly 70 percent of adults in San Francisco do not have school-aged children, a dynamic that both affects volunteer service and reduces most residents' information about the schools to what's presented in the media. Spinali asked Hurst for help and Taproot responded by supplying a professional team from Wells Fargo to help design an education awareness campaign. The team started with polling and other research to gain critical insight into current public opinion, and used that insight to advise the coalition on effective messaging. The campaign began at the start

(Continued)

of the school year in 2009, with a focus on transparency in school performance. "The Wells Fargo team created an incredibly powerful product," Spinali says. "We would never have been able to achieve what we did without them."[47]

The process of matching volunteers with work that interests them has always been labor-intensive. Local affiliates of national organizations like United Way, Hands On America, and the American Red Cross help find the right matches. A few years ago, Jean Case, CEO of the Case Foundation and at the time chairman of the President's Council on Service and Civic Participation, suggested to the board of CNCS that Web 2.0 tools could expand service by dramatically reducing the difficulty of recruiting and placing volunteers. In 2009, demonstrating the predicted vitality of such platforms, a group of technology providers with encouragement from the White House produced All for Good—a powerful national portal that creates a deeper and more robust platform for matches. The additional volunteer service or individual philanthropy that the new platform enables has the potential to catalyze dramatic change inside delivery systems.

A terrific example can be seen in the work of Nina Zolt and her husband, Miles Gilburne. Their ePals and In2Books technologies connect millions of students across the globe and match reading mentors to grade-schoolers. As with many other entrepreneurs, personal experience and observation motivated Zolt and Gilburne's civic breakthrough.

In 1997, Zolt took a break from her law career to attend some art classes, where she noticed how much difficulty the younger students had with writing. Eventually, she became the class literacy coach. In visits to elementary schools, Zolt saw how much a personal library meant to the younger children. She also learned that surmountable barriers limited the number of willing adults who were matched to young learners. Many schools were ill-equipped to integrate "strangers" (outside volunteers) into the school day, despite evidence that doing so would achieve better results. Finally, Zolt sensed that many individuals wanted to help children but could not easily schedule the time.

These insights and Zolt's experience with digital media and learning products led to the creation of In2Books and ePals, which now connects more than 600,000 classrooms as teachers and students worldwide help one another. *The New York Times* has described ePals as "an unusual combination of a business and a social venture."[48] In2Books connects carefully screened adult pen pals who each year read five books with young students who read the same books and then exchange six letters through the ePals site. Teachers use the site to reinforce class discussions.[49]

The persistent and engaging practice of In2Books has driven four out of five participating students from low-income schools to achieve grade-level literacy. An evaluation concluded that at every grade level, students in In2Books classrooms scored significantly higher than students in comparison classrooms on the nationally normed SAT-9 Reading Assessment Test. This evaluation attributed the In2Books's success to "authentic, challenging work, the actualization of a learning community, and engagement."[50]

As an online platform connecting reading mentors directly with young learners, ePals provides one example of how technology can catalyze sweeping change in volunteerism. Two other examples illustrate the power of personal discovery and the potential of online matchmaking. After teaching in a public school, Charles Best was familiar with the generosity of public school teachers, who spend roughly $1 billion annually—almost $500 each—of their own money on supplies and equipment for their students.[51] He also knew that a lack of supplies and equipment prevents students from accessing both basic and cutting-edge lessons. Best thought he could create a much better market for microphilanthropy by connecting the classroom needs of teachers with people looking to donate money to meaningful causes via the Internet.[52] As of spring 2009, the platform he created, DonorsChoose, had benefited 1.4 million students by serving as the channel through which more than $24M was contributed to more than sixty thousand school projects. Partly because DonorsChoose utilizes volunteers to review all incoming requests from teachers before posting them online, 100 percent of a donor's contribution goes to the project.[53] DonorsChoose shows how a simple idea can fill crucial gaps in our existing service delivery systems.

Like Best, Keith Taylor wanted to give generous individuals a direct way to help families who need just a little help for unexpected expenses such as car repair or for rent after a layoff. Having relied on the generosity of friends and family as he made his way through college and graduate school, Taylor decided to tithe 10 percent of his income to help people in a bind. ModestNeeds, the site he developed to reach possible recipients, grew quickly and exponentially—among both people submitting requests and people who wanted to make donations.[54] By 2009 those donors had reached seven thousand individuals or families, with grants averaging more than $500. But, Taylor argues, it is about much more than the money. "The giving culture is just as important as the grants," he says.

Zolt, Best, Taylor—all three opened up a large supply of volunteers by building a much more efficient pipeline—and the volunteers in turn (when mixed into an existing service system) often provided just the right catalyst for success.

Bringing It All Together: The Nehemiah Foundation

One organization stood out among the hundreds that benefited from the federal government's Compassion Capital Fund, which we discuss at greater length in Chapter 3. Faced with economic distress and a staggering 100 percent divorce rate, the business, civic, and faith communities of Springfield, Ohio, came together in 1993 to start what they called a "spiritual venture capital fund"—the Nehemiah Foundation. Nehemiah quickly became a powerful force in Springfield and beyond, not as a provider but as a funder and convener focused on fixing serious social problems. Wally Martinson, the founding director of the foundation, explains that when faced with an issue that the community identifies, such as family instability, Nehemiah plays the role of "traffic cop . . . trying to get leaders around the table to say, 'How are we going to deal with this?' It doesn't make a difference from whom the ideas come. How are we going to do this together?"

Martinson calls the thirty local nonprofit organizations in his portfolio the "street saints." Most work directly with their neighborhood youth and families.

> "They're the best delivery system the government can have because they have relationships with these people," he says. "These ministers are going door to door every week in forty different neighborhoods in Springfield. . . . The beauty of the delivery system we have is that it works. . . . The school systems understand that, the courts understand that, the local government understands that, even at state government level they understand that. They know that programs don't work, relationships do."[55]

In Springfield, as in most communities, nonprofits often claim to collaborate, but most will not willingly change their core businesses to fit a community need. Instead, they work in isolation as they struggle to fulfill the demand for services and to ensure that bills are paid and payroll is met. Collaboration is also stymied by a perceived zero-sum environment in the nonprofit sector, where agencies believe that they must compete against one another for grants from foundations and public agencies. Instead of focusing on a shared mission or shared outcomes, nonprofit providers focus on sustaining their own organizations. In this environment, it is no surprise that incumbents view new organizations and programs as threats rather than as potential allies. Lack of collaboration also means duplication of services. In Springfield, Martinson points out that despite 120 food pantries, hunger persists. The consequences of duplication, obvious at a systemic level, might not be apparent to individual providers. Not only are the clients ill-served, but providers often wind up on the losing end, especially when donors become frustrated by inefficiencies and poor results.

Nehemiah's innovation was to address these problems head on. Martinson brought the street saints together in a new entity—the Ministry Leader Forum. The forum is built on two beliefs: that the street saints are closest to the problems in Springfield and know how best to solve them, and that Nehemiah needs to hold the street saints accountable. Martinson explains:

> "You can't just tell 120 food pantries to work together. You set a higher goal. We said, 'We are not going to fund you guys unless you work together, unless you come to these meetings. We're going to pray together once a month and we're going to meet together every other month and we're going to talk about our lives, we're going to build relationships with each other, we're going to figure out what we can do together that we cannot do by ourselves; we're not going to care who gets the credit.' Those were some painful years early on. People were about ready to walk on us. We said, 'Look, you walk, you're not getting your support check. You figure out what your end game is together, and it cannot be outputs, it has to be outcomes.'"[56]

Martinson and his street saints decided their goal was a mature, responsible Christian . . . whether somebody was doing a home for unwed moms or an after-school program for grade school kids or working with gang kids. They were all in it together in terms of producing mature, responsible citizens.

Martinson articulated an overarching goal and demanded that the agencies join together to achieve it or lose their funding in order to force attention away from organizations and toward individual and community transformation. This position allowed Nehemiah to implement new programs across the collaborative—as when, for example, it received $1.5 million in public funding for a fatherhood initiative.

As director of the Ohio Governor's Office of Faith-Based and Community Initiatives, Krista Sisterhen worked closely with Martinson. She calls Nehemiah "the best model I have seen of a faith-based intermediary working with government and other private funders to make life better in their community."[57]

Simply inserting an intermediary, which we explore in the next chapter as a means of reducing the administrative burdens faced by smaller, newer providers, is not civic realignment. Some intermediaries merely accommodate and incorporate the failures and successes of the participants. Others, like the Nehemiah Foundation, act as civic realigners that, through position and money, force changes in the system. Nehemiah shows us that innovation and change can foster results when the entrepreneur as civic realigner facilitates an overarching community agenda, applies a common outcome metric, and rationalizes resources by forcing consolidation, new outreach, or both. For example, Martinson says, "We've actually seen ministries combine buildings because they knew that their end game wasn't getting served by . . . having their own building with their own shingle out front."

Conclusions

Whether struggling or middle class, individuals live inside complex social networks of friends, family, neighbors, colleagues, and others. It is counterintuitive to assume that a single program or activity by itself will make all the difference. However, in this chapter we suggest an intentional discovery process that asks how a new intervention could substantially alter the results of that network. Badly needed social change can be accomplished by mixing something new into the current brew of existing providers that dramatically changes the approach, operation of a program, or interaction between existing players.

While I focus primarily on civic interveners who develop a new structure or technology or pipeline, there is another option for providing the missing catalytic ingredient in a local delivery system: The civic entrepreneur can import rather than invent the solution. Education reform expert Michael Fullan writes, "The main problem is not the absence of innovation in schools, but rather the presence of too many disconnected, episodic, fragmented, superficially adorned projects."[58] Indeed, when the Knight Foundation first funded our Harvard Executive Session discussions, we set out to bring together some of the country's most creative civic entrepreneurs. These attendees represented a dazzling array of interventions, yet often they had not heard of one another. They began to identify how components of one solution could add value to another. Innovation must, of course, remain dynamic, and it constantly benefits from access to new ideas—whether "invented here" or imported.

In this chapter we see that these new ideas, whether technical or human resource breakthroughs or different ways of integrating and arranging the missing pieces, can produce renewed progress and even transformative change.

Civic Actions: Chapter 2

A transformative innovation does not have to be a new tool or program model; it can be any catalyst that will dramatically improve performance across the system.

Discovering the Missing Catalyst

- *Civic Discovery:* Map and understand the institutional assets in the system.
- *System Discovery:* Explore the relationships between actors.
- *Personal Discovery:* Listen, closely observe, and experience.
- *Predictive Discovery:* Use data and decision-support systems.

Typologies

1. Civic Realigner
   - Develop a coherent rationale for new roles.
   - Capitalize on crisis or high-profile events to bring people to the table.
   - Leverage credibility to take on the status quo and create a culture of collaboration.
   - Force realignment through focus on proven models and metrics.
2. Technological Glue
   - Identify the inflection point for infusing technology as a catalyst for change.
   - Design a technology to unleash latent potential within the system; for example, optimize relationships between field workers and clients.
   - Work closely with users to integrate technology into daily routines.
   - Seek feedback to refine the technology as it is utilized.

3. Filling the Management Gap

- Become the management answer that turns around an existing organization.

- As incumbent provider, find management partners who will share resources, knowledge, and talent.

- As consultants, match skills with providers to help build capacity for transformative impact.

4. New Volunteer and Donor Good Will Pipeline

- Identify an unmet need and/or untapped goodwill.

- Unleash people's energy with activities they find meaningful and productive.

- Bridge barriers as matchmaker, navigator, and/or informational guide.

Part II

MARKET MAKER AS CIVIC ENTREPRENEUR

3

OPEN SOURCING
SOCIAL INNOVATION

"The key was to remove as many barriers to social
entrepreneurship as possible, and to provide some
of the enablers where they were absent: finance,
networks, support, and development, so that the
other invisible hand could do its work."

Geoff Mulgan

It startled me when I heard Michelle Rhee, the new chancellor of the D.C. Public Schools, declare her primary responsibility as educating the city's children and not running a school
system. For twenty years I had experienced a quite different
reality.

During my twelve years as prosecutor, I had watched with dismay the continuing deterioration of Indianapolis public schools and thus hoped for bold reforms as mayor. Early on I approached the head of the local teachers' union, who had endorsed me for mayor. Fresh from a terrific meeting with some of his members, who wanted more site control so that they would have more freedom to teach, I suggested to him that we should team up against the hapless school bureaucracy and give entrepreneurial teachers the right to band together to start charter schools. The thought of one set of teachers with a totally different set of work rules from the rest was anathema to him. Those dedicated union teachers had no chance against the independently elected school board and its bureaucracy without the help of their union, and thus Indy struggled on, year after disappointing year, chained to its top-down, rule-driven, one-size-fits-all model.

The contrast between D.C. and Indianapolis reminded me of a gentle rebuke I once received from the great economist Milton Friedman. We were in his home discussing government reform when I offered a comment about Indianapolis's public schools. Friedman, to emphasize the importance of open competition in the provision of public education, immediately corrected me by saying that I was describing not our "public schools" but, rather, our "government schools"—those run by the government. Government plays multiple roles in education and in other areas, adding a level of complexity to reform. It can be an operator, as is usually the case in K–12, or it can be a purchaser of services, as in charter schools, mental health, drug treatment, homelessness, and more.

Government also acts as standard setter in these areas. Achieving the right standards, without allowing the process to be exploited by groups that may benefit from high barriers to entry or adding undue costs, is a challenge. The tension between what government must do to guarantee health, safety, and performance and what government actually does—in terms of prescribing activities and limiting entrepreneurship—provides the backdrop to this chapter.

Open and competitive sourcing of service provision and innovation requires incentives from both the supply side and the demand side. By "demand" we refer to those funders who configure the market by essentially purchasing social services for others and who could give clients more choices by forcing providers to respond to real client interests. Promoting innovation through the demand side involves complex challenges, because no leader controls all the parts or sufficient resources. Thus creating space for breakthrough change requires a leader whose credentials and rhetoric inspire a community around an important social goal and then, through the right combination of persuasion and forcefulness, cause it to occur.

We look at five specific ways that government leaders—with the support of, over the objections of, professional associations, incumbents, and large-scale organizations—can provide social opportunity. Together, these approaches lead to a new path for disrupting existing provider and funder webs and more openly sourcing social good.

Breaking Down Protectionist Barriers

In social services, barriers to success come in all shapes and sizes. The most egregious of them are over-regulation and bias toward government and a tendency to maintain the status quo. By committing to a range of client options among providers, innovative public officials have the power to mitigate policymakers' and government funders' practice of protecting incumbent providers and their associations. This calcification generally arises not from nefarious political plots but from relationships that develop over time and then serve to bar new entrants.

In Indianapolis I saw how vested interests used every opportunity to turn licensing and credentialing processes into shields against competition, invariably claiming that repeal would endanger health and safety. I first walked into this battle when I proposed to remove the limit on the number of taxis in order to better serve neglected neighborhoods. The incumbent cartel fought back, claiming the new taxis would be unsafe. Credentialing tensions also surfaced when we fought with state regulators over which organizations could help neglected children, and whether the state could reimburse effective faith-based drug treatment groups that did not require master's degrees in social work. Building codes can limit options as well, which I observed when state codes requiring contiguous outdoor playground space obstructed my efforts to encourage more child care options downtown.

Government, of course, discharges an important role in ensuring the safety of children—whether on the premises of commercial or public enterprises. It should also articulate standards so that parents can determine whether a provider prepares children well for school. But how state and local governments carry out their regulatory functions has critical public policy consequences. As rules extend beyond safety and outcome standards and into prescriptive inputs such as teacher training, certification, curriculum, and class size, they become more likely to be used by entrenched interests to reduce competition. For example, as curriculum standardization and unaffordable child/teacher ratios are established in pre-K, the breadth and diversity of options is reduced.

Tightening the rules to limit competition also limits parental choice, which in turn reduces quality. As states expand funding in early childhood education, they remain aware that parents prefer choice. Surveys by the advocacy group Pre-K Now show that more than 80 percent of parents support choice over public school–only options.[1] Further, competition among different providers helps improve educational quality. With market pressure, both private and public schools appear to respond to the incentives of competition.[2] Social service advocates, pointing out that some clients, such as abusive parents, do not make good choices, often argue against choice for all parents. But not all consumers need to be equally savvy to create sufficient competitive pressure. Informed marginal shoppers can influence quality across a delivery system. Like marginal consumers, the most involved parents visit schools, ask questions, and evaluate performance criteria in order to choose a school for their children.[3] Their behavior has a positive effect across the entire delivery system as schools strive to respond.

Market competition also motivates providers to differentiate their products. The research on what works for young children continues to evolve, but we do know that different approaches work for different children. Yet public education's administrative and political structures tend to rely on a narrow set of standardized approaches to teaching techniques and curricula.

Such prescriptive rule setting brings unanticipated consequences. Some states require that preschool teachers have a four-year college degree on the assumption that this makes them better teachers. On its face, this rule makes sense, as do so many other barriers. Yet no private provider—whether church basement or large national for-profit organization—could afford to staff its centers exclusively with college graduates. And some question whether the requirement, even if affordable, produces true value. Pre-K expert Dr. Susan Landry of the University of Texas suggested, during a tour of her facility, that preschool teachers whose two-year degree programs are supplemented with structured hands-on training often perform better than teachers with a four-year degree (whom providers may employ after they've failed to get a job in an elementary school).

This regulatory process can be quite opaque to the public. States concurrently increase mandates and decrease subsidies, an intentional combination that tilts the competitive balance toward parents who can afford private choices or toward public schools that subsidize their offerings with tax dollars. For example, the Wisconsin legislature, dealing with related issues in K–12, was caught between the popularity of Milwaukee's voucher program and the hostility to choice from public school advocates. It chose to take indirect aim at parental choice by mandating additional costs for private providers while simultaneously reducing funding.[4]

Regulators approach their work with different motives. Some advocate the toughest possible standards regardless of cost. Others view their efforts as an indirect way of forcing children or clients into professionalized, unionized, or government-provided services. Others, interested in bringing innovation and performance into the delivery system, set threshold standards for safety and learning, encourage a diversity of providers, and publish performance results to ensure both quality and an informed consumer.

The points above regarding pre-K illustrate a set of critical principles. First, government should regulate health and safety. But it must explicitly determine whether the purported "safety" might be achieved in some less expensive manner that does not price lower-income clients out of the market. Second, government should proceed cautiously when moving from health and safety to regulate credentials, curricula, or specific approaches to instruction. I remain nonplussed by the fact that I can teach at Harvard but cannot teach government in the Indianapolis public schools. Career corporate scientists cannot teach physics, chemistry, or biology in many public schools. Further, government plays a critical role when it supports informed consumers by assembling, disaggregating, and plainly communicating the maximum amount of performance data possible to clients, legislators, program officers, and others.

The demand for social services of all types exceeds what either government or individuals can provide. Equity requires that we not drive up costs for those who can afford to pay at the expense of those who cannot.

Finally, one sure way to limit innovation and choice is to set up a process biased against it. Not even hard-core trade protectionists would advocate allowing GM to decide how many cars Honda can sell or letting a North Carolina textile manufacturer decide how many shirts China can ship to the United States. Yet this is exactly the process often used in educational services. Several years ago, Texas authorized pre-K funds to the Houston and Dallas Independent School Districts, allowing them to either set up pre-K classrooms or contract them out. Eighty percent of the dollars were spent internally. No Child Left Behind appropriated supplementary tutoring dollars for Title I children, allowing school districts to decide the rules and control whether these funds could go to outside providers. At first, few districts administered the funds in an open fashion because they could also use the dollars themselves.

We do not make a detailed argument here about what constitutes high-quality pre-K. Rather, we use the pre-K clash to illustrate the many subtle ways in which the social equivalent of trade barriers create rigidity, protect incumbents, and reduce opportunities for innovation. Innovation requires breaking down protectionist barriers to allow in new ideas from the outside. This open sourcing of ideas works best when the authorizing agency is not also in the business as a competitor.

Opening Space for Innovation

Invention requires imagination but also access to information and capital—financial and political. Networks themselves are another resource that can either inhibit or promote entrepreneurship. As Mark Casson and Marina Della Giusta point out, "Although the popular perception of entrepreneurship is very much that of an individualist . . . entrepreneurship is, in fact, socially embedded in network structures."[5] As we see with civic realignments like Communities in Schools and Blair Taylor's Neighborhoods@Work, network learning can in fact lead to discoveries that not only make a program better but also cause the network itself to perform at a much more effective level. Together these ingredients can create room for experimentation and risk, providing greater latitude for new approaches.

So how might community leaders open up space for breakthrough civic accomplishments? They can do so by promoting a culture of innovation, providing information and forcing transparency, sponsoring events that create opportunities for social discoveries, and offering protection for those whose efforts, whether successful or not, challenge the status quo.

In addition to these critical steps, public and private policy actors can catalyze innovation by strategically injecting new sources of funding. Such is the plan of President Obama and his Social Innovation Fund. Even after institutional, cultural, and legal barriers are removed, growth and impact require funding. What we might call catalytic capital helps fertilize new ideas that can in turn leverage other resources for better results. This catalytic capital can be private or public, from local or outside sources. Indianapolis has often benefited from the willingness of the Annie E. Casey Foundation to fund new approaches to urban poverty. My administration's neighborhood empowerment strategy of microfinance and community leadership training and my successor Bart Peterson's charter school efforts (discussed below) occurred because of Casey's willingness to take risks.

New York City's Center for Economic Opportunity (CEO) provides an exciting structure for public innovation capital. Housed in the Mayor's Office, CEO seeks out and funds innovative, performance-driven initiatives to help lift families and individuals out of poverty, with an emphasis on personal responsibility. The city deposits $125M a year into an innovation fund, and private foundations invest another $25M. Providers compete for funds through competitive bidding, and CEO combs through applications, looking for creative initiatives that hold promise for strong results and that propose leveraging other government and philanthropic efforts.

CEO funds each initiative as a demonstration—long enough to give the program an opportunity to succeed or fail. Rigorous external evaluations help the center decide which initiatives will continue in an expanded form and which will be scaled back or terminated.

Today, the CEO Innovation Fund supports more than forty initiatives, with particular focus on serving the working poor, young adults, and children. Deputy Mayor Linda Gibbs and Director Veronica White manage a twelve-member staff that continually looks for national and international models to emulate and to help guide their priorities. The programs they fund are diverse, ambitious, and pragmatic. They fill service gaps, meet the needs of underserved populations, and improve education, skills, and job opportunities for low-income New Yorkers.

The government's record in the United Kingdom demonstrates how catalytic public capital, as part of a deliberate strategy that also includes policy, leadership, and advocacy, can open delivery systems to entrepreneurs and innovators.

In the late 1990s, the government launched two of its earliest social investment funds, and in 2000 it established a Social Investment Taskforce to develop recommendations for improving social finance. In 2002, it introduced a Community Investment Tax Credit and two more social investment funds to test venture capital–style financing in small businesses and community enterprises. From 2002 to 2005, the government improved tax incentives for investment and philanthropic donations, creating a legal structure for social enterprise and encouraging traditional banks to work with communities in need. It also sought to encourage volunteerism and increased philanthropic giving among UK citizens.

The UK government continues to support a social investment "marketplace" in order to improve access to capital to support innovative solutions to public challenges. Its own social

Leveling the Playing Field in the UK

Tony Blair ushered in a new era for social enterprise in the UK. Blair embraced a robust third sector that would provide more innovative and effective public services. He specifically increased support for businesses led by social entrepreneurs with primarily social objectives, seeing them as chief drivers in creating a more community-focused public sector.[6] At the same time, Charles Leadbeater published his book *The Rise of the Social Entrepreneur*; leading entrepreneur Michael Young founded the first School for Social Entrepreneurs; and Geoff Mulgan, now heading the Michael Young Foundation, joined the Blair government as a chief adviser on social policy.

By the end of 2005, the UK's third sector had become critically important in the government's public service delivery strategy. As the government worked to open space, innovative providers responded. Public service in the UK evolved as earned income—largely from government—increased from under 25 percent to over 50 percent of total third-sector revenues from 2001 to 2006.[7] These providers have grown from small, scattered grant recipients into significant partners with the government who have a greater role in policy decisions.

The UK experience demonstrates how catalytic capital investments and policy changes can create the space for innovation for third-sector organizations—and distinctly social enterprises.

Of course, this deepening relationship between the sectors was not without tensions—some of which continue today. One challenge has been ensuring that multiple voices from the sector, not just those of the national advocacy groups, are represented in negotiations and policy decisions with government. Additional concerns include whether the third sector's growing dependence on public dollars will impede its ability to voice concerns and whether eventually it will possess the capacity to handle an increasing number of contracts for public services.

The UK government eventually created an Office of the Third Sector (OTS) in 2006, with a mandate to "support the environment for a thriving third sector (voluntary and community groups, social enterprises, charities, cooperatives and mutuals), enabling the sector to campaign for change, deliver public services, promote social enterprise, and strengthen communities."[8] The OTS is led by the Cabinet Minister, who works closely with central and local governments and with representatives from the sector. Third-sector and government policy leaders now participate in discussions on such issues as charity laws, regulations, and funding; community action; volunteering; and reducing barriers to involvement. OTS also supports and leads research efforts on critical issues in the field.

About the UK's support of social enterprise, Mulgan has written that he advised Blair not to go with a "grand plan" or to pump too much into the field too soon, but, rather, to take an evolutionary approach: "The key, instead, was to remove as many barriers to social entrepreneurship as possible, and to provide some of the enablers where they were absent: finance, networks, support, and development so that the other invisible hand could do its work."[9]

investment portfolio includes grants, loans, equity, and other emerging investments made available to large and small social enterprises. Recently, the UK has launched new social investment funds specific to health care and community building which provide risk capital for new ventures. Its social investment strategy reflects two important lessons from a decade of efforts: government funds should act as a catalyst and not replace or "crowd out" capital from other sources; and government should support organizational capacity building by combining funding with assistance.[10]

Currently, the OTS is working with private-sector partners to develop a social investment bank, a social stock exchange for social enterprises, and a new center focused on defining standards for social returns on investment. These efforts raise important definitional issues, because a broad array of for-profit organizations provide some social value. It will be interesting to see how politicized the definitional process becomes.

One other UK innovation deserves attention. The Department of Health established two funds to stimulate front-line staff members to develop and launch their own social enterprises and to create a culture for innovation. The first two years brought only mixed success, because front-line workers didn't understand how to create social enterprise opportunities from the fund. Future efforts should improve as the funds are paired with strategic advisory services from two leading foundations that advocate for social innovation and innovation in public services. These funds can also facilitate the use of 2.0 tools to connect volunteers, neighbors, and collaborative organizations in the production of social services.

Applying open sourcing concepts to front-line workers can generate significant contributions. In Indianapolis, after we gave union employees consulting assistance and the funds and time to be creative, they produced significant reforms, sometimes in government, sometimes with outside partners, and occasionally by proposing a "leveraged buyout" of their own public enterprise.

The UK experience demonstrates "the total package" of government tools—leadership, advocacy, regulation, tax policies, and financing—and serves as a model not only for the U.S. government but for local and state officials as well. As our government at all levels begins to embrace social innovation and determine strategies on how best to encourage innovative cross-sector solutions, the UK story underscores government's potentially powerful role as a catalyst, partner, and collaborator with civic entrepreneurs.

Wherever we find bold social change efforts, we find a strong actor willing to carve out the financial or political space for innovation inside a highly bureaucratic and often calcified system. Mayor Michael Bloomberg and Prime Minister Tony Blair both played this role. Louisiana Lt. Governor Mitch Landrieu has set up an Office of Social Entrepreneurship under the direction of Executive Session member Brooke Smith. And Virginia's Phoenix Project has relied on support from Governors Mark Warner and Tim Kaine to train and inspire social entrepreneurs across the commonwealth. An official whose support transcends vested groups is often the only force able to disrupt the political economy that protects entrenched interests. The democratic mandate derived from a popular election is one obvious source of the requisite authority and support to implement the steps outlined below.

Leveling the Playing Field

The faith community provides a huge source of civic commitment, innovation, and energy in social services. Religious congregations can transform lives and communities. While, of course, faith-based providers vary in quality, they can dream up, organize, and implement programs in ways that government cannot. Yet how government solicits and regulates partners can provide either substantial incentives or insurmountable barriers for faith providers. I have seen private donors and government alike help drive social progress by nurturing, rather than restricting, faith interventions. Yet, historically, foundations, corporate philanthropists, and government turn away from faith groups, especially smaller community-based ones.

In Indianapolis, our effort, dubbed The Front Porch Alliance, unleashed innovative vitality in hard-pressed neighborhoods through almost five hundred faith-city partnerships. These civic innovators did not scale in the organizational sense, but they did grow in terms of aggregate impact. We used funding, authority, convening power, and the bully pulpit to support their efforts to improve communities. The Front Porch Alliance staff literally went door to door asking faith leaders what they needed to expand their social service and redevelopment efforts.

We pressured city government agencies to stop ignoring faith-based organizations (FBOs) and to consider them viable partners. As a result, city land use and code enforcement officials removed barriers to the conveyance to FBOs of contiguous vacant property that could become playgrounds or rehabilitated homes. We also used the bully pulpit to encourage foundations, businesses, and individuals to take FBOs seriously and support them financially.

These successes helped frame the White House Office of Faith-Based and Community Initiatives. John DiIulio brought his unique combination of academic and community organizing skills to the office as its first director. His report, *Unlevel Playing Field*, found that, although FBOs provided significant social services, they received a disproportionately small percentage of applicable government dollars. It also highlighted the need for more outcome-based funding and deplored the entrenchment of status quo providers.[11] Barriers experienced by grassroots efforts, both religious and secular, included limited access to information, burdensome regulations and requirements, complex application processes, and bias toward incumbent providers.[12]

President George W. Bush ordered the federal government to "update policies to guarantee a level playing field for faith-based organizations and set clear, constitutional standards for government partnership with them."[13] The changes mandated that agencies not discriminate "for or against" organizations on the basis of religious affiliation or require FBOs to "forfeit or change their religious name, mission, or governance." Still, when a community- or faith-based organization approaches government it may use the word "partner," but almost always these relationships contain enough characteristics of a "principal and agent" that they can threaten the integrity of the nongovernmental players.

I raise these issues because by organizing, personalizing, or augmenting the other fragmented services available in a community, combining them with the right message of hope, FBOs can transform a neighborhood or a family. Therefore, open sourcing to these local providers will encourage thousands of such organizations to add even more value.

Yet simplifying the administrative burdens identified in *Unlevel Playing Field* can extend only so far in the face of federal procurement rules. Compliance costs and the complexity associated with even small grants preclude participation by many social inventers. However, with the help of an intermediary to reduce administrative burdens, these small entities may be able to effectively blend government money with other sources.

Ohio received the first federal Compassion Capital Fund (CCF) grant of $750,000, directed at building the capacity of faith- and community-based providers to compete for federal and other large grants. CCF relied on intermediaries to help FBOs develop their capacity by distributing mini-grants from $5,000 to $75,000 and providing one-on-one technical assistance and training sessions.[14] CCF helped small organizations increase their reach,[15] but more incrementally than transformatively.

Social innovation expert Geoff Mulgan's description of the UK efforts, in which he was central, closely match our faith-based efforts: Provide little new money and instead focus on identifying and removing barriers to existing funding streams; build capacity of the new providers; and force change in regular procurement mechanisms. One thing that the faith-based effort lacked was attention to supporting innovation. In the UK efforts, Mulgan writes, "There has also been a strong emphasis on innovation—the use of zones, pilots, public venture funds . . . and the encouragement of constructive rule breaking like the clause in the Education Act which allows head teachers to ignore national rules if they think they can do better."[16]

Mulgan and DiIulio both knew that a closed delivery system reduces an inventive entrepreneur's chances of introducing an idea that truly makes a difference. Rigorously removing barriers—as we did in Indianapolis and as was done by the White House Office of Faith-Based and Community Initiatives—helps level the playing field for innovation. Such efforts need not be partisan. The Obama administration both created a social innovation fund and retained the faith office, pledging to use it to make an impact on policy issues including poverty, family stability, and "interreligious dialogue and cooperation."[17]

Inviting the Exceptional

Successful open sourcing starts with the passive step of opening the door to new ideas but eventually requires active solicitation. As Mulgan says, for the purposes of social entrepreneurship, the best governments are not only open and accessible, but also "engage with civil society" and actively support civic participation.[18]

"Positive deviance" provides one important example of how one might go about such a solicitation. The positive deviance process looks for success stories that stand out—what Jerry and Monique Sternin of Tufts University call "positive deviants, whose uncommon but successful behaviors or strategies enable them to find better solutions to a problem than their peers."[19] This fascinating approach to social innovation grew out of nutrition and public health initiatives at Tufts University. After identifying the exceptional behaviors of the positive outliers, the civic entrepreneur attempts to mobilize the community to adopt the behaviors more broadly.

Because the solutions come from within the community, they tend to be feasible, culturally appropriate, and affordable. They also tend to bring quick results. The benefits of positive deviance appear to be ongoing and widening. The Tufts team has found that communities that have engaged in the process will, for example, mobilize to solve other problems or to demand better social services from the government.[20] The positive deviance approach appears to be working in places with severe social problems, such as the poorest neighborhoods of Worcester, Massachusetts. There, the University Park Campus School has reduced the dropout rate to almost zero, and nearly every student continues to post-secondary education. Although it partners with nearby Clark University, the school succeeds without additional financial resources. University Park, which credits its success to "an exceptional school culture and academic program that refuses to let any student fail to achieve high standards," is now sharing its model across the country.[21]

When facing a social system that does not welcome innovation, a public leader can create an alternative delivery system and invite in outside innovators. Former Indianapolis Mayor Bart Peterson, faced with a deteriorating school system, both lobbied for the right to issue school charters himself and invited in proven school innovators.

Peterson was determined to force improvement in the long-languishing Indianapolis Public Schools (IPS). In 2005, 83 percent of the system's 39,000 students qualified for the federal free or reduced price lunch program.[22] IPS had a four-year graduation rate of 30.5 percent, ranking forty-ninth of the fifty largest school districts in the United States.[23] Peterson, a Democrat, laid the groundwork for an idea first introduced by the Republican state senator and long-time charter school advocate Teresa Lubbers. The threshold innovation was a pioneering form of charter authorization, with the mayor playing the central role. The charter schools would be tuition-free and open to all children, and would receive per pupil funding from the State Department of Education. Critically, charters would be granted not by the school district but by the mayor, on whose shoulders responsibility for their success squarely sat.

With this new authority granted by the state legislature, Peterson created an Office for Charter Schools in the Mayor's Office and instituted an application process and an accountability framework to create a system of high-quality new public schools. These schools have shown impressive growth and promising signs in raising student achievement. Sixteen charter schools opened in 2006–2007, serving 3,855 students, with more than a thousand students on a waiting list.[24] By the end of that first school year, 82 percent of parents expressed satisfaction with their children's charter schools.

The public transparency and data enabled Peterson to show skeptics that charter schools were getting better outcomes than traditional district schools. In fact, the evidence on academic performance and parent and staff feedback accumulated from reports, reviews, and expert site visits, coupled with annual public reports, provided important support when the mayor needed to revoke the charter he had issued to a popular but underperforming school.

Peterson followed with a second innovation equally important to understanding how entrepreneurial communities are created. The mayor expressed concern about both the pipeline of high-quality charter school operators and the lack of attention from national civic entrepreneurs who would assist IPS. The shortage of robust human capital for leadership in educational reform posed a real risk, threatening to impede progress by dampening policymakers' enthusiasm for educational entrepreneurship.[25]

To address the city's need for more education entrepreneurs, Peterson asked his education and policy adviser David Harris to help him recruit to Indianapolis national education programs with track records of extraordinary results in other cities.[26] They started The Mind Trust, a nonprofit incubator and venture fund. Peterson serves on the board as chair alongside the superintendent of IPS and the senior leaders of local universities, businesses, and prominent community groups. Since its inception, The Mind Trust's venture fund has helped channel nearly $2.9M to recruiting three exceptional organizations to work in Indianapolis: Teach For America, The New Teacher Project, and College Summit. The organization also funds fellowships for those interested in a career in charter school management and leadership.[27]

The Peterson experience also illustrates how open sourcing can catalyze better support networks than traditional closed,

hierarchical models. With city sponsorship and buy-in, charter schools were able to access other public resources and assistance.[28] For example, the mayor helped schools acquire facilities
financing through the city's Bond Bank and pieced together
support services from the Indianapolis Housing Agency and
its Health and Hospital Corporation. The effort also attracted
support from national sources, such as the Bill and Melinda
Gates Foundation, the U.S. Department of Education, the
Annie E. Casey Foundation, and the Local Initiatives Support
Corporation.

Forcing Cultural Change

A strong public official can also try to force a change in culture
in order to open room for innovation. This top-down process
involves identifying the agencies and departments that fund
social services; using authority or other tools necessary to ensure
that all corners of the organization embrace innovation; requiring cooperation or partnership with new providers; and reforming the procurement and payment processes that threaten new
players.

Krista Sisterhen, the first director of the Ohio Governor's
Office for Faith-Based and Community Initiatives,[29] incorpo-
rated her deep understanding of the tension between government and faith providers to deftly force cooperation and bring
social innovation to urban Ohio. Sisterhen, who helped me set
up The Front Porch Alliance in Indianapolis, facilitated competition, performance-based contracting, and new cross-sector collaborations in the city's social service delivery networks.

In Ohio, Sisterhen says, she took a "very pragmatic" approach
to the faith initiative: "We have these tremendous needs, and
we're looking for ways to address them."[30] She viewed her charge
as simplifying "doing business with government" for smaller providers; encouraging, supporting, and inspiring partnerships among
public agencies and faith- and community-based providers;[31] and

developing the capacity of FBOs to measure and report on their work. This last goal, Sisterhen insisted, would both improve the performance of the FBOs and demonstrate which direct service grants actually improved outcomes.

Supported by the Governor's Office, Sisterhen took important early steps to level the playing field. She identified the stumbling blocks preventing FBOs from competing for government funding, including burdensome administrative processes for applying for grants and a bias toward larger providers. Because grants and contracts tend to exclude smaller providers, Sisterhen's office distributed much of its funding through intermediary organizations that carried the administrative burdens "so that smaller subgrantees could just do the work."[32]

Sisterhen understood that internal change would be critical across the board and that it would not come easily. "We're not a grantor," she notes. "We're a facilitator."[33] This was clear from the start, because Sisterhen had an annual budget of slightly more than $300,000—just enough for administration and staff. But she knew from her time in Indianapolis that her role in forcing change across the system would have more impact than distributing any new dollars allotted for faith-based or community providers. "The larger challenge is busting through the idea that we're doing the best we can," she says. "I don't think we are. There are new opportunities. And I see that as the mission of this office: to create an opportunity for new partnerships and a new way of doing business that might have a better effect."[34] Sisterhen often asked herself and her staff, "How do we incentivize delivery networks to come together?"

Sisterhen's efforts extended to changing the practices of other state cabinet agencies as well. She understood that because most of Ohio's safety-net dollars go to the counties, county executives needed to endorse the FBO partnerships. Sisterhen used persuasion and a small amount of discretionary funding to help convince county officials of the value of procuring social services on the basis of performance.[35]

Wally Martinson, who leads the successful Ohio intermediary the Nehemiah Foundation, urged Sisterhen to push decision making down to the local level and to "not hold back on putting people's feet to the fire as far as producing outcomes." Martinson said, "Don't hamstring us with reporting and don't instruct us on what to do in Springfield from Columbus. We know what to do. Give people the benefit of the doubt that there are some social entrepreneurs in each of these cities."[36]

Local leadership counts especially when someone needs to call the community together around broad civic goals. DiIulio confirms, "You really can't affect those partnerships, given the intergovernmental character of the way in which virtually all grants and contracts are administered, unless you have active partnership from the mayor's office. So we did get a hundred or so mayors in 2001 to sign on to creating their own equivalents of the Office of Faith-Based and Community Initiatives."[37]

Interestingly, Sisterhen went one step further—connecting directly to citizens. Ohio introduced a voucher mechanism for mentoring older youths aged sixteen to twenty-one, mainly in order to open up space for social innovation by FBOs as well as others. "We picked the field of mentoring because there isn't an organized lobby to go fight with," she says.[38] The mentoring program aimed to reduce out-of-wedlock pregnancies among girls, many of whom were "leaving juvenile detention facilities or foster care, and lack resources or traditional social supports."[39] This model gave girls the freedom to pick a provider, including an overtly religious provider—for which public dollars would otherwise be unconstitutional.

Another of Sisterhen's many innovations was the creative use of public dollars to drive change. Sisterhen persuaded the governor to set aside 1 percent—about $11M—of Ohio's TANF block grant for an area in which she and some experts thought long-term, important gains could be produced: "programs that help to rebuild families such as reducing out-of-wedlock birth rates and encouraging marriage." She not only moved money from treating symptoms to addressing the cause, but she did it in a way that allowed new organizations to participate.

The lessons from Ohio are especially important when a public official needs to call together a wide array of resources, most likely organized in narrow verticals, around a brighter or new civic aspiration. We knew when the White House set up the faith office that it would produce little real change unless it had a change partner in all the relevant agencies. The president thus directed cabinet agencies to establish their own offices to ensure that they would no longer "discriminate against faith-based organizations based on their religious characters" and would establish new outcome-oriented standards.[40] The White House charged each agency with revising its grant application processes, including retraining staff and informing FBOs of their rights and responsibilities as grantees. Results varied, but at the Department of Health and Human Services, for example, the value of competitive grants won by faith-based organizations increased from $477M in 2002 to $818M in 2007. Under Welfare-to-Work grants in particular, faith-based organizations increased from 2 percent to 11 percent of total funded providers.[41] Ohio's use of TANF funds mirrored this success in improving access for new faith providers. The Ohio example presents important lessons on how to open innovative space for new organizations, whether they are faith-based or not.

At the community level, tight cadres of social service providers exist outside the government bureaucracy, yet many are funded directly with city dollars. Procurement processes act as another fearsome institutional barrier to entrepreneurial city officials who are looking to engage innovative and high-performing organizations. We invited a couple of the country's best procurement officials to participate in our Harvard Executive Session discussions and suggest ways to restructure contracting to make room for civic innovation.

David Gragan, chief procurement officer for Washington, D.C., says that the public procurement process is designed to be as much a controlling as a facilitating process.

"The centralized control that governments exercise over expenditures is meant to ensure the public 'gets what it paid for.' These central financial controls in government embrace and support the concepts of public trust, deliberation, full and open competition, and the primacy of process. Focusing on process at the expense of results is shortsighted . . . . If we could really write a prescriptive contract or grant, we would—in essence—have already solved the problem we are seeking help in solving. If we want to solve intransigent problems at the fully operational level, not simply proof-of-concept or pilot programs, we must recognize that inventive programs thrive in the nonprofit sector and that our most viable solutions will likely come from that entrepreneurial arena."[42]

Government procurement represents the ultimate in rule-driven, prescriptive processes. The procurement function itself has been created to ensure that all bids respond to the same detailed set of specifications, thus preventing the abuse of discretion. Procurement complexity and administrative requirements stipulated in government requests for proposals also discriminate against small or all-volunteer providers and favor larger organizations. Imaginative officials try to mitigate these barriers to innovation by reducing start-up investment costs for small-scale providers, asking for results instead of activities, and eliminating slow pay, high bonds, and severe risk shifting in the procurement process.[43]

Another procurement officer, Jason Whetsell of the federal Office of Personnel Management, offered an excellent explanation of the value of intermediaries, acknowledging that government often represents "unenlightened buyers" who cannot understand how to price risk in complex social service areas. He suggests that government could procure with the advice of a third-party intermediary like New Profit, with its expertise in evaluating risk and reward, whose involvement would reassure the mayor about the quality of the choice.[44]

These structural and cultural shifts, plus openness to new ideas, must include not only procurement, of course, but also the operating and human resource agencies of government. We now return to Chancellor Rhee in Washington, D.C.

Structurally Creating White Space

We need to find a way to clear space for innovation that seems less personal to the incumbents. Public officials might consider adapting a reform from other areas of government. Sunset legislation creates an institutional mechanism for redesigning or ending programs and agencies. Sunset clauses—now found in half the states—establish an automatic review of results, no matter how close the relationship has become between provider and funder. The Texas legislature's Sunset Commission has since 1978 abolished more than fifty agencies and consolidated another dozen, saving the state roughly $800M. Such a process applied to social service agencies and all their third-party contractors would reduce the political capital needed to take on a specific nonprofit by subjecting all the contracts and relationships to regular review.[45]

Bringing It All Together:
The Enlightened Monopolist

In early 2009, I moderated a conversation at New Profit's annual conference between D.C. School Chancellor Michelle Rhee and Mayor Adrian Fenty. Chancellor Rhee articulated her mission as providing quality education—by whatever delivery mechanism works. She started with a straightforward principle that drives innovation and quality: "I would *never*, as long as I am in this role, do anything to limit another parent's ability to make a choice for his or her child. Ever."[46]

Remarkably, the civic entrepreneurs Rhee partners with do not just run charters but participate in all her internal reform efforts as well. Rhee and Fenty show that open sourcing education can bring meaningful change and options for parents that closed systems will find hard to equal.

Fenty had pledged during his mayoral campaign to take control of the schools. He interpreted his sweeping victory as a demand that he "take ownership of education." "We had in Washington, D.C.," Fenty recalls, "career superintendent after career superintendent . . . . We did not need to hire another career superintendent who was an expert in the bureaucracy. We needed someone who was an expert in how to teach kids and who would find any bureaucratic reason why you couldn't teach kids to be something that needed to be rolled over."[47] Both he and Rhee knew that when government dominates a service area, bold leadership, both elected and appointed, is needed to create room for social innovation. In football terms, Fenty provided the blocking, and Rhee found the room to run for change.

In Fenty, Rhee found the type of leader she had always hoped for—someone who shared her vision, believed in bottom-line results, and apparently had no fear of making tough decisions. She also found someone who pledged to support her no matter how hard things got. Rhee recalls that in their first meeting, Fenty said, "As I walked door to door across this city, the one thing that every citizen was in agreement on was that we had to change the schools. So he said, I don't care about the political noise. I don't care about the opposition. As long as you're operating in a way that you think is going to make the schools better, I'll give you whatever you need."[48] Taking the reins at the D.C. Public Schools, Rhee found comfort in what she describes as a "brilliant new school governance structure," in which "the ability to act quickly, both on the policy and the implementation front, is unprecedented."[49] In this structure, Rhee reports directly to the mayor instead of to a school board.

As I wrote at the start of this chapter, Rhee views the District's 78,000 students—not its buildings or bureaucracy—as her clients and her cause. She therefore risks controversy and confrontation daily to bring in all possible resources. To meet her goals, Rhee is aggressively removing barriers that impede deep and meaningful reform, actively engaging charter options, and recruiting civic entrepreneurs—such as The New Teacher Project (TNTP), Teach For America (TFA), New Leaders for New Schools, and City Year—as partners in her work.

To fully understand why and how Rhee has opened her doors so widely to these entrepreneurial providers, we have to travel back more than a decade to her roots as a civic entrepreneur. In 1997, after serving as a TFA corps member, Rhee launched an organization dedicated to bringing more quality teachers into the public schools through alternative routes. She believed in TFA's mission and saw the need for more organizations doing similar work, but she also wanted the organizations to emerge in a different way. As Rhee recalls, "When I started The New Teacher Project, Teach For America was still very much a lightning rod." She wanted to avoid similar opposition for at least the first few years of TNTP. "We did things purposefully so that every program that we created had the identity of the city— Teach Baton Rouge or the New York City Teaching Fellows," she recalls. "Each was very much seen as an initiative of the district," rather than as a national organization sweeping in and telling the locals what to do.[50]

In her work at TNTP, Rhee and her colleagues learned how hard it can be to break into school bureaucracies. They learned to develop what she calls "nonnegotiables," a tool she now employs in her work as superintendent. As TNTP expanded into new cities, Rhee would insist on a set of nonnegotiables and a champion from the high ranks of the school district. The champion, whether superintendent, mayor, or school board president, "had to want us there, be willing to expend political capital to get us there, protect us once we were in, and assign a key point person tasked with making sure we got what we needed."[51] TNTP faced opposition in pursuing this strategy, although Rhee notes that it came far less from teachers unions than from the human resource directors inside the school systems' central bureaucracies.

With these experiences under her belt, Rhee recognized that as chancellor she had to bring in better talent and improve the skills of those who taught, led, and worked in the district schools. "My major focus coming in was human capital at all levels," she says, "at the central office, the principals, the teachers." To make room for social invention, Rhee needed to move aside recalcitrant central office staff. She had to make sure her human resource team would welcome new hires from outside groups like TNTP, TFA, and New Leaders. "Smart HR directors conclude, 'I'm going to bring these people in, and then everything they do is going to be my win,'" Rhee says. "The best ones set it up like that. But the not-so-savvy ones set it up as a competition, which always ends up as a disaster."[52]

Above all, Rhee wanted a senior-level team that shared her vision and had the talent, skills, and drive to help fulfill her mission. She knew that by shaking things up centrally, she could begin to spark a much-needed culture change throughout the system. She says, "I essentially sent a clear message to people that this is the new culture—knowing that cultures don't change overnight. So you're either on board, or you're not."[53] What happened to those who weren't on board? Rhee took action to fire them and promptly walked into a political firestorm. A tough battle ensued to get legislation passed making the staff at the school district's central level at-will employees. Rhee remembers the struggle and the key role Fenty played in helping her win this early fight. "I started doing what I think any CEO in a transformation situation does," she says. "I started to fire people. My general counsel at the time came running into my office and he said, 'Chancellor, you have got to stop firing people.' I said, 'Why? If people are not good, then we move them out and we bring better people in.' And he said, 'Welcome to D.C. public schools, where we never fire anyone.'"

Rhee could not succeed without her own team and the authority to hire and fire. She vividly remembers the mayor's response: "If we don't like the rules of the game, then we change the rules. We will introduce legislation to make all the central office employees at-will employees."[54] This relationship between the mayor and the chancellor provides an invaluable lesson for communities that want social change. The executive leading reform and the top politician need to be closely aligned—and prepared to expend political capital.

Rhee also took immediate action on hiring and firing principals. For this she did not need a change in the law, but she did need some serious political will. Rhee used her executive power to freeze the hiring of all principals as soon as she arrived in June. This move stopped preparation for the coming September dead in its tracks and allowed her to hire interim-only principals. It also gave her a full year in which to bring in New Leaders for New Schools to help find and train recruits.

Rhee invited national civic entrepreneurs into the D.C. public school system. Her changes in principal recruitment and hiring provide powerful lessons about breaking down barriers and operating in new ways. Rhee knew and believed in the work of New Leaders for New Schools. She saw in that organization an opportunity to find talented recruits, and she trusted the caliber of training that New Leaders would provide. Because New Leaders and Rhee are like-minded in their philosophy and approach, it was likely that these recruits would share her view of the role and responsibilities of a school principal. Once she had built this partnership, she says, "a very significant percentage of our new principal candidates came through New Leaders. I'm good to have them do it—it's their core competency. Why would I ever want to touch that?"[55]

With the help of New Leaders and her senior team at central headquarters, Rhee began to reshape the principal corps. In less than two years, she replaced more than 30 percent of the District's principals. After the first year, reading and math test scores increased by about 10 percent across the board at the elementary and secondary levels, and the achievement gap between students of color and their white peers narrowed by

11 percent. Rhee credits her principal strategy and the shift in culture and focus it brought.[56] But she had also taken steps to improve the overall quality of the teaching force. For this, Rhee turned for help to Teach For America and The New Teacher Project, which together supplied half of D.C.'s new teachers. About these two organizations, Rhee says, "We know that they're bringing quality projects. Almost without fail, when I go into a class with a TFA teacher, it's incredibly exciting and energetic, and the kids are engaged. That makes a difference."

The TNTP/D.C. schools teamwork illustrates how deep such partnerships can go. It's not just about bringing in good teachers. According to Deputy Chancellor Kaya Henderson, who joined Rhee's leadership team after working for both TFA and TNTP, these organizations provide support, training, and certification. TNTP helped the District radically overhaul its teacher recruitment and hiring processes, and the D.C. schools have hired a handful of former TNTP employees to run their teacher recruitment. Changes included reorganizing the human resources department, instituting major hiring reforms to broaden choice in teacher staffing for both principals and teachers, moving up the hiring time line so that the district could secure higher-quality candidates, and instituting major technology and data management improvements.

In addition, beginning a few years ago, TNTP helped meet a district demand for more data-based evidence for changing teacher policies, pushed the envelope on teacher-quality reforms, and instituted collaborative discussions among the D.C., NYC, Chicago, and Denver school systems.[57] Rhee's ambitious proposals in teacher contract negotiations in 2009 were also a direct result of TNTP's policy work and collaboration. In these and other endeavors, notes Rhee, "They have a perspective that nobody else does on these union questions. And their connections on the Hill and beyond make them invaluable."[58]

Rhee has also cultivated other civic entrepreneurial organizations, including City Year, to make substantial contributions inside the schools. Having consolidated twenty-three schools that were among the lowest performing in the District, Rhee was concerned about how DCPS would turn them around. She asked City Year whether it could help. The organization proposed to put a "critical mass" of ten corps members in each of the four lowest performing of the consolidated schools to help to shift the culture at the school. "It's been an unbelievable partnership,"[59] Rhee says. Now DCPS and City Year are piloting a host of new initiatives in those four schools to increase school capacity.

Rhee's open approach to innovation allows an infusion of enthusiasm and invention, but it is not without controversy. A heavy reliance on organizations like TNTP, TFA, and New Leaders has drawn criticism from people who see the talent and nature of these organizations as elite and not of the community— with the possible exception of TNTP's Teaching Fellows program, which endeavors to cultivate a home-grown presence and talent base. In addition, many of those recruited by the three partner organizations have little previous teaching or school leadership experience. Even with excellent training and organizational support, these recruits—particularly the principals—may be unable to meet the challenges of working in some of the nation's toughest schools.

I present this process not necessarily as the recipe for education reform but as a remarkable road map drawn by a government official committed to change and innovation by removing barriers and incorporating outside innovators in remarkably comprehensive ways. Listening to the mayor leaves little doubt that he and Rhee are confident they will reduce dropout rates and improve graduation rates, school attendance, and test scores.[60]

Soon after this Rhee-Fenty panel, I had dinner with a well-known mayor who claimed to have a 75 percent approval rating—but whose city is known for its poor schools. I was tempted to suggest that he should invest some of his popular approval in helping someone like Rhee create transformative change in his schools.

Conclusions

In *Good Capitalism, Bad Capitalism*, Robert Litan, Carl Schramm, and William Baumol suggest three conditions necessary to generate the most innovative private sector entrepreneurship: ease of starting and growing an organization, the presence of motivational "rewards" (or the flow of resources toward entrepreneurial activities), and "disincentives for unproductive activity." They believe in institutionalizing innovation, because today's small start-ups are tomorrow's corporate giants, and today's established firms were yesterday's entrepreneurs and innovators. They suggest that constant competition—protected by antitrust or anti-monopoly rules and by opening the borders, so to speak—is key. In social services, government too often fills the role of monopolist, rather than anti-monopolist. Social and educational programs, dominated by government rules and funding, impede the above conditions.

Social service clients rarely have the choices that the free market provides. Incumbent providers, funders, and decision makers often subvert competition and choice by placing a regulatory and contractual thicket in the way of new providers. These iron triangles must be broken to allow social progress. New York City's CEO, Indianapolis's The Mind Trust, the UK's Office of the Third Sector, and the other efforts described in this chapter seek to represent clients who have no choice and little voice. They help the system overcome these barriers to innovation by inviting and supporting civic entrepreneurs to seek funding for better solutions.

We will see in the next chapter how private and government funders acquire or procure social services matters. Truly competitive, results-driven procurement can create a marketplace for innovation. Ironically, perhaps, Mayor Peterson's greatest accomplishment was closing a community-supported but ineffective charter school. Government must be pushed to allow more open competition—even if it results in failure—as long as poorly performing entities can be closed and their funds repurposed.

Civic Actions: Chapter 3

Start with opening a system or organization to entrepreneurship and innovation.

Break Down Protectionist Barriers

- Measure government's important safety and quality standards against both their intended and unintended costs.
- Proceed cautiously when regulating inputs that narrow offerings; limiting competition can limit quality.
- Support informed consumers and separate the "make or buy" decision.

Build the Political and Community Will for Innovation

- Provide the financial resources for "social R&D."
- Secure civic leadership to face opposition and overcome risk aversion.
- Identify and publicize barriers to strengthen the mandate for change.

Level the Playing Field for New or Outside Providers

- Eliminate unnecessary rules that prevent small providers from entering the system.
- Utilize intermediaries to reduce administrative burdens and barriers.
- Fund capacity building so that smaller providers can enter regular procurement streams.

Identify and Invite in Exceptional Innovators

- Identify and incubate local exceptional actors (positive deviants).

- Import new expertise into the organization or community.
- Sunset underperforming providers or require performance-based accountability.

Force a Cultural Change Across the Entire Organization or Bureaucracy

- Go where the money is; identify gatekeeper agencies and departments.
- Use authority to ensure that all agencies and actors embrace innovation and encourage future cooperation.
- Reduce start-up costs in procurement and do not shift all risk onto providers.

4

TRADING GOOD DEEDS FOR MEASURABLE RESULTS

"It's not enough to just save one child; we must save large numbers of children, one child at a time."

Judge James Payne

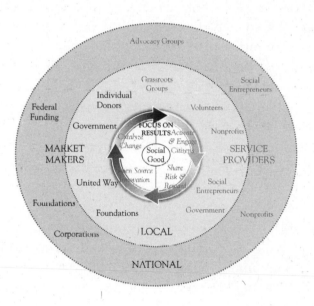

When President Obama signed the Edward M. Kennedy Serve America Act, which demanded that grantees set out measurable performance goals,[1] I thought back to some of my more unfortunate moments in undertaking "evidence-based" social programs.

As a prosecutor I proudly applied empirical research in deciding which policies could effectively reduce crime, prompting an invitation for me to speak to a group of researchers in the ornate auditorium of the National Science Foundation. I bragged about how I relied on the results of longitudinal studies of juvenile delinquency to shape policy. Unfortunately for me, the first "question" came from the noted expert Marvin Wolfgang, who was responsible for maintaining and analyzing the data I referenced. I still remember his comment: "If I had any idea someone like you would use the data in this fashion, I never would have done this work in the first place."

A gentler caveat came a few years later when Lisbeth Schorr visited Indianapolis to talk about her important book, *Within Our Reach*. I told her of my efforts to organize performance-based social initiatives. Her unanswerable question has affected my work ever since. She asked me whether I thought youthful participation in an inner-city church choir would be worthwhile in the neighborhoods we targeted for renewal, and if so, how I would measure the success of that participation.

A difference of opinion in 2008 with the Office of Management and Budget (OMB) on how to measure the CNCS program Learn and Serve, which combines service and classroom work for high school students, brought both of these experiences to mind. OMB told CNCS that the standard of success would be high school graduation. This may be one of the most important metrics in a community, but can we really say that Learn and Serve should be held responsible for this outcome, regardless of teaching quality, violence, or other factors?

Chapter 3 showed communities and organizations how to open the door to entrepreneurs; this chapter will help funding organizations, whether public or private, create an environment in which the most effective innovations have a chance to grow. Executing change across a social service delivery system starts with recognizing that one must shift some assets away from ineffective incumbents—unsuccessful programs, irrelevant goals, and inefficient practices—and toward goals and providers better suited to the needs of those you are trying to serve. Although a process must be developed to challenge mediocre results, in many cities defining efficacy and performance remains quite daunting, especially when a "system" contains so many actors doing different things.

Current Funding Limitations

Americans generously support causes they believe will improve the lives of others. In 2004, about seven out of ten households gave to charitable causes.[2] No other country has a tradition of private philanthropy like ours. This generosity equals big dollars. Total private giving from all sources—individuals, foundations, and corporations—surpassed $300 billion in 2007 translating into $1,000 in annual charitable giving for every American.[3] Although recently the recession has taken a toll (in 2008, charitable donations declined in real terms for only the second time in forty years), over the past three decades the number of foundations and their assets grew significantly. From 1964 to 2001, philanthropic foundations in the United States grew in number from 15,000 (holding $16.3 billion in assets) to 61,180 (holding $480 billion in assets). Foundations in 2005 collectively made grants worth $36.5 billion.[4]

Despite this generosity, private philanthropy must invest wisely to transform a social service delivery system in which government provides much of the funding.[5] In 2006, federal spending on Medicare for seniors and social service programs alone totaled $1 trillion. This amount excludes other federal entitlement programs such as Medicaid and Social Security as well as all federal spending on education and public safety. Thus, private dollars, which often serve as the venture capital for social funding, will create meaningful change only if they are invested in a way that leverages improved performance across a varied system of loosely connected actors.

Indeed, at times it appears that both private and public funding come with too many accountability mechanisms—prescriptive requests for proposals and intense reporting requirements—and too few results. In addition to being maddeningly bureaucratic, erratic, risk-averse, and overly political, funding tends to flow toward need rather than toward success, be delivered in isolation from other factors, and carry too many conditions. Funding decisions commonly reflect the following problematic traits.

Irrational

Management expert Jim Collins, in applying his *Good to Great* concepts to nonprofits, contrasted the irrational capital of philanthropic funding with the rational capital of the private sector.[6] Consider the typical philanthropic model, in which a foundation funds an organization for three years, hoping it will succeed, and then pulls the funding, in contrast to a venture funder who stays in once success is proved. In the philanthropic exit-strategy syndrome, success is most often determined by whether or not government steps in and takes on the role of funder. This might make sense in terms of sustaining a provider's funding, but it reduces the chances of truly disruptive, productive social transformation.

Stove-Piped

Bill Drayton, the father of the modern social entrepreneurship movement, also points out the need to transform funding mechanisms. "Institutional financial services remain overwhelmingly in the hands of stove-piped governments and foundations," he writes. "[We] need investors who value new ideas, and are okay with ideas that cut across fields and categories and disciplines. . . . The citizen sector's most valuable resource, its cutting-edge entrepreneurs, spend over 70 percent of their time and energy chasing small fractions of what they need."[7] Drayton argues that these changes are necessary to spark our latent potential for citizen-driven social change.

Prescriptive

Program, legislative, and regulatory professionals can inadvertently limit civic entrepreneurship by asserting a technical definition of "the right approach." The idea that a few smart program officers can design a solution and issue contracts governed by a set of rules misses the point entirely when we confront today's increasingly complex and interlocking social problems. The invention process relies on civic discoveries—from both the targets of help and the other providers that touch them—that are translated into a new product, intervention, or means of delivery. Since no true market for social innovation exists, transformation depends on the people working inside the system to tease out and understand feedback from clients. The discoveries that drive progress rely on a limited number of courageous funders and regulators to see a different way.

Conflicted

Yet another issue undermining a tight performance-driven funding model revolves around the fact that active neighbors may support an underperforming intervention. The leaders of neglected communities, rightly suspicious of outsiders, often conclude that a mediocre effort today may be worth more than an unfulfilled promise tomorrow. What if officials cease current funding altogether? Failure and underperformance rarely drive change when political forces, rather than the market, choose the suppliers of services. During our Executive Session discussions, Mark Moore directed the group to the work of social scientist Paul DiMaggio, who underscores the tension between perceived value and empirical results by pointing out that organizations pursue legitimacy, not performance. Legitimacy comes from doing the thing everybody thinks is the right thing to do, even if in practice it turns out to be ineffective.[8] Community and peer support should play a critical part in the delivery of services, of course, but giving them primacy instead of recognizing each as one component of performance privileges legitimacy over results.

A number of very smart and dedicated people, in and out of government, labor every day to make a difference with the funding available to them. Certainly no simple formula for transformative success exists. In this chapter, we suggest four questions, derived from our interviews and some inspiring examples, that funders interested in social change might ask in order to create a re-orientation toward the scaling of measurable success across a social production system.

What Public Value Are We Purchasing?

If we want to unlock substantial value, we can start by asking two key questions: What exactly is the public value we are trying to create? What is the market failure that we need government or philanthropic participation to correct? Getting this right is much more difficult than it may sound.

Last year Shirley Franklin, then Atlanta's mayor, came under attack for almost exactly the same step I had taken ten years earlier. She had reduced funding for one homeless shelter, provoking cries of hardheartedness. Why had she done this "awful" thing? Debi Starnes, who spearheaded homeless issues for the mayor, responded, "The reason their funding dried up is because of the lack of results. There is no excuse for why people should languish in the shelter."[9] Is shelter care the public value in Atlanta, or is it something else? A recent experience in New York City helps answer the question.

Anyone who believes that entrepreneurship cannot occur inside government should meet New York City Deputy Mayor Linda Gibbs. I became aware of Gibbs's initiatives in the late 1990s, when she teamed up with Commissioner Nicholas Scopetta to turn around the troubled New York City Administration for Children and Family Services. In both 2006 and 2009 Gibbs won Harvard University's Innovations in American Government Award, the second time for a program she helped develop for Mayor Michael Bloomberg as an incubator for social innovation.

In both instances, Gibbs succeeded not simply by doing a public act better but by rethinking the public goal itself. An important Harvard Kennedy School teaching case[10] shows how Gibbs put her finger right on this issue when she pushed New York not to just serve the homeless but rather to concentrate on ending chronic homelessness. Most Americans are pained by the presence of homeless individuals and families. Our compassion leads us to assist them —at soup kitchens, in homeless shelters, and on the streets. But do these good deeds solve or perpetuate homelessness? Do they address its root causes or simply alleviate its effects?

In 2002, with more than 33,000 homeless people in New York City shelters in any given month, Mayor Bloomberg appointed Gibbs as commissioner of homeless services. A combination of factors, including the prevalence of HIV/AIDS, the closing of mental health institutions, a shortage of low-income housing, and litigation created a maze of complications for the city.[11] New York City's Emergency Assistance Unit, a makeshift stop for homeless families without shelter placement, was overflowing. People slept on floors.[12] Gibbs noted that the Department of Homeless Services (DHS) had made shelters its centerpiece, which perversely perpetuated chronic homelessness rather than reducing it. As Gibbs later observed, "We were smart enough to know how to help the clients' underlying needs. But you put them in the shelters and suddenly the shelters became the solution, which is turning the world upside down."[13] DHS was producing an almost perfect example of what economists call moral hazard—when well-intentioned public policies encourage the very act that the policies are attempting to address. Once homeless, individuals and families jumped to the top of affordable housing lists, allowing them to choose among various types of shelter. In effect, the homeless had more choices than people working to pay rent.

With Bloomberg's backing, Gibbs redefined the agency's goal from serving the homeless to ending homelessness. This step forced the DHS to take preventive actions before things got worse. The agency shifted its focus from supposedly temporary, stop-gap shelter to permanent housing with supports. DHS could now intervene by redirecting resources toward helping people they identified as at risk of becoming homeless stay on their feet. Gibbs next engaged the Vera Institute of Justice, a respected research-focused nonprofit, to conduct a comprehensive analysis of the causes of homelessness.[14] Vera helped DHS learn about the specific pathways that lead families into the shelter system, so that DHS could develop targeted, preventive strategies. For example, the Vera study identified the neighborhoods families came from immediately before entering shelters. A competitive request for proposals was released to provide homelessness prevention services in the six communities with the highest demand for shelter. DHS in consultation with major private foundations forced the nonprofit providers to focus on prevention rather than shelter.

The new program, Homebase, reflected the urgency Gibbs gave to accomplishing her three main goals: (1) preventing homelessness; (2) helping families find immediate alternatives to temporary shelter or, failing that, shortening their time in shelters; and (3) preventing repeated stays.[15] Homebase extended its reach well beyond housing concerns. It provided clothes for job interviews; funded job training; and secured child care, mental health care, education, and employment services. It even provided mediation for family and landlord disputes.[16] The impact on the families and communities served was significant. By July 2008, more than 90 percent of the 10,042 households served by Homebase had stayed out of shelters for a year after being served.[17] Moreover, from July 2004 to June 2007, Homebase showed a 10 percent difference between the increase in the rate of shelter entry in its six communities and in a "control" group. In 2008, given the success of the pilot, DHS expanded the program beyond the original six communities to make it citywide.

Faced with an expensive underperforming public hospital, former Mayor Tony Williams of Washington, D.C., used this same approach to determine whether the goal of his administration should be a better public hospital or better public health. The question led to an increase in the number of community health centers.

Government exercises its authority in many ways—from taxation to land use regulation—but few such exercises are more vivid than when a judge enters an order. Judicial authority often extends over organizations that furnish services to children under the control of the court. For years as prosecutor I saw abused and delinquent young adults rotate through ineffective programs—but this all began to change when Jim Payne became the presiding judge of the Marion County Juvenile Court. After a few years, Payne could no longer tolerate the poor results of the overactive, underperforming system of controlled chaos known as juvenile justice. The four courtrooms under his jurisdiction held between two hundred and three hundred hearings a day, amounting to nearly ten thousand cases per year. Payne's budget included millions of dollars for service delivery, ranging from placements at group homes run by nonprofit providers to a 144-bed juvenile detention center. Payne depended heavily on the overwhelmed state-managed child welfare system, which had oversight for neglected and abused children, but he did not control it.

This sorry system and others like it had been in place for years, but strangely, few leaders demanded change. An iron triangle of government bureaucrats and legislators, allocation committee members of United Way, and board members and executives of not-for-profit service providers concentrated on securing resources to keep the existing organizations afloat. Everyone in this triangle intended to help children, and none saw disruption as possible or beneficial.

Well-intentioned organizations with considerable volunteer and financial support found serving children with fewer issues more fulfilling than assisting deeply troubled youth, which left too few effective services for youths who needed them most. Moreover, too many small operations suffered under the management of inexperienced individuals. To be effective, the system needed to attract and redirect resources to more entrepreneurial and higher-performing providers. Payne had something that I lacked as mayor—the judicial authority to order a specific treatment for a child. He could and did use that authority to disrupt the status quo.

The judge forced the juvenile system out of its slumber and into an entirely new approach that directed more resources, earlier, to the most troubled or endangered children. He forced the state to rebid services in light of a new mission that focused these interventions on how best to benefit the child, demanding reforms in four categories: service uniformity, timeliness, cost, and outcomes. By instituting a new bidding system, he also ensured stringent financial accountability and introduced performance measurements into the system. In addition, Payne added new programs to meet the most serious needs and adjusted existing policies for sentencing and treatment.[18]

This system disruption created a new market for civic entrepreneurs eager to serve youths and children. Predictably, the changes also elicited resistance from entrenched service providers, who worried that they lacked the operational capacity to place bids and would be elbowed aside by new nonprofit or for-profit providers. The other corner of the iron triangle, foundations and funding intermediaries like the United Way, also opposed the changes, believing that the organizations in their portfolios would be hurt.

Judge Payne rejected the idea that a package of good deeds that helped a single child counted as success. "It's not enough to just save one child; we must save large numbers of children, one child at a time," he said.[19] He used his authority from the bench to force service providers to change their behavior and to persuade foundations to follow suit.

Gibbs's and Payne's redefinitions of value demonstrate that when government puts its money and authority behind a big idea, it creates seismic change across a social service delivery system.

Are the Funded Activities Still the Most Relevant?

Some established philanthropic and nonprofit organizations resist civic change, unwittingly spending their money and energy to cling to obsolete tactics. Their efforts fail "the irrelevancy test": Look at an organization's mission, and look at what it does. If the organization's activities do not further its purpose, making a tangible, measurable difference in the community, it runs the risk of obsolescence. It may be large, it may be influential, and it may be invited to all the right gala fundraisers—but it is irrelevant. Other national organizations are catalysts for change because their reputations and credibility influence others, making their impact disproportionate to their size. If they discover a new and better approach, others take note.

We do not assume here that small means new and entrepreneurial, and old means large and lethargic. At the Corporation for National and Community Service, the results of the relatively new civic entrepreneurs we funded, organizations such as JumpStart, City Year, and Teach For America, impressed me. Seeing so many dynamic young ventures succeeding, I fell into the habit of assuming that civic entrepreneurship was restricted to the new. Michael Lomax disabused me of this notion.

Lomax possesses credentials and experience that allow him to challenge almost anyone.[20] Successful in both the private and public sectors, since 2004 he has led the United Negro College Fund (UNCF), a venerable institution in the world of social change. During one of our Harvard Executive Sessions with civic entrepreneurs, mayors, and other national leaders in community change, Lomax put to rest the idea that established organizations could not innovate. Without the slightest defensiveness, he told us that, despite UNCF's efforts, when he took over, it was not making a difference in a critical area: in the students' educational development leading to college.

Lomax was quite familiar with the concept of social entrepreneurship. Ten years prior, he had begun to see similarities between established nonprofit efforts like UNCF and start-up civic entrepreneurial efforts. Both were motivated by serious inequities that, in his view, have led to two Americas. Lomax also saw that both types of organizations were "led by unreasonable people with intolerance for excuses and objections." He saw in civic entrepreneurs "an attitude reminiscent of the fiercest student activists of the 1960s." Further, their ideas were working, attracting new resources and providing innovative models.[21]

Lomax explains why he developed relationships with organizations like Teach For America: "My personal strategy over the last ten years has been to align myself with social entrepreneurs. I mean actually get out there and look at them, figure out who they are, and," he adds jokingly, "insinuate myself into their organizations."[22] Civic entrepreneurs began asking Lomax to intervene on their behalf by talking to skeptical school board members or mayors. "They needed allies," he says. In 1999, Lomax joined the board of Teach For America, which connects thousands of motivated recent college graduates to two-year teaching stints in urban and rural school districts. Later, he also joined the board of directors of the KIPP Foundation, which operates sixty-six charter schools in low-income neighborhoods.

Its graduates are four times as likely to go on to college as high school graduates nationwide, on average.

For more than six decades, UNCF had worked toward a singular mission—to provide operating support for private historically black colleges and universities such as Xavier University, Morehouse College, and Tuskegee University.[71] But enrollment at some of these institutions, particularly the rural ones, was declining. Further, many of the students that UNCF supported were inadequately prepared by the K–12 education system. Lomax notes that 60 percent of African-American students who go to college require at least one year of remedial course work.[24]

As president of Dillard University in New Orleans for seven years, Lomax had seen close up "that the pipeline was not working." Too few students of color were adequately prepared when they came to Dillard or other universities. Many were not even graduating from high school; 25 percent fewer African-American students than white students graduate from high school.[25]

Lomax knew that unless UNCF "engaged in fixing the pipeline," it would never achieve its goal of helping students of color earn a college education.[26] No matter how many excellent deeds it supported, it would still lose ground. And so he engaged in that critical first step of moving from good deeds to better results: recognizing when you are on the wrong track in the effort to meet your goals and steering yourself onto the right one.

"One of the things that we learned about our brand was that it is highly esteemed and highly differentiated, but not viewed as relevant," Lomax explains. "We were not actively engaged in the issue getting the most discussion—the failure of public schools."[27] UNCF would have to rethink the environment in which it operated and reshape its mission, with a new emphasis on ensuring a seamless transition both to and through college. Lomax's challenge became redeploying UNCF's institutional assets—credibility, esteem, and trust—toward repairing the broken K–16 pipeline for students of color.[28]

To do this, UNCF staff first asked some fundamental strategic questions: "How can we influence youths to stay in school and prepare for college academically and financially? Can we raise college graduation rates by improving college readiness programs? Can we help meet the financial gap so that kids can go to college? Once they are there, can we provide more social supports such as mentoring?"[29] Lomax eventually convinced his organization that taking a larger leadership role in K–12 education reform was necessary to achieving its mission. Teach For America and UNCF now enjoy a close relationship. According to the UNCF annual report, "Two UNCF member colleges, Spelman and Morehouse, lead the nation in the number of African-American graduates who have joined Teach For America."[29]

What Change Does the Community Want and What Assets Can It Mobilize?

The United Way in Indianapolis has long enjoyed strong leadership and broad community support. It has raised and awarded an impressive amount of funding to local service organizations. Nevertheless, when I, as mayor, started to demand that the municipal financial support to social service organizations be based on measurable evidence of performance, I found myself at loggerheads with the United Way leadership, which supported the general operating costs of most of the same groups.

In 2008, I made this observation to Brian Gallagher, the talented head of United Way of America. Gallagher acknowledged that United Way had been in the wrong business for years, viewing itself and its affiliates as fundraisers. He insisted that the United Way of the future should be a community change organization. To accomplish this goal, he shifted its mission to make United Way a problem solver rather than a program funder that remained obligated to more or less the same providers year after year, regardless of performance. He recognized that its greatest asset was not the money it had become known for raising so proficiently but the capacity to work locally within communities to address some of their most pressing needs.

Gallagher's revelation about United Way was hardly obvious. Started in 1887 in Denver, the first United Way raised about $20,000 in its first year. By 2007 the national organization and local affiliates were raising more than $4 billion annually.[30] These fundraising successes led most people—including those inside the organization—to think of United Way as a fundraising machine. But according to Gallagher, the organization's biggest asset had become its greatest liability—money. "It didn't matter the problem, we showed up with the same tool."

Gallagher was poised to bring new thinking. In January 2002 he took over as president and CEO of the national hub of the 1,300 local branches in the United Way network, having risen through the ranks of the organization, working in at least five different branches across the country over the previous twenty years. His experiences in the mid-sized United Way of Central Ohio in Columbus, for example, led him to realize that the model needed to change to one of solving a community's social problems rather than funding them.

The business community had approached Gallagher about moving the homeless community off a parcel of land intended for development. At the same time, Gallagher, like Gibbs, was looking for a new solution to rising homelessness in the community—one that did not involve expanding the complex existing shelter system. He responded to the business leaders in typical civic entrepreneurial fashion: "Let's share in the benefits. If you'll support this new approach to homelessness, then we'll support your plan." Business and service groups lined up behind a supportive housing proposal. Funding came from all sectors—private philanthropy, the business community, the mayor, and the county. Gallagher brought on the YMCA, HUD, the police department, and the mental health board. Over the next seven years, Columbus developed one thousand units of service-supportive housing and zero shelters.[31]

Experience facilitating community-based solutions taught Gallagher that United Way's approach needed to shift. He says:

> "United Way is at the intersection of individual interests in a community, business interests and labor, political interests and private sector, white people and people of color, urban residents, suburban residents, rich people and poor people. That's our differentiator. So we decided to use it because community change is a political change, and you cannot make political change without individual interests locking arms to try to act collectively. So everything we now do is with that differentiator in mind."[32]

Gallagher remembers what he considers some of the best advice he ever received: "If you're serious, set your goals so high it forces everybody to change, most importantly you." He took this advice to heart, and learned that no organization can turn itself around and repurpose spending from old activities to new until people start thinking beyond their own organizations and to the community.

Unfortunately, community mobilization and performance do not always point in the same direction. In the Indianapolis United Way story above, many in the community wanted to retain funding for community centers, even though they could demonstrate no tangible outcomes. Such tensions can be accommodated but not erased. To some extent, if the community responds positively and enthusiastically to a project, that in itself is one form of positive performance measurement. What, then, if the community rallies around a service or an organization that it believes produces value, even if the numbers cannot back that up? Performance must include both lives changed and the intangibles that make up a vibrant neighborhood.

Are We Funding a Project or Sustainable System Change?

The large organizations we profile in this chapter drive results and change by using intangible assets and strengths in addition to their money. The path-breaking social venture fund New Profit Inc. demonstrates that success results from its careful combination of funding with tight investment selection and management assistance. The fifty-odd philanthropists brought together by New Profit's president and founder, Vanessa Kirsch, have contributed more than $90M over the past eleven years for the organization's work.[33] This may be a modest amount compared to total private philanthropic giving, but it has produced a hugely disproportionate impact. People and ideas, not money, count most.

The story of how Kirsch landed in the middle of an impressive cadre of civic entrepreneurs begins with her own entrepreneurial efforts. In the 1990s, she listened to youths on midnight basketball courts and college campuses across the country talk about their views of citizenship and public service. She landed in Washington, D.C., walking door-to-door to see whether she could identify the young adults who would become the city's future public leaders. "I felt that there was a need to call young people to a sense of higher purpose and that they would serve, if called," she says.[34] Kirsch started Public Allies with eighteen young people working in public service for one year.

Kirsch's efforts to grow Public Allies through affiliates introduced her to the irrational funding process for inventive nonprofits. For example, after Barack Obama joined her board, Kirsch recruited his wife, now First Lady Michelle Obama, to run the Chicago effort. Interestingly, their subsequent successes demonstrated that funding processes needed to change. "Chicago outperformed any of our other cities and grew rapidly, because Michelle is so impressive," Kirsch says. "But when our executive director hit her goals, nobody wanted to give her more money to scale. I began to realize the ultimate internal culture of the nonprofit sector. Reward the needy, not what works."

Another listening tour connected Kirsch's experiences in growing innovations to a new understanding of philanthropic capital. Kirsch and her husband, Alan Khazei, traveled the globe, meeting 350 social entrepreneurs from around the world.

"There was an innovation to solve every problem you could imagine," she says. "We would get to a village in Vietnam and there'd be this nutrition program that was saving lives, while in the village right next door, kids were dying. And yet both villages had Coca-Cola. What is it about the private sector that takes innovation down the Mekong Delta, and why can't we do that?"

Kirsch took these lessons home to Boston and started a social venture fund. She would capitalize on a new generation of venture philanthropists who sought to increase their personal involvement and direct accountability for performance, in contrast to the practices of traditional foundations. The American Association for Museums describes venture philanthropists as "living donors who choose to influence how their money is used" and "question the efficacy of old-style giving."[35] Or, as Mark Kramer of FSG Social Impact Advisors writes:

> "Funders have a powerful role . . . by becoming directly involved and taking personal responsibility for their results, these donors can leverage their personal and professional relationships, initiate public-private partnerships, import projects that have proved successful elsewhere, create new business models, influence government, draw public attention to an issue, coordinate activities of different nonprofits, and attract fellow funders."[36]

Kirsch pooled a number of these new philanthropists and created New Profit to further the "concept of invest, measure, and invest. Double down on what works and pull out of what doesn't . . . let's constantly encourage competition and make sure that we're directing resources to what's working." A second aspect of her original vision was to fund new organizations— what Kirsch calls the "innovation space"—as opposed to proven models. New Profit, operating as a venture fund rather than as a grantmaker, insists on rigorously examining business models and leadership before funding. The key, Kirsch maintains, is: "You've got to invest in people, not just ideas."[37] Early portfolio members included civic entrepreneurs like Wendy Kopp of Teach For America, Sara Horowitz of Working Today/Freelancers Union, J. B. Schramm of College Summit, and Jon Schnur of New Leaders for New Schools.

Further, New Profit seeks "a transparent relationship" with its portfolio members whereby both sides agree on the portfolio organization's growth strategy and the metrics that will be used to measure their results. A New Profit representative sits on portfolio members' boards.

New Profit looks for organizations that generate innovations with the potential to transform a problem or field and to deliver high-quality social impact.[38] To identify and attract the nation's most exciting civic entrepreneurs, New Profit asks potential portfolio members, "What is the problem? What is your entrepreneurial insight? What is the system you're trying to change?" They must aspire to scale their ideas and, eventually, have a vision of what systemic change would look like. The venture fund seeks to determine whether a civic entrepreneur still in the earliest organizational stages will not only dream big but also deliver results. New Profit has learned over time "to bet on a set of characteristics" inherent in effective civic entrepreneurs. So in addition to having an innovative idea and a transformative vision, the person is both a "great leader" and a "good learner."

New Profit concentrates on organizational growth that transforms both lives and social service delivery systems. The two do not always go together. As Kirsch says, "You have great organizations that touch many lives, but they're not really in the system-changing business. We are trying to push our entire portfolio into the system-changing business, about which we have become much more precise."[39] New Profit uses its dollars carefully and explicitly to push results, not just good deeds, by requiring as part of its unique investment selection process that an applicant explain its model for change and demonstrate its effectiveness.

What Will We Measure?

For twelve years as a prosecutor heavily involved in collecting child support for working poor mothers, I never met a mom who could not use a bit more help. Later, as mayor, when I had a hand in distributing limited public resources to address important social needs, it seemed almost immoral when a public dollar did not drive maximum social impact. This opinion, however, failed to insulate me from controversy when we began an unpleasant but necessary effort to redirect funds away from nonprofit groups whose inadequate results did not correspond with their good-hearted efforts.

Ten years later, when I was serving as chair of CNCS, I accompanied President Bush to an event hosted by Save the Children that was designed to highlight our joint good work. At the event, the president and one of our AmeriCorps members read a story to an elementary school child. The event went off as planned, and I was feeling pretty good about everything until a few minutes after the president had finished. He turned to me and shared his frustration that the AmeriCorps volunteer herself could not read very well. He then asked me point blank: Is there any evidence that this activity produces real results?

I was now being asked the type of question that I used to ask as mayor. If it is hard to ask such a question, it is infinitely harder to field it, especially when it comes from the president and you do not have a good answer. The question is tough but essential for progress—and for equity. How can government and private funders force more good deeds that produce real outcomes? Measurement can be difficult for logistical reasons; using performance data to influence an organization's operations is equally thorny. As a result, most donors and governments today claim to fund performance, but few of them really do. Instead, they end up fighting normative, operational, and political battles.

Often funders, particularly government, equate accountability with increases in reporting requirements. They hold providers accountable, but for the wrong things—inputs and activities instead of results or outcomes. Shortly after President Obama announced the stimulus funding with an emphasis on accountability, I convened the top policy advisers to mayors of the country's largest cities, which collectively house millions of citizens in need of help. Asked what they thought Washington most wanted from them during these difficult times, the city officials responded, "Financial documentation." The message: Be careful, do not take risks with start-ups, and spend lots of time on financial tracking and reporting. "Innovative responses to the country's economic distress" was barely mentioned.

This tension between accountability and innovation is neither new nor easily resolved. For example, at CNCS accounting for grant dollars trumps purpose and outcome results. Alan Khazei once told me that City Year, a CNCS funding recipient for many years, spent more than twenty-five cents of every grant dollar on compliance and reporting costs.

Of course, funding performance presents enormous challenges. No one makes a grant that omits performance as a criterion. But how does one define or measure performance? If longitudinally, then over how long a period of time? Are all providers in the network responsible for results? How about critical actors outside the network? Will evaluation alone be enough, or does accurate assessment require an expensive controlled experiment? In the hope that this enormously complicated issue will not dilute efforts to drive transformative civic progress, we suggest the following principles:

Do not let the perfect be the enemy of the good. Expensive, well-conducted research certainly helps, but funders can choose more practical and easily verified performance metrics as well. As Lisbeth Schorr responded in a discussion about evidence-based social interventions, "We have reached the point that the late MIT organizational theorist Donald Schon described as 'epistemological nihilism in public affairs'—the view that nothing can be known because the certainty we demand is unattainable.

And we have done so at a time when richer, more inclusive ways of determining what works are available."

Do not let a provider blame its poor results on someone else. An excuse contagion sets in when providers believe that they are performing well but others are not pulling their weight. Each group of actors concludes it needs more resources to overcome outside issues or systemic failures. Gallagher and I both remember hearing from nonprofit providers on many occasions, "My program is working; look at my metrics." Gallagher's response: "Yeah, but look at the metrics in your neighborhood."[40] I could not agree more.

Do not neglect to measure social or community effects. Gallagher approached his work with the understanding that "what makes community policing work is the leverage of getting citizens involved in things you never count."[41] In Indianapolis, when I started imposing performance measures on the police department, the early metrics looked good for the department but not so good for community safety. For a patrol officer, time spent working with a community organization to build up positive police relations in the neighborhood often represented time away from other activities that he could count—arrests, traffic stops, drug busts, and so on. As Schorr recently wrote, "The interventions that turn around inner-city schools, strengthen families, and rebuild neighborhoods ... are sprawling efforts with multiple components, some of which may be proven experimentally, but many that can't be because they require midcourse corrections and adaptations."[42]

Use competition to drive continuing innovation (and change for change's sake). The comfort of long-term relationships often undermines entrepreneurial opportunity. In Massachusetts, for example, the Operational Services Division describes the Commonwealth's process in this way:

"The nature of most services being purchased in the Massachusetts human and social services system has always been predicated on a long-term relationship existing between the state purchaser and the private provider. However, this relationship has historically been operationalized by having contracts that were 'renewed' on an annual basis over an extended period of years, almost since the inception of this industry."[43]

Incumbent service providers grow skillful at nurturing the political and philanthropic contacts necessary to sustain their model, regardless of performance. Gallagher references this principle from his Columbus work:

"Columbus had a deep, rich history of settlement houses, and we were trying to move away from this program funding. Because United Way funded agencies and then funded programs, we taught everybody to get behind a program. The settlement houses were designed to care about an entire neighborhood, no matter the issue, but they had learned to become the best program funding recipients ever. They knew politics: how to get to a city council member. I went to the godfather of the seven or eight settlement houses in the city and said, I will go to my board and get a guarantee that you will get $750,000 or $850,000, and it will not be at risk over the next three years, if you will agree to [accomplish specific] neighborhood-wide goals. He couldn't do it. Couldn't get his head wrapped around it. Why would I do that? Well, because that's your legacy, that's your mission, that's who you are. We're the ones who turned you into program junkies."[44]

When I challenged the settlement houses in Indianapolis, the political uproar unleashed a cascade of problems. These neighborhood-based groups told their clients that the mayor intended to close them down (an exaggeration). The city councilors from the affected wards were even blunter. The settlement house advocates were "great street fighters," Gallagher says. "They knew how to win." I agree. The lobbying gets so intense because the providers and their boards firmly believe in the work they are doing.

Ask the client and the community. Another area of opportunity involves using social media to garner feedback directly from clients themselves. Take, for example, sites like RateMyProfessors. com and RateMyTeachers.com, where students can anonymously evaluate teachers and professors for other students to see. These sites are gaining in popularity—each claims more than ten million ratings as of summer 2009—and in significance. In its 2009 ranking of "America's best colleges," *Forbes* magazine gave considerable weight (25 percent) to the student evaluations of a college's professors on RateMyProfessors.com.[45] Similar sites allow citizens to evaluate city services.

Accounting for Change

In 1992, the Council for Excellence in Government and the Harvard Kennedy School brought together dozens of former high-level federal government officials who had transferred to the private sector. Their charge was to reflect on their own experiences dealing with the tensions between innovation and accountability. The conventional wisdom was that accountability in the public sector, as compared with the private sector, is marked by inconsistent and constantly changing values; slow, expensive, and inconclusive evaluation efforts; little emphasis on the need for innovation; and great personal and reputational risk in the event of failure. Yet the discussions, brought to light by Mark Moore in a short but inspired book called *Accounting for Change*, found a number of important subtleties.[46]

Most relevant here is Moore's critical observation that accountability mechanisms have both a technical aspect (performance measurement, reporting, auditing) and a managerial aspect (using data on processes and outcomes to influence operations). Moore also identifies a good accountability system as one that prioritizes stakeholder interests in its guiding values; reassures those above (principals) that their subordinates (agents) are achieving the stated objectives, motivates agents to perform while giving principals enforcement capability if objectives are not met; includes an appellate process for renegotiating terms; and minimizes costs in terms of "resources claimed, initiative blunted, and controversies ignited."

Bringing It All Together: Linda Gibbs

Complex policy interventions can be difficult to evaluate. Even randomized trials are often not sufficient to do the job. These interventions have many moving parts, require local discretion and flexibility, rely on human relationships and social capital, and often are too new and innovative to have been rigorously evaluated. So how can we keep our focus on measurable results? Schorr suggests using a range of methods that combine research and theory, individual or collective experience, and evidence (including randomized trials) when appropriate.[47]

We saw how Linda Gibbs reoriented New York City's Department of Homeless Services around performance-driven contracts. She emphasized the managerial aspect of accountability, paying Homebase providers for successful diversions of a family that remains out of shelter for one year. The current Homebase contracts are based 50 percent on achieving performance outcomes. I was not surprised to learn from Gibbs that New York City's efforts to measure the impact of homelessness prevention have been challenging. Once the program had been expanded from a pilot in six communities to serve families citywide, it was no longer possible to measure the impact of communities served by Homebase against control communities. When these difficulties were revealed in 2008, DHS responded with programmatic adjustments and enhanced evaluation plans. In 2009, Gibbs also hired an outside firm to measure individual outcomes and community impact through a randomized design study.[48]

In Mayor Bloomberg's groundbreaking CEO office, Gibbs promoted conditional cash transfer experiments in which families and students would receive cash incentives for various educational and health accomplishments. This bold and controversial program, organized with the active support of Dr. Judith Rodin, president of the Rockefeller Foundation, has significant policy implications if in fact small payments can change behaviors. Thus, it is the subject of an extensive, and expensive, evaluation by the leading third-party evaluator MDRC. New York City demonstrates the principles of pragmatic performance contracting, using varying levels of rigor as appropriate and affordable.

Conclusions

Institutionalizing innovation itself can drive measurable success. Absent market forces, funders that set up processes conducive to continuing innovation can create a cultural shift that provides the room for civic entrepreneurs to add value. We see this play out in different ways.

In *Social Inventions*, Stuart Conger catalogued thousands of social innovations through history. He observed that the most entrepreneurial systems that produced major social innovations exhibited "a basic philosophy, organization structure, and risk capital that favour experimentally adopting new methods," making them more likely to innovate and change over time.[49]

In converting United Way's culture from leading with money to forcing community change, Gallagher took on the need to produce results and not simply fund good deeds or more activities. He drove this goal by encouraging a more entrepreneurial culture in his affiliates. This is a departure from tradition, in which the United Way network spent much of its time looking for scale through compliance rather than achieving scale by relaxing the rules to unleash innovation. "We didn't know who would figure it out, who would actually change the allocations process and invest in things that they would never invest in before. Who would, for example, create a partnership with the mayor's office that nobody had ever created before? But we knew it would happen."[50]

These ongoing creative and collaborative responses to new community-generated statements of public value should indeed produce a continuing stream of innovations and not just activities. This is especially true if the community generates clear outcome goals and funders solicit open and competitive proposals.

Key actors focused on performance can also change conduct across the social system. Michael Lomax knows that to achieve the broad, systemic change necessary for satisfactory results, civic entrepreneurs, whether leading new local organizations or established national ones, must influence the other actors in the delivery system. He says, "Together, we can reenergize, retool, reengineer, organizations and institutions that have powerful equity and scale, yet are large ships that will be difficult to turn around: United Way, UNCF, Boys and Girls Clubs, and HBCUs."[51]

Linda Gibbs made system change a key piece of her leadership. She insisted that nonprofit partners adapt to her new mission or lose city funding. Gibbs's work vividly demonstrates some basic lessons. First, government funding drives nonprofit action. Second, trying to solve the problem with good deeds took so much time, money, and energy that for years no one stopped to ask whether they were actually doing the right thing. The urgent preempted the indispensable. Gibbs, a civic entrepreneur located in government, used her authority to transform the city's response.

In the end, the biggest challenge is not adopting performance measurement in principle but, rather, implementing it. The difficulties of enforcing performance measures multiply when an organization uses its influence to turn the assets of other actors within a system toward a new goal, such as creating interdependent delivery systems. Enforcing accountability through performance-based contracts; constantly checking whether goals, strategies, and metrics are aligned; and being willing to resist a culture of compliance within the organization are helpful.

In choosing cases for this book, we have elected to pro-file entrepreneurs whose work evidences a high likelihood of continuing success on the basis of leading indicators. Leading indicators for high school graduation, for example, would be on-time grade promotion, test scores, and whether a child attends class alert, healthy, and interested. Such interim results are a good place to start our search for performance metrics, even though we might not know for years whether a child will actually graduate.

There is no doubt that Americans are generous and caring. We have lived through decades of good deeds and govern-ment and philanthropic funding, but not of better civic results. Significant social progress can be made if philanthropic, corpo-rate, and government funders of services all insist on seeing results for their money and ideas. The results must be those that help cit-izens become engaged, productive members of their communities. This chapter shows how funders and others who exercise author-ity over organizations delivering, or individuals receiving, social services can deploy strategies, advocacy, and interventions to drive transformative social results. In the next chapter we intro-duce the role of citizen choice—and voice—in demanding a focus on results when entrenched political interests stand in the way.

Civic Actions: Chapter 4

Ask these questions in order to drive innovation and measurable results through the community or organization.

What Public Value Are We Purchasing?

- Avoid incentivizing the behavior you are addressing, taking preventive action instead when possible.
- Seek out services that put clients and services first.
- Repurpose dollars and persuade others to do the same, creating a new market for better services.

Are the Funded Activities Still the Most Relevant and Material?

- Rethink the environment in which you are operating.
- Leverage the new mandate to reinforce and sustain willingness to repurpose assets.
- Use all assets, including credibility, to influence others, making impact disproportionate to size.

What Change Does the Community Want and What Assets Can It Mobilize?

- Look to the assets of your organization, sphere of influence, and beyond.
- Align assets inside the system with your new goal.
- Articulate and collaborate on shared goals, creating coalitions.

Are We Funding a Project or Sustainable System Change?

- Fund what works, rigorously evaluating both the person and the business model.

- Seek entrepreneurs with the potential to transform lives and transform systems.
- Form a close, transparent relationship between funder and provider, agreeing on a growth strategy and metrics.

What Will We Measure?

- Do not let the perfect be the enemy of the good.
- Reject providers that blame poor results on someone else.
- Value and measure social or community effects.
- Use competition to drive continuous innovation.
- Ask the client and the community to evaluate service providers.

Part III

SERVICE PROVIDER AS CIVIC ENTREPRENEUR

5

ANIMATING AND TRUSTING THE CITIZEN

"There are a great many guardians of the status quo.
But there is just no adequate defense for restricting
people to a series of bad choices. . . . At this stage,
there needs to be more disruption."

Michael Lomax

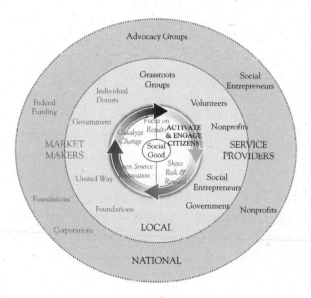

As my deputy mayor and chief operating officer in Indianapolis, Skip Stitt uncovered much serious inefficiency in city government. I knew when he called one day promising a shocking government performance statistic that it had to be really bad. The State of Indiana had asked for proposals to modernize the process of helping residents more efficiently establish their qualifications for health, welfare, food, and disability benefits. Stitt discovered that struggling Hoosiers made 2.5 million unnecessary visits a year to county welfare offices—millions of hours of missed work, riding on buses, and finding child care by the very residents who could least afford it.

Could any of us imagine going back to a fast-food restaurant again and again to place our order before we finally got the right hamburger? Of course, such inconvenience would lead us to drive down the street to the next option.

In a consumer market we make our expectations and demands known with our dollars. Moms cannot do that in a government monopoly. In social service delivery systems, clients rarely have choice. Even Indiana's problematic outsourcing to improve families' self-sufficiency was an effort to make a monopolistic system more efficient. Nevertheless, we found civic entrepreneurs who, by amplifying expectations, needs, and demands, succeeded in breaking through these performance barriers.

Chapter 4 presented the challenge and necessity of performance funding and measurable results. Absent a market, who actuates this demand for better quality? Government funding is by definition part of a political process, while philanthropic funding is often based on relationships and/or established practices. Change comes only when the public—whether as clients, taxpayers, or concerned community members—both expects better results and acts on those expectations. In this chapter we focus on the citizen and his or her voice and participation. We depict citizens, however, not as victims who should be lobbying government for money but as engaged participants in improving themselves and their communities. We see citizens operating inside a network of valuable relationships in their communities, perhaps supported by government services—not as isolated clients receiving a prescriptive set of programs from a designated professional.

During my public career I preached citizen engagement but found achieving it quite difficult. As professionals, whether in government or in the broader social sector, we look for ways to apply our skills in making a difference. Accommodating input or interventions from citizens can easily seem burdensome, noisy, and unnecessary for the most sincere of reasons.

The first part of this chapter addresses citizens as engaged neighbors active in problem solving and as concerned individuals demanding political and civic attention to serious issues in need of innovative and effective solutions. We look at mobilizing public demand for better outcomes, not as a definitive approach to organizing but, rather, as it relates to the approaches taken by civic entrepreneurs we interviewed about how they had created the room for innovation. The second part of the chapter looks at citizens as "clients" who should be trusted to make more of their own choices in a complex world in which bureaucrats by definition are ill positioned to make decisions for others. The third part looks at how successful civic entrepreneurs engage the citizens they serve at a higher level, expecting and receiving more from them as part of the solution.

Balancing the Professional with the Public

For decades Nathaniel Urshan, pastor of the inner-city Calvary Tabernacle Church, stood out in Indianapolis as a voice for good and a provider of services to struggling individuals. Despite his conservatism, Urshan was not opposed to government partnership and once visited me in the White House Office of Faith-Based and Community Initiatives, looking for ways in which the international church he by then led could provide more assistance with domestic violence and shelter needs. I attended his funeral some years later, and was struck when one of the pastors present said in his eulogy: "I really appreciate Pastor Urshan because he fought against the curse of professionalism." The expression has stuck with me ever since. Urshan and his church had spent time, energy, and money trying to persuade government regulators that results should matter more than credentials or prescribed approaches. Government officials often convince themselves that they know the best way to deliver services and who should deliver them, disregarding input from the very people they purport to help.

The curse of professionalism can affect anyone in the system. Workers in these fields want to help. Often they consider almost any possible source of assistance except the person they are trying to help. Government officials, this author included, can be guilty of designing formulaic policy interventions. The curse of professionalism can also unintentionally crowd out volunteer participation. Harvard University's Robert Putnam, social capital expert and author of *Bowling Alone: The Collapse and Revival of American Community*, calls attention to another consequence of professionalism:

> "Kindergarten reform was brought to the U.S. at the turn of the last century and was initially a great source of social capital, entirely nongovernmental in sponsorship. (The 'teachers' were all passionate volunteers and they sponsored classes and clubs for moms while the kids were attending the classes.) However, once the program was transferred into the public school system, the professional pressures from regular teachers led to the kindergarten teachers having to become more 'professional' and less sensitive to the social dimensions of what they were doing, and ancillary activities (mothers' clubs and so on) were greatly reduced."[1]

The curse underlies three other characteristics that often plague social service production systems: misdirection, growth stunting, and entrenchment.

Misdirection

Effective solutions require information and feedback from clients. Every time I start to think, "If I just get the right experts in a room, I can solve a tough civic problem," I am reminded of one of the first times Harvard's Kennedy School invited me to a policy discussion during my term as prosecutor. I explained with pride—to a group that included urban anthropologist Mercer Sullivan—how Indianapolis had crafted an array of juvenile justice activities with the right mix of punishment and constructive alternatives. Sullivan looked at me and asked whether I had any real idea how urban teenagers processed the messages my office directed at them—whether through prosecution, treatment programs, or public pronouncements. He suggested that young people interpreted these messages in a context quite foreign to my own. Sullivan also suggested that meeting with the youths whose behavior we wanted to change might yield quite different assumptions. Civic entrepreneurs need to make sure they do not replace one powerful arbiter of value with another—unless it's the client or citizen herself.

Growth Stunting

Another negative feature of the typical social service production system is the inability to grow an innovation on the basis of whether people actually want it. The power of the market to force new products through old systems—and the demise of outdated products or services—does not exist in the social service world. Here's an insight from Joseph Schumpeter, the champion of creative destruction in the marketplace:

> "Most new firms are founded with an idea and for a definite purpose. The life goes out of them when that idea or purpose has been fulfilled or has become obsolete or even if, without having become obsolete, it has ceased to be new. That is the fundamental reason why firms do not exist forever . . . the "natural" cause

[of death], in the case of firms, is precisely their inability to keep up the pace in innovating which they themselves had been instrumental in setting in the time of their vigor."[2]

In Schumpeter's world, a firm succeeds if its product attracts customers. The social or civic sector has no analogous incentive or disciplinary mechanism.

Entrenchment

When a new idea shows positive outcomes, in order to grow it, the civic entrepreneur must beg government to redirect tax dollars away from old providers or models to his new model (and possibly new enterprise). Political success, not consumer success, drives social service delivery systems. This reality requires the inventor to excel at the political level. But Schumpeter's creative destruction is not tolerated because even failed programs almost always have vocal and strong constituencies. A program in a delivery system not based on market choice can creatively construct a new opportunity but not so easily destroy the old program. Social innovations most often layer themselves on top of older programs of dubious value.

According to David Osborne and Ted Gaebler in *Reinventing Government*, "The single best way to make public-service providers respond to the needs of their customers is to put resources in the customers' hands and let them choose."[3] This chapter looks for ways to give voice and centrality to the citizen.

In a system in which third-party funders, not end-users, set funding priorities and set supply decisions, existing relationships and the curse of professionalism create entrenched cadres of connected incumbents. This incumbency advantage does not result from some wicked political plot but, rather, is the logical outcome when individuals are understandably convinced they are making a difference and do not wish to be subjected to unnecessary disruption or risk. In *Governing by Network*, I wrote of the need for carefully configured networks of service providers to overcome the fragmented nature of service delivery. Yet if government and foundations do not force these networks to compete with one another for the right to provide services, they will lose the imperative for responsive change.

Building a Public

During one of our Harvard sessions, Mark Moore challenged the group with a question: "Where does the 'public' in public will or public demand come from?" He referenced John Dewey's statement that the "problem of public leadership is calling into existence a public that can understand and act on its own interests."[4] It reminds us that an engaged, well-informed public that can reliably instruct government must be called into existence; its presence cannot be taken for granted.

Someone must make this call; it could be the civic entrepreneur proposing a new solution, a public or foundation leader, or a group of civic activists with a mission to create space for improvement. Yet too frequently the leaders within social service delivery systems—donors, community foundations, and government officials—are part of a community or professional network that restricts the incentives for disruptive change. Notwithstanding his experience at the Bradley Foundation, which we discuss below, William Schambra, an expert on philanthropy, notes that foundations have been involved in public policy for a long time, but few of their boards choose to risk political and personal controversy over topics opposed by local political interests.

Civic progress requires that those who advocate for new interventions build a community of engaged citizens with the power to demand change in social-political systems. This is true whether the barriers come from iron triangles, bureaucrats, unions, or incumbent providers. Civic entrepreneurs enter the social realm to make a difference—to perform—and their passion and talent are often distinct from the legitimacy enjoyed by incumbent providers or the political support enjoyed by the well connected. Change advocates might try to rally citizens by appealing to their rational side—for instance, by publicizing studies that demonstrate a program's lack of results. But as we will see, capturing and amplifying the voice of the underserved can be more effective in making underperformance politically untenable.

The greater the challenge (the larger its scope, the more controversial a solution, the more opposition to change) the greater the amount of political will and number of intense advocates needed. Some civic entrepreneurs help by developing or building movements. Conger paraphrases sociologist Herbert Blumer in writing that social movements originate in broad changes in people's values, including perspectives on their own rights and responsibilities. These same changes can and should elevate citizens' expectations of themselves and their communities. Yet the very social service institutions closest to the community tend to restrict individual and collective action when middle-class public officials design services for struggling individuals.[5]

We do not here assume that a civic entrepreneur must play all of the necessary roles. Some civic groups may specialize in advocacy, others in policy development, and still others in growing a service delivery organization. Blumer identified four stages in the development of social movements, and, he found, each stage requires a different style of leadership. Stage 1, restlessness and unease, needs an "agitator." Stage 2, popular excitement and unrest, requires a "prophet or reformer." Stage 3, mobilizing, needs someone to employ "tactics and discipline." And stage 4, fixed organization, calls for an "administrator." The civic entrepreneurs who shared their experiences with me fall into these categories. Although few represent all four styles, when acting together they cause system change. An entrepreneur might push open space in a community to take her initiative to transformative scale, or she might take advantage of the space created by another entrepreneur's movement. Michael Lomax, for example, relies on his experience in the civil rights movement, along with the organizational reach of UNCF into the homes of aspiring minority students, to agitate for fundamental educational change. Lomax lobbies the actors in the public education system to improve the infrastructure. Himself a civic entrepreneur, he makes space for other innovators through his advocacy of K–12 reforms, including more-rigorous academics for all students, more creativity, and experimentation. Lomax also advocates more options for families and better teacher preparation, but he's "agnostic" about specific interventions or solutions.

UNCF works to inform and activate students, their families, and eventually the public to demand change. "The right solution will be found by an informed consumer base," Lomax says. "We've been influencing influentials for enough time. It's not changing things. I believe that in a democracy, an informed electorate is where the power is."[6] As a first step he mobilizes parents and families around the notion that something is wrong "by demonstrating what it looks like, and feels like, when something is right." Here is where civic entrepreneurial organizations like TFA and KIPP and others play an important role in Lomax's vision—not only in generating new models but in demonstrating what a high-performing school looks like.

Iris Chen is president and CEO of the "I Have a Dream" Foundation, which, like UNCF, promotes opportunities in higher education. Like Lomax, Chen sees the need for higher expectations among parents in driving reform. She writes, "Often our end consumers in the social change sector have only seen the services they are stuck with and therefore don't know what 'better' looks like. For example, post-Katrina, when New Orleans students were displaced to Houston public schools— which were by no means stellar but were better than the schools back home—their families were reportedly outraged to see how much better public education could be than what they had settled for back home. With more equal information, we might drive up demand."[7]

In the pages that follow, we focus on calling the public into existence by giving voice to three groups of citizens: those who need the help, those who want to give it, and those interested in how their community responds to its challenges.[8]

Tapping into a Shared Identity

For Sara Horowitz, who had grown up in a union family in Brooklyn, the plight of the working class was hardly abstract. After many years in labor law and organizing, Horowitz understood that although unions represented employees in organized sectors such as education, health care, and building trades, an increasingly large segment of hard-working, relatively low wage workers in unorganized sectors were falling through the cracks. These freelancers, consultants, independent contractors, temps, part-timers, contingent employees, and self-employed people make up about 30 percent of the nation's workforce.

Horowitz perfectly exemplifies the first step in calling forth the public: tapping into a shared identity or interest. Early on, her biggest challenge was literally finding freelancers—no factories to stand outside of—and then organizing individuals that do not "necessarily think of themselves as a group." In building her organization, Working Today, Horowitz fell back on an earlier lesson that people are complex and have multiple identities, not just a single, well-defined identity, whether it be "steelworker or Catholic or Midwesterner or gay or of color." Horowitz explored the question, "How do you activate a web programmer or massage therapist to also identify as a freelancer, an identity that they might not have realized?"[9]

As a first step, she needed to focus on a common interest identified by the community itself. Communities are animated by word of mouth. The freelancers chose health insurance as their top priority. Horowitz began there and added other benefits relevant to the evolving world of an independent workforce. By 2009, Working Today's national membership had grown to 120,000, of whom 20,000 had bought health insurance.[10]

Immigrant communities often possess a natural cohesion that can stimulate the demand for better services. Suzanna Valdez, chief of staff to Miami Mayor Manny Diaz, suggests that schools occupy a key position with immigrant parents whose children are interpreters, educators, and navigators for them. Educators tend to have significant authority and credibility among immigrants. Organized properly, Valdez explains, schools can reach out to parents, first involving them in their own education at the school—perhaps in a course on financial literacy—and then structuring their involvement with their children's education. The parents can then be mobilized as a constituency group that advocates for school improvements.[11] The model works unless, of course, the local school itself is the problem—in which case the parent-teacher conduit reinforces the status quo rather than advocating for change.

Gaining Trust and Commitment

As Working Today grew, Sarah Horowitz continued to nurture her relationships with its members, moving from leveraging the common health interest to mutual trust. She did this in part by solidifying her reputation for reliability and creating a strong infrastructure and service model. Once Horowitz had an established and cohesive organization that was providing health benefits, she started a 501(c)(4) organization to increase her constituents' advocacy efforts. It tackled the double tax for freelancers. "We've been able to parlay that cause into action," she says. "We have a bill that has passed the New York State Assembly which will reduce the double tax on freelancers in New York City, which is incredibly regressive against low-wage freelance workers. That progress occurred only because we have 70,000 members in New York, and are the fourth largest union in the state now."[12]

I initiated management reform in Indianapolis city government because we had to wrestle down the operating costs of
government in order to fund the capital investment in long-
neglected neighborhoods. Predictably, the operating changes
churned up significant opposition from legislators, public bureaucracies, and labor unions that cared deeply enough to resist me
mightily (at least initially). Meanwhile the majority of voters,
including those who favored the reforms, were not passionate
about them. Anticipating this engaged opposition—and casual
support—as a political stumbling block, we quantified the savings and pledged to invest those dollars in specific projects under
the umbrella of Building Better Neighborhoods. Residents of
long-neglected neighborhoods witnessed their wins and became
the face of change. Subsequently, when we took on the state's
child welfare bureaucracy with aspirations to transfer some of its
functions to community-based nonprofit providers, those same
neighborhood residents helped us lead the change. Looking
back, I have no doubt that building that trust and commitment
among community residents provided the building blocks for
success.

The Indianapolis story reflects one way to develop citizen
trust—responding to engaged residents who demand better services and then participate in their delivery. The other sections
of this chapter deal with funders trusting citizens in need to
make the right decisions for themselves, whether with vouchers or in how they participate in solutions that reflect higher
expectations.

Animating the Face of Change

In June 1996, 250,000 people gathered in Washington, D.C.,
to "stand for children." The event, inspired by Jonah Edelman
and organized by the Children's Defense Fund, called into existence a public committed to advocating for education reform.
Edelman, encouraged by the event, started an organization

called Stand for Children in Washington State. As of 2009, Stand for Children had expanded to Massachusetts, Oregon, Tennessee, and Colorado, operating both a 501(c)(4) membership organization and a 501(c)(3) training and leadership development organization.

Stand for Children combines traditional grassroots campaigning with the strategic thinking and the measurable-impact-orientation of a civic entrepreneur. Its work illustrates another step in leveraging public action: Once you have activated a group, give its members the tools and direction to build broader public support by amplifying their voices and shining a light on the realities of poorly performing actors and systems.

Edelman mobilizes citizens—especially the parents of schoolchildren—to hold their elected officials accountable around education issues. This group becomes the face of change—turning it into something more tangible and familiar that citizens can mobilize around.

Edelman's strategies include leadership training and mentoring for community members around how to mobilize a statewide grassroots campaign to hold incumbents accountable and help elect officials with friendly agendas. "Our notion is that we can combine best practice research that's out there with the energy and passion of the constituents needed to make those changes happen," he says. "People don't just sit down in their homes or church basements or school libraries and say we really need to improve teacher quality by improving schools of education, holding schools more accountable, etc."[13]

Stand for Children also stresses careful issue identification. "We have overarching issue criteria," Edelman says. "We won't take on any issue unless it's broadly and deeply felt, non-divisive, achievable, immediate, easily explained." In Portland, Oregon, for example, Stand for Children has helped to pass—through the city council and then through a referendum—a property tax levy that has benefited more than forty thousand children through new pre-K and out-of-school-time programs. Edelman chose to avoid more partisan and divisive issues, at least until he had gathered the strength and the size to take on both statewide and local campaigns.

Data, too, helps to mobilize public support for change. In Portland, the Stand for Children staff used research from the New Teacher Project to demonstrate problems in the existing hiring system. Stand for Children members then partnered with the New Teacher Project to advocate for a school-based hiring system, which indirectly resulted in the seating of seven new school board members sympathetic to the reforms.

Edelman understands that politicians and policymakers convert a public expectation for results to actual change inside social service delivery systems. Indeed, Stand for Children was the first advocacy or mobilization organization that New Profit brought into its portfolio of civic entrepreneurs. As Kirsch explains, "We need to get the demand side to be pulling for these innovations. The way Stand for Children has organized it, because Jonah's an entrepreneur at heart, provides more of an emphasis on ensuring that there's a demand for innovation."[14] Edelman fundamentally believes in "the power of marshalling the collective capacity of citizens so that there's a shift in the balance of power." He says,

"The social entrepreneur world has yet to fundamentally figure out how to get from here to there. The charter school notion is that we're just going to get enough charter schools going and somehow it's going to change the public education system. There's that theory of we're just going to shame the union into performing or we're going to show what's possible. But there's no cause and effect there. What's missing there is a political question—what's actually keeping the system from changing and what would it take to effect change?"[15]

Teach For America understands the importance of the link to the political so well that it has launched a major initiative to develop political and educational leadership among the TFA alumni ranks. TFA knows that its teachers alone cannot change the system; thus it seeks to build a force of political leaders who have the conviction and insight that come from teaching in low-income communities. John Gomperts, the president of Civic Ventures, suggested to me that perhaps TFA's most valuable contribution will turn out to be that of its alumni, who use their positions of authority as superintendents, dedicated civic leaders, and the like to promote innovation through charter schools, fellowship programs, and other creations. This important observation challenges us to think about how a program can scale up through grassroots action. TFA's Political Leadership Initiative shows the organization's dedication to system change through knowledgeable life-long civic leaders as well as by strong teachers.

Similarly, Alan Khazei, cofounder of City Year, has created an advocacy organization called Be the Change that utilizes a grassroots and "grasstops" approach to policy change. Public support for this organization's mission, however, comes from mobilizing the voices of those who are moved to serve rather than those who are affected. Be the Change recently pushed (successfully) for a reauthorization and expansion of national service programs like AmeriCorps. Khazei mobilized thousands of citizens through a network of hundreds of service and voluntary organizations. He also organized a national event that drew presidential candidates Barack Obama and John McCain, providing further support for his cause.

As Khazei understands after two decades as the country's leading advocate for national service, creating demand for social change requires that the civic entrepreneur build political will among either the elites who control the assets of the delivery system or the citizens who call the elites to account—or both.

Growing a Movement

In Miami, Florida, I learned how a civic entrepreneur rallied the public—similar to DiIulio and Goode's efforts for the children of prisoners—to invest in an unmet need. In the 1990s, Governor Lawton Chiles recruited David Lawrence, Jr., the publisher of *The Miami Herald*, to his bipartisan Governor's Commission on Education and, subsequently, to chair the task force on school readiness. Lawrence, who had little experience in the field, quickly grew passionate about early childhood development. "I became so enthralled with what I thought was important for the future of my country and my own community that I decided to retire to work full-time on this."[16]

Lawrence read everything he could get his hands on and traveled the country asking questions of experts in high-quality early childhood development, care, and education and in movement building, from those at the Yale Child Study Center to Lisbeth Schorr. "Any talents or strengths I have as a journalist, I used," he says. Within months Lawrence began leading an impressive—and ultimately successful—campaign for statewide and free pre-K schooling for all four-year-olds and for The Children's Trust, a dedicated funding source for early intervention and prevention programs in Miami-Dade County. His approach to mobilizing support for The Children's Trust involved strategies and messages that together represented another step in building public demand—understanding your audience and opposition well enough to know how best to engage them in a broader movement of diverse constituencies.

Residents approved both The Children's Trust and universal pre-K in fall 2002 by wide margins. The pre-K initiative became a national model for parental choice. "Parents of four-year-olds ought to have a choice of public, private, and faith-based settings," says Lawrence, "provided that they meet quality standards. I don't know how you would do that without a voucher." The impact has been tangible. In 2009 almost 160,000 of Florida's four-year-olds were enrolled in the program.

Lawrence focused not on "those" children but on "our" children, while realizing, of course, that some children need a lot more help than others. In order to increase public support, he added a sunset provision and an independent board and, most important, a name, The Children's Trust, that said it all. "We are certainly on the side of the angels," Lawrence says, "but we needed to make the case with voters that this was about practical investment in children's lives and futures and that voters could feel that their property tax dollars would be prudently, honestly spent."

"In an issue campaign," Lawrence says, "it's not the same as running for mayor or senator or governor. I think the secret in an issue campaign is to have no opposition." Lawrence called on all the relationships he had built with Miami's civic and business leaders while heading *The Miami Herald*—city and county officials, community leaders, health and education leaders, faith leaders, children's advocates, and more. He also mobilized the public around this issue by combining listening to people with appealing to their interests. A true civic entrepreneur, Lawrence understood that "calling a public into existence" is necessary not only to shake up entrenched incumbent providers, but also to drive new resources toward an unmet need—with the potential to positively impact hundreds of thousands of lives.

Leveraging Social Media for Change

Lawrence deftly used the media to motivate Floridians on behalf of social change, but this effort to expose an unmet need does not come easily. Even when the impact of poverty or violence is clearly visible, providers and government funders often use opaque processes or confidentiality rules to hide poor performance. Increasingly, social media tools allow individuals to mobilize their fellow citizens in a way that grabs the attention of government and service elites. Imagine citizens virtually marching on city hall. We saw this when Ashton Kutcher and Kevin Rose asked their two million Twitter followers to demand a response from elected officials about ending malaria.

These tools not only change how advocacy efforts occur but also fundamentally democratize news gathering and reporting, following a trend of devolving control over information from authoritative experts to citizens. Social media will continue to produce opportunities for creatively constructing a new model of citizen participation. Paula Ellis, the Knight Foundation's vice president for strategic initiatives, a member of our executive session, and a former reporter, suggests the upside of this lack of boundary between citizen and journalist. Ellis prefers the wisdom of the crowds because, "I'm never sure that the arbiter of value, whoever it is, is acting in my self-interest or the self-interest of people I care about."[17]

Alberto Ibargüen, also a former publisher of the Knight-owned *Miami Herald*, who today serves as the foundation's president and CEO, points to the Knight Community Information Challenge as a key example of the foundation's focus. The Challenge provides $4M a year in grants to community foundations to "find creative uses of media and technology to help keep communities informed and their citizens engaged."[18] An engaged citizenry, according to Ibargüen, needs to be able to pursue what he calls "their own true interests."[19] The way Ibargüen and Ellis think about the role of community in nominating problems and fashioning solutions closely parallels Brian Gallagher's rethinking of the role of United Way—using community learning to transform how we solve community problems.

However, we add another step—activating citizens who will pressure funders to redirect underperforming resources toward higher-value solutions. Such pressure comes, for example, when community-based reporters or bloggers comb government data, make sense of them, and broadcast the information to force change. Thus, mobilizing citizen demand for transformative social progress via social media requires access to performance and financial data, plus an engaged community that will post reactions to programmatic involvement.

In the absence of a consumer market for social services, community leaders need to more effectively capture and organize citizen feedback. I am reminded of a visit some time ago to a group of mothers in an orientation room at the pay-for-performance job trainer AmericaWorks in New York. I asked the thirty women present to raise their hands if they thought the city welfare department had helped them. After a little laughter, just two people responded affirmatively. Today, texting, Twitter, and other 2.0 tools would allow that room full of people needing help to digitally "blow the whistle."

Dominic Campbell, a leading proponent of using 2.0 tools to promote third sector involvement, contributed to my understanding of the potential of social media when he filled a small conference room above a London café with social technologists. Among the varying approaches to engagement they shared with me, one simple application best illustrated how citizen interest could be amplified. AccessCity encourages London residents to travel the city and post pictures, text messages, and "tweets" about the worst public spaces in the city for persons with disabilities. This interactivity allows citizens to spot a public problem and demand a solution at the same time. The site uses mashup software that requires no new hardware; citizens use their own cell phones equipped with cameras and video recorders. According to AccessCity organizers, the site "shows that what meets the needs of official accessibility targets does not necessarily meet the needs of the people using the city on a daily basis."[20]

Ben Hecht is an experienced civic entrepreneur who now leads Living Cities, a coalition of some of the nation's largest philanthropic foundations and financial institutions. Hecht argues that the Internet's potential to "wholesale social change" will supplement philanthropy's capacity to drive social progress. The sector must, however, provide the legitimacy and financial capital to create space for both experimentation and the growth of civic entrepreneurial efforts that leverage social media.[21]

Former Ashoka fellow Steven Clift provides another example. His e-democracy.org has fifteen years of experience engaging the public online. Because most online efforts fail owing to lack of participation, e-democracy.org invests heavily in outreach and recruitment. And, consistent with what we found earlier, Clift first engages people on their close-to-home interests in neighborhood-based "Issues Forums"—the most successful of which daily engages 10 percent of all residents in one Minneapolis neighborhood.[22]

Similarly, Ellis approaches her work at Knight with the assumption that community engagement relies on an emotional attachment to place; on information and the meaning you assign to that information; and on opportunities to participate. But Ellis wants more evidence and a tangible understanding of community engagement. Is a more engaged community going to do better? What makes a community more engaged? She searches for what civic and community leaders can do to engage more citizens in improving their communities and, by extension, their lives in a measurable way.

While we explore above options for emulating market pressure for constructive change, we also consider how organizations can better communicate information to alert and activate citizens. However, the very information fragmentation that many complain about carries with it great promise. Because the public agenda is so much more difficult to shape now, change in any system must enjoy broad networks of support. And it must have the support of those whose lives will be most affected. According to Ellis:

"Too often 'experts' believe they have the rational answer founded on evidence. They ask the public to trust them. They miss the 'wisdom of the crowd' and solutions flounder because they lack a true empathetic understanding of each stakeholder's perspective. To thrive in these times of rapid change, we need the time and talents of all citizens. We need to create more pathways for their engagement. We live in a time of deinstitutionalization. The time is ripe for a citizen-centered agenda."[23]

"Client" Choice

Describing the individual as the central mover of civic progress can mean many things. As discussed in the first half of this chapter, individuals advocate for what is in the best interests of their community—in effect raising the public's expectations for the quality of services provided in our society. We also trust the citizen when we give him responsibility and the freedom to choose where to get help. It also means trusting that with the right encouragement and expectations, individuals will act responsibly, and become productive members of civil society. This is the transformative power of personal responsibility, which can lead to a cultural shift toward higher expectations among individuals and within a community. Success breeds success.

A brief return to pre-K shows why parental/client control through choice produces value. To a professional school administrator, pre-K appears to be exclusively an education decision. But a four-year-old's education cannot be configured separate from other essential family concerns, such as child care, transportation, the child's individual characteristics, and sibling issues. When parents make school choices, they take on greater personal responsibility for their child's future, and often can find better options for him or her.

A competitive system will correct itself more quickly than a system without choice. KinderCare, for example, views itself as among the highest-quality providers available. Its concentration on curricula, building design, parental involvement, and feedback impressed me. But because it has more than 2,500 centers, some parents would inevitably have a bad experience. When that happened, the company took action or the parent took the child and walked—to a neighbor's at-home child care, to a religious center, to a private competitor, or perhaps to a public school. No one in the company could order the parent back. The market, when regulated correctly, enhances quality.

It is no surprise that choice also produces substantial controversy. Some people oppose school choice because they claim it undermines public (government) schools; others resist because of well-documented challenges to successful implementation. For example, the National Center for the Study of Privatization in Education at Columbia University lists the potential risks in voucher systems, including increased inequality, limited choices, increased costs, and loss of education as a matter of public discourse.[24]

Nowhere do we see that controversy more alive than in efforts to pursue private school choice, or vouchers, in K–12 education, but scholars on both sides of the debate have identified helpful lessons. Political scientist Jeffrey Henig cautions against over-exuberance for choice, but suggests that school choice can play two important roles: as a "safety valve for motivated families seeking immediate relief from unsatisfactory conditions and as a social indicator that can help public authorities identify problems and target responses."[25] The steps to effective implementation of choice include making information on existing options more transparent and available to parents; making choice available at the right age; being intentional about the differences between school options; and involving the community in decision making.

Choice can be a powerful mechanism for putting decision making back into the hands of clients or parents, who force us to pay attention to the voice of the citizen. Here we do not seek to engage in the political arguments around choice, namely whether to apply choice as a means for holding social production systems accountable for performance. Rather, we advocate for its use to ensure that the voices of clients are heard.

Michael Joyce, while he was president of the Bradley Foundation, trusted parents to make the best decisions for their children. At a dinner in Indianapolis organized by neighborhood activist Bob Woodson, I heard Joyce's unwavering passion for this cause; he had no interest in hedging his bets or balancing his investments. He wanted choice. Led by Joyce and William Schambra, Bradley championed a fight nearly two decades long for school vouchers in Milwaukee. In doing so, the foundation took on political controversy almost unprecedented for a philanthropic organization. We go into some depth on the campaign not solely because of its commitment to vouchers, but because it shows the deft use of a broad array of tools by an unusually policy-committed foundation interested in creating space for the innovation it favored.

Joyce joined with Michael Holt, editor of Wisconsin's largest African-American newspaper, to encourage Governor Tommy Thompson to support a pilot voucher program. The coalition had accomplished the first step of engaging people around a shared interest. The state responded with support for a limited school choice system capped at a thousand children.[26] Bradley followed with extensive grants to build capacity in participating schools.[27]

But with religious schools barred from participating in the pilot, the number of private schools involved (seven) was so low, and the number of quality schools involved so limited, that only 341 students took part in the first year. In response, Joyce gained Mayor John Norquist's support for privately funded vouchers for Catholic schools and joined forces with business and other leaders to help form an education innovation group called Partners Advancing Values in Education (PAVE). In 1992, with the help of a $1.5M grant from Bradley and $2.5M from local businesses, PAVE made a three-year commitment to pay half the tuition for 1,900 students who wanted to attend private schools or religious schools.[28]

The local business community, seeing a strong link between better public education and its need for skilled employees, began to put the full weight of its lobbying power behind proposed legislation to expand choice in Milwaukee schools. Bradley's investment and its continued advocacy work paid off. In 1995 Wisconsin passed legislation authorizing school vouchers for about seven thousand students, and religious schools were included in the program.[29]

The local paper and most community leaders still opposed choice. The ACLU filed a lawsuit against the new legislation, and the state supreme court issued an injunction to stop the program just days before the start of the new school year.[30] Ironically, Schambra calls this the action that tipped public opinion toward supporting school choice. *The Milwaukee Journal-Sentinel* ran a front-page story accompanied by a photo of a distraught mother who had just heard that her two daughters would not be attending the school they had signed up for. Thousands of other parents had signed their children up for new schools. People saw the woman's despair, and public opinion shifted dramatically. Under the leadership of PAVE, Bradley and others raised funds to replace the money lost by the court injunction. The community rallied around the effort to support the affected families, with the local newspaper reporting regularly on how much money the community had raised. Schambra remembers that the "anti-school choice forces became anti-poor and anti-education, while supporters became the good guys." In the end, PAVE provided the funds for 4,650 students to attend their schools of choice.

When the state Department of Instruction tried to limit the program by heavily regulating participating schools, the leadership at Bradley organized a cadre of lawyers to "beat back the regulations," easing the burden on schools that might otherwise have opted out. By the 2001–2002 school year, the number of vouchers exceeded the number of slots available in Milwaukee's private schools by four thousand. In response, Bradley Foundation stepped in again, with its largest gift ever—$20 million to PAVE to help Milwaukee's top private schools expand capacity.[31]

We present the Bradley story not just to make the case for choice but as an exemplar of how a foundation interested in change might go about creating the conditions for reform by catalyzing the interests of the clients. As Schambra describes it, "The virtue of funding the voucher system was to give parents a taste of choice, an example of personal power and responsibility which they had not had. Their choices had always been dictated to them. And choice in education is a most critical choice."[32]

The Bradley Foundation's effort provides a road map for any funder, left or right, looking to drive social change. It funded a broad range of tools available to foundations looking to drive change: research, public official awareness, grassroots grants (in this case vouchers), capacity building at schools, parent organizing groups, and litigation support.

But both choice and community engagement, online or off, require that professionals and bureaucrats be confident—and willing to accept—that individuals do not require that these decisions be made for them and that some people will make bad decisions. This confidence in most people to take advantage of opportunity leads us back to J. B. Schramm and the expectation gap.

Curing the Expectation Gap

Mitch Roob, Secretary of the Indiana Family and Social Services Administration, recently told me with genuine exasperation, "We are spending $9B a year on poverty and not moving the needle at all." He then recounted his conversation with a leading social service professional who told Roob his job at the state was not to solve the problem but to help provide for people who are poor.[33]

The American dream will be relevant to more children only if we lift our expectations of them and of those working in the systems that deal with them. I took up this inquiry during an interview with J. B. Schramm in his crowded office in an improving Washington, D.C., neighborhood in 2009. I asked him to explain College Summit's extraordinary success at increasing the number of high schoolers going on to college. He responded that his primary product is developing a college culture inside a school such that it grows from within—through peer leaders, for example. Schramm sees real power in changing student behavior by creating what he calls energy or optimism that says, in this school, "going to college is what we do."[34]

College Summit succeeds in getting schools to seek this cultural transformation by developing a peer leader program and equipping teachers with enough information to be "college positive" and "college savvy." College Summit relies on teachers to "nag" students about application deadlines and the like—something that students in suburban schools expect but urban students receive neither from counselors nor at home, especially in families in which they will be the first to attend college.[35]

Schramm's straightforward "let's simply raise the bar" response reminded me of two similar observations. I once asked Jerry Miller, who had started a pay-for-performance welfare-to-work company after leaving Michigan state government, to explain his success. My question came at a time when similar government efforts were struggling. Miller explained that his company simply expected, and insisted, that individuals go to work. By aligning performance pay to this expectation, he permitted no exceptions and radically changed the culture.

Years earlier, during a tour of the Indianapolis juvenile detention facility, I noticed the prevalence of graffiti and grime. In response to my question about the center's appearance, the manager made some gruff retort about the quality of the people who stayed there. Shortly thereafter, I visited the juvenile facility in Louisville, Kentucky, and saw not a mark anywhere. I asked the facility's manager how he kept the place clean and he responded that they simply did not allow the alternative.

While prosecutor, I had the opportunity to spend some time with George Kelling learning about the "broken windows" theory that Kelling and James Q. Wilson first published in 1982.[36] If you pay attention to small problems, fix them immediately, and thereby encourage others to take similar responsibility, small problems will not grow into big ones. Kelling and Wilson's breakthrough discovery became a key crime-fighting strategy. To me, it also provides an important lesson about expectations—proof that individuals and neighborhoods respond to new norms and tipping points. Schramm and the manager of the Louisville juvenile facility both understood that lower expectations become the broken windows of social service, leading providers to accept lower performance and greater dependence.

In this sense, curing the expectation gap involves values, both personal and civic. However, when values become less widely held—as with, for example, marrying before one has children—public-sector navigation around them becomes more problematic. Isabel Sawhill, an expert on domestic poverty, tries to bridge the divide between the structural or economic forces that underlie poverty and its cultural or behavioral components. As Sawhill writes, "If you stay in school, work hard, marry, and have a reasonable number of children, you may struggle financially, but you will not be destitute." But she believes that effective interventions "must be both generous enough and sufficiently tied to desirable behavior to be effective."[37]

Predicating transformative change on values like personal responsibility creates substantial dissonance. In Indianapolis, when we added into our child support enforcement an effort with faith-based and other providers to convince young men and women that out-of-wedlock teenage childbearing was a bad choice, our campaign sounded too judgmental to many. So our local service providers, who tended to be deeply tolerant individuals intrinsically motivated to help others, shied away from discouraging bad choices.

For example, I became concerned that child support enforcement focused too much on money and not enough on fatherhood. But when I proposed that some fathers be forced back into the lives of their children, the social service system responded with considerable alarm. When I was mayor, my office asked the Superior Court judges and the county prosecutor to give men who were failing to pay child support an option: They could participate in a combined job training and fatherhood initiative instead of receiving the normal sanctions, which included jail. Some time later I attended one of these fatherhood/job-training sessions with men who "chose" the program as preferable to jail. These supposedly "incorrigible" fathers radiated optimism and commitment to their new responsibilities to work and their children. High expectations, the right supports, and clearly shared values produced results.

Bringing It All Together: Family Independence Initiative

Traditional programs may have a good idea but low expectations of what their clients can do. Maurice Miller, an exciting civic entrepreneur from San Francisco, demonstrates how to use elevated expectations, personal responsibility, and social networks to realize transformative social change.

Miller had experienced the top-down intervention efforts that typify social service professionalism throughout his career in youth services. Public and private funders dictated the supply of providers ("We only want one service center in that neighborhood"), while social workers often treated clients in isolation from their networks of family and friends. Clients rarely controlled services or exercised choice because they did not have money to pay private providers.

Miller started his service career teaching construction to San Francisco youths involved in gangs. He observed the influence of meaningful relationships—gangs, friendships at the work site, and even "the positive things that happen to these kids when they got in with a good woman; she stabilized them." Miller saw these relationships as more important to the youths' success than his teaching, and he became invested in keeping dating relationships stable, because they kept the young men on an even keel.[38] He believed so strongly in the power of relationships that he seriously considered closing down the training program in order to start a dating service.

Instead of launching the dating service, however, Miller spent twenty-two years as executive director of a multi-service community development agency in the San Francisco Bay area. He hired 120 employees, including social workers, case managers, employment specialists, and other professionals, as his Asian Neighborhood Design grew into a $10M operation. His agency even caught the attention of President Clinton, who invited Miller to his 1999 State of the Union address.

After a number of years running the successful agency, Miller grew dissatisfied. "I was filling in the pieces I assumed were missing in their lives," he says. "I had housing programs, employment programs, organizing programs, you name it, trying to fill these gaps. But my program staff only dealt with that individual." These youths had other relationships outside the agency, but funders would not give Miller money to leverage relationships—only to "do something" with (or to) the youths. In other words, no dating service.

Most people in Miller's program did not need services as much as help building healthy and stabilizing relationships with those closest to them. The biggest challenges Miller found in his work came not from participants but from the social service delivery network in which he was operating. The traditional social work model ignored parents and significant others—or, even worse, distanced clients from them. Family "should be the first line of defense for everybody," Miller says. "You always go back to family and community. And if you can't find it, then the state may have to come in." Miller wanted to go through the family and friendship networks to reach individuals, in effect to provide families "with a way to help each other."

A needs-based approach distrusts citizens and restricts their progress. In the traditional service model, the more one hurts, or the greater the need, the more resources are dedicated to the client. In this framework of distorted incentives, Miller says,

"We actually reinforce the negative." He sees rewarding positive behaviors as a powerful way of raising people's sense of responsibility and their expectations for what is possible. "What we need is a different system to help people become middle-class," he says. "You can't reform a needs-based system. You set up another system that people can jump to." Miller used these discoveries to establish a system based on citizen choice, personal responsibility, natural relationships, and positive incentives.

Miller's approach relies at its core on the program's ability to stabilize individuals by recruiting and involving family networks. He says, "We go through either churches or social service programs that know the families in a community. I'd been in San Francisco for twenty years and knew a lot of the families." As he did with the girlfriends of the young men in the construction training program, Miller bases his success on enhancing family and peer relationships. Miller serves the working poor—those earning up to 30 percent above the poverty level—not homeless or broke, but living paycheck to paycheck and at risk of failing. These families sometimes receive a little support from government programs, but they are not totally dependent on them.

Miller also looks to identify networks of friends and incorporates these connections into FII's (Family Independence Initiative) work. Families in the program are asked to come in with five or six friends to be interviewed together. "If they can't produce those five people, then you know they're not sufficiently connected," Miller says. He knows that most benefits materialize when families have a reasonable amount of social capital in the neighborhood. "People within this sector don't see much peer success. So if somebody succeeds, people pay attention. . . . We don't take the ones that are likely to succeed, mostly because they won't create a ripple." Once the family group has been identified, each member signs an agreement to report monthly to the FII, attends orientation, and gets a computer. "Their responsibility is to give us stories and access to whatever is going on," Miller says. "Our responsibility is to send them a check once we verify all of that."

Individual households report on positive behaviors—each of which earns them $25. There are hundreds of positive actions to report, from taking a class to participating in an after-school program. "We just want them to make sure that they give us the data on what they have done," Miller says. "Every third month we audit what they reported. So we're going to see report cards if they report that their kids' grades went up. We're going to see that their savings did go up. We total it all up and give up to $500." The program staff intentionally creates space for the participants to learn from one another and to come up with solutions. As the participants receive more checks, they step up to fill the leadership vacuum. Gradually the power dynamic changes, and the participants are no longer asking the staff, "What do you want us to do?" as the traditional service model has programmed them to do.

The model illuminates the motivational effect of family and friendship networks on individual behavior—the power of relationships that Miller identified early in his career. But it also influences collective behavior. In other words, the benefits spread throughout the participating families' communities. Because FII works with lower socioeconomic levels, among immigrants characterized by large family networks and tight communities, its support extends to the wider circle connected by culture and language. "We know that they don't talk to just the four or five other families in their core group," Miller says. "They have other friends. So we said, 'If you think this would be helpful to your friends, start recruiting them. But you need to understand that if you bring them in, you're responsible for them,'" Each participant typically refers more than ten addi-tional families from his social network.

Miller likens this effect to the immigrant model whereby the first family settles in a neighborhood or gets into a partic-ular line of business, and others in the community follow. A youth's behavior affects his parents and then his peers. "It then starts spreading," Miller says. "Your expectation of not just your

Political Cover and Incentives

New York City serves as the focal point for the conditional cash grant program, a particularly interesting and controversial anti-poverty effort that pays individuals who accomplish certain activities—making and keeping dental appointments, improving grades. One program rewards exemplary school performance with cash. As Bloomberg explains it, "In the public sector, we believe that financial incentives will encourage actions that are good for the city and its families: higher attendance in schools, more parental involvement in education, and better career skills."[39] New York's experiment has triggered a debate about whether paying individuals for things they are expected to do anyway enhances or undermines responsibility. Early results suggest that these incentives work; but, importantly, the debate shows the need for investing not just financial but political capital in order to facilitate civic entrepreneurship. Deputy Mayor Linda Gibbs describes this program as "too controversial, in our opinion, to start with public funds." She says, "We have created the program entirely with foundation support. We've engaged those foundations as our partners in arms to sell and defend the program, expanding the protective force around it."[40]

household but also your friends starts changing. It's that change in expectation that serves as a catalyst for higher expectations. Others in the community need to see themselves in the family that is succeeding."

Participating families experience clear benefits. In two years among the San Francisco cohort, households increased their income by an average of 20 percent; half the school-age children improved their school performance; three out of five households reduced their debt; and three out of four increased their savings. Word spread quickly. In just six months of recruiting by the initial sixteen households, two hundred new families contacted Miller. Yet the model is still young, and Miller considers it a learning project. Remembering his experience at Asian Neighborhood Design, Miller says, "I can give you figures that we always succeeded. It didn't change anything. Every nonprofit shows you figures that they succeeded, but nothing really changed." FII helps those in its programs succeed in a market-based economy by relying on their personal abilities rather than the support props of the traditional welfare system.

Many existing social service providers find themselves frozen in the status quo by their own frames of reference—they assume that their clients cannot live without them. This view becomes a self-fulfilling prophesy as those who need help look increasingly like problems to be managed rather than people with unrealized potential. Miller acknowledges that the most difficult cases—people in crisis and living alone—will need substantial publicly funded services. But he also believes that others in crisis who have connections to family, friends, neighborhoods, or religious institutions can be helped by drawing on their social networks.

Conclusions

By definition, civic transformation requires citizen activism, and it requires government and other funders to support and not accidentally supplant that activism. Trust can be predicated on citizen choice as in a voucher-based delivery system that forces more responsiveness to clients. It can also come from a competitive delivery system based on results, as suggested in Chapters 3 and 4, which makes the systems quicker to respond to client needs.

Continuous improvement requires an open environment and a demand for performance. Yet incumbent organizations resist change in a social delivery system, often overwhelming the fragmented interests of individuals who would directly benefit from reform but either do not know or do not believe they will benefit. That is why the entrepreneurs in this chapter worked so diligently to animate parents and other stakeholders.

In the same way that citizens must expect more from social production systems, those systems must expect more from citizens. For example, citizen trust produces breakthrough results when service providers radically raise their expectations of what their clients can achieve, or when people providing help condition it on important values of work, family, community, and faith. The elevated expectations that civic entrepreneurs have of themselves and others are more than just hopeful enthusiasm. They powerfully influence how those people view their work, allowing them to see potential and opportunity in people and their communities where others see only risk.

Civic Actions: Chapter 5

Engage individual citizens both in identifying problems and in solving them. To fight against the curse of professionalism, call into existence an engaged, well-informed public.

Tapping into a Shared Identity

- Activate citizens by tapping into a shared goal or interest.
- Meet people where they are—such as church or school—to tap into existing identity.
- Mobilize families around the notion that something is wrong by showing something right.

Building Trust and Commitment

- Solidify a reputation for reliability.
- Furnish the activated group with tools and direction to build broader public support.
- Hold elected officials accountable.

Animating the Face of Change

- Build broader public support by capturing the voice of those most affected.
- Amplify that voice by demonstrating something tangible around which citizens will mobilize.
- Shine a light on poor performance and ineffective processes.
- Understand both your audience and your opposition.

Leveraging Social Media for Change

- Provide new, attention-grabbing ways for individuals to mobilize fellow citizens.

- Devolve access to information from "experts" to citizens.
- Gain access to and post providers' performance and financial data.

"Client" Choice

- Allow choice to promote greater personal responsibility and engagement.
- Promote competition to incentivize and enforce quality.
- Address the challenges of choice programs, especially in education.

Curing the Expectation Gap

- Raise expectations for individual lives and the communities in which clients live.
- Leverage the power of social networks.

6

TURNING RISK INTO REWARD

"We are betting the Los Angeles Urban League on this model. Why? Because I don't see the choice, and you can't continue to have a deteriorating status quo for the least among us and somehow think that that's acceptable."

Blair Taylor

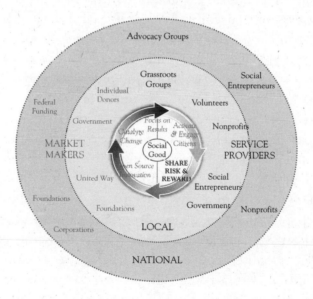

In the early 1990s I did not know the term "civic entrepreneur," but I certainly needed someone to fill that role. The Indianapolis economy, although relatively strong, did not work well for young African-American men. Neither the market nor government worked for these young men: local job training efforts produced

no value and the business community lacked enthusiasm—
presumably because many of these potential employees looked,
spoke, and behaved differently from the rest of the workforce.
I needed someone who could remove the hiring risk perceived
by local employers.

AmericaWorks offered to bring its pay-for-performance
approach to the city. It would employ hard-to-place workers and
contract them out to businesses. Because AmericaWorks knew
much more about these candidates than did the businesses, it
could better evaluate risk, inject assistance where needed, and
place the young men as temps. An employer could observe a
candidate in a work situation before actually putting him on the
payroll. In other words, AmericaWorks took a risk and social-
ized it for a fee paid with tax and philanthropic dollars.

Most commercial employers cannot easily price the operational and public/political risk in civic initiatives and thus shy
away from them. When entrepreneurs cultivate business models
that bridge the risk between social programs and a hard-to-
access market, room for social gain opens up.

In the previous chapter, we focused on the dynamic role that
citizens can play in helping shape more responsive and effective
social delivery systems. This chapter focuses on a key charac-
teristic of entrepreneurs of all kinds—the ability to understand
and underwrite risk in a way that unlocks value. The first part
of this chapter looks at civic entrepreneurs who create value
by understanding market risk and then enhancing participation for marginalized populations in such areas as employment,
housing, and retail shopping. The second part looks at how creative officials contribute to civic progress by taking on political risk in government-dominated systems like education and
public safety.

The entrepreneur in both cases starts by doing his own
analysis of the potential rewards and the risks associated with
the communities and individuals he seeks to serve. He gathers

as much data, formal and informal, as possible about the population, environment, and existing service delivery system in his area of interest. A critical component of this analysis is the entrepreneur's willingness and ability to process the information in a way that often contrasts with widely held perceptions, allowing him to see greater potential and fewer risks than most and to begin to envision creative ways to capture that potential.

The civic entrepreneurs we profile below use that superior knowledge to assume or mitigate economic or political risks in a way that produces financial returns, political credit, and improved communities.

Seeing Opportunity Where Others See Liability

Suzanne Boas of Consumer Credit Counseling Services champions the cause of low-income families whom she sees as exploited by the markets. "Low- and increasingly middle-income folks lack money," she says, "but more than that, they are indentured . . . they have taken on so much debt that they can't get out until they work off what they have taken on."[1] The numbers prove Boas's point: One in four Americans has zero or negative net worth.[2] Boas's client families work multiple jobs (and often travel on public transportation for basic errands like grocery shopping) and possess insufficient financial information. Together with language problems, these factors exclude them from mainstream credit markets.

Consumer Credit Counseling Services assists some six hundred thousand people every year. But for many, the real value occurs when the service helps them negotiate the refinancing of mortgages and other debt. In effect, Boas uses her deep understanding both of her clients and of credit providers to facilitate changes in mainstream lending markets.

Meanwhile, Andrea Levere, president of the Corporation for Enterprise Development (CFED), applies her knowledge of underserved populations to restructure incentives in a way that facilitates savings. She views her low-income clients not as hapless consumers but as potential producers. Her organization helps them build wealth through innovative programs that encourage saving. Like Boas, Levere plays a critical market-making role by helping mainstream financial institutions overcome stereotypes by providing them with more-accurate information about potential. As it seeks to bring low-income communities into the financial markets, CFED demonstrates and documents innovative products, programs, and policies that change the perceptions of these institutions. With the data from her previous success in creating matched savings accounts (called children's development accounts), Levere demonstrates to banks that low-income households save at higher levels than might be expected.

CFED takes a broad approach to its mission, also working to implement federal, state, and municipal policies that both build and protect assets. In addition, she provides financial education and the right incentives to help in asset-building efforts. For example, CFED is currently designing a pilot project with UNCF, Citi Foundation, and KIPP schools to employ their asset-building experience in promoting college enrollment and success for students from low-income families by connecting matched savings, financial education, academic counseling, and scholarships. She hopes these steps will produce positive outcomes similar to those realized by early savings plans for young children, which have been shown to actually improve parents' expectations for their children's future.

Taking First Risk

In some situations it takes more than information and training to facilitate urban markets. In these instances, the entrepreneur recognizes that she must take on the larger role of bridging the gap with a unique service or product and, like AmericaWorks, be the first to take a risk she considers overpriced by the market. Here, civic entrepreneurs evaluate the potential of particular actions in light of their deep knowledge of the people who need help and then borrow the necessary financial or political capital or use their own to accomplish a transaction.

Baked Good

Most participants in our Harvard Executive Sessions represented either government or nonprofit organizations. Thus, it felt jarring when one of the members introduced himself with this commercial: "Greyston Bakery hires the unemployable to produce the best-tasting brownies that you'll ever have."[3] Greyston Bakery is a fascinating hybrid—a for-profit company with a double bottom line—profit and social good. A religious group started the bakery in the Bronx in the early 1980s "to produce quality, locally made products that would give the group a sustainable, satisfying livelihood." It soon expanded its vision to become "a socially responsible business extending opportunity to others." The bakery supplied restaurants across New York City and then added ice cream makers Ben & Jerry and Haagen-Dazs to its list of clients.[4]

The Greyston Foundation owns the bakery, allowing it to work in housing, youth services, and health care without complete dependence on contributions. Julius Walls, president and CEO of Greyston Bakery, grew up in a public housing development just minutes away from the bakery. The absence of African-American businessmen or -women in his neighborhood made an impression on Walls. After many years in the chocolate business, both as an executive and an entrepreneur, Walls came to Greyston in 1993 as a volunteer. He was soon hired as a consultant and, within just two years, named CEO.[5]

Walls feels strongly about Greyston's mission to help people achieve self-sufficiency and economic security, which he defines as "being able to cover your base needs without fear, have some level of active savings, safe housing, and . . . a living wage. If you are fearful of missing a paycheck and that results in you not being able to eat tonight, then you are not secure."[6] The bakery employs people from the poorest neighborhoods in Yonkers, the fourth-largest city in New York State. Walls describes his recruitment pool as the "bottom of the pyramid—people whom the system, whatever system, the school system, society in general, has failed." Four out of every five Greyston employees have at some time been either arrested or incarcerated, did not graduate from high school, and possess limited literacy.[7]

In other words, for most of Greyston's hires, mainstream employment markets are inaccessible. Those markets do not recognize the potential Walls uncovered when he undertook his risk analysis. "There is a gap between their skill set and the value they bring to the business and what the business needs to be able to pay them," he observes.[8] I do not think I could describe what Walls puts in the brownies any better than I could describe what, exactly, he adds to make this all work for so many with so few marketable skills—but he succeeds.

Walls emphasizes three keys to his approach. First, anyone can walk in, fill out an application, and add his or her name to a waiting list—no questions asked. Most employees heard about the opportunity from family and friends. When his or her number comes up, a new hire starts as an apprentice, making about $7 an hour with no benefits. "We give feedback on a biweekly basis around attendance, attitude, productivity, and punctuality. We are trying to give people that first level of legitimacy in the workplace. If you perform, you have a job. If you don't perform, we ask you to leave."[9]

The open hiring process reflects an understanding that neither an interview nor a background check can predict success. Anyone who interviews well may have simply taken a course that taught him how to interview—but not how to work. Walls says, "I could cite you example after example of people who become significant leaders in our organization that you would have never hired by any standard of hiring."[10]

The program also recognizes that people in low-income communities often lack the social networks that the middle class turns to for advice on banking, investing, legal issues, and the like. Walls calls these services "HR for life," which he provides as the second part of his formula.

> "We have an HR department that provides them a support system for all the other things that go wrong that influence whether or not they are able to maintain their jobs, and so we provide those levels of support . . . that's what we choose to do with our profits."[11]

The Greyston Foundation, which sustains itself from profits from the company, helps struggling individuals find housing, child care, health care, after-school programs, GED prep, and tutoring.[12]

Greyston insists on quality, strict accountability structures, transparent internal processes, inclusivity, steep demands of everyone involved, and extensive supports. We see this, for example, in the work ethic and commitment to quality that Greyston demands of its employees. Walls tells the story of standing in line at the local Department of Motor Vehicles and hearing the man behind him say, "I need a job." His companion replied, "You should go down to Greyston." The response? "I'm not going there; they make you work."[13]

As CEO, Walls trusts that people can succeed if provided the opportunity and right supports; but he also understands that they need a structure that requires actual effort. He makes it clear that he expects a lot once someone is in the door: "The person coming in must deliver a value fairly quickly or we don't have the ability to pay him," he says. "Certainly we are not sustainable if we have people working for us who are not performing at a value higher than what we are paying them."

Ways to Work

In 1984 Minneapolis's McKnight Foundation asked strug-gling single parents what they needed to succeed financially or to become self-sufficient. Consistently, they responded: access to credit to buy a car for work and family needs. McKnight responded with its Family Loan Program.

Now called Ways to Work, the program has had a major impact on thousands of single-parent families. Since 1984 more than 28,000 families have received more than $52M in loans. The program is operating in thirty cities.

Under the Ways to Work program model, local social service agencies make low-interest loans of as much as $6,000 to low-income families without access to credit, primarily to buy used cars. In addition to servicing the loans, non-banker social service workers provide borrowing families with financial literacy educa-tion and other support services. The two-year repayment rate is better than 90 percent.

The results have been significant: Families enter mainstream financial markets while increasing their self-sufficiency and over-all quality of life. A national study found that the income of the average recipient grew by more than 40 percent, credit scores rose, and less than 12 percent of successful borrowers returned to cash assistance within two years.

Operating funds come from charitable donations and govern-ment funding, but the loan capital is entirely non-governmen-tal—secured from national lenders and through program-related investments by national foundations.[14]

A few years ago, ABC News profiled Greyston and asked one employee with a criminal record, "Why is it working now?" When he replied, "Well, they gave me a chance," the reporter asked, "But haven't you been given a chance before?" The man explained, "The difference here was not just being given a chance, but being given trust and resources." As Walls tells this story:

> "By trust he meant that the assumption we make with employees is that they can succeed, and so when we talk about an apprenticeship, most employers talk about a probationary period which involves watching whether or not the person could fit in and make it. We talk about an apprenticeship, where it's a place for you to come and make it; here are the resources to go succeed. And so he said that we gave him an opportunity, training, and resources and trusted that he would be successful."[15]

Greyston produces more than $5 million annually from its wholesale business, along with transformative financial and social opportunity for its employees. Walls accepts a different kind of up-front risk when he hires entry-level employees with little experience or education. He sees opportunity where others see liability.

Fresh Food

I did not know what to expect on my visit with civic entrepreneur Jeremy Nowak. Although I wanted to find out about his role in creating inner-city supermarket opportunities, I knew him only as the lemonade stand guy—the person whose heart and energy turned Alex's Lemonade Stand into a charity that has raised more than $25M to fight children's cancer.

Nowak operates exceptionally well at the intersection of public purpose and market discipline, striving to remove the barriers that reduce neighborhood and personal opportunity. Supermarkets faded away in much of urban America as middle-class consumers moved, and developers found suburban opportunity more inviting. Urban retailers confronted a long list of costs to overcome, including recruiting and training employees, public safety, insurance, security, and the difficult process of aggregating land controlled by multiple parties and often plagued with environmental issues. In addition, the narrow profit margins of grocers made it difficult to succeed, even though low-income communities possess more buying power than most retailers think.

Mayors, including myself, have worked to overcome these obstacles, often without success. Nowak took on these issues in Philadelphia, the city with the second-lowest number of supermarket stores per capita of major cities in the nation.[16] He studied not just the market obstacles but also the extremely limited access to fresh produce in many low- and moderate-income communities, almost one-third less access than in high-income communities.[17] Citizens suffer a health penalty, and neighborhoods incur losses of jobs and tax revenues.

Nowak saw potential where most before him had seen only obstacles. He figured out how he could get the market to work for these stores. He needed some government support—but not a typical prescriptive government program, and not in a system in which politics and not the market determined location. Every possible site presented its own list of problems. He needed public capital and the flexibility to use it to overcome these barriers to doing business in the city, and he needed a public figure to do the blocking for him. The Commonwealth of Pennsylvania supplied the capital, and an activist state legislator, Dwight Evans, provided the blocking.

Pennsylvania legislators began by holding hearings to explore the "grocery store gap." They went on record that the detrimental impact on low-income rural and urban residents required government's attention. The Philadelphia-based Food Trust, which promoted healthy eating and better food availability, recognized that teaching about healthy eating would not solve the problem if children and their families had nowhere to purchase more nutritious foods.[18]

A forty-member task force, representing experts and officials from all sectors including supermarket owners, recommended "policy changes [that] would create a more positive climate for supermarket development and create jobs, prevent diet-related disease, and contribute to the revitalization of Philadelphia."[19]

Local and state officials met with Nowak's Reinvestment Fund, and together they crafted a plan to close the grocery gap across Pennsylvania. The Reinvestment Fund would lead the effort, together with the Pennsylvania Department of Community and Economic Development, The Food Trust, and the Greater Philadelphia Urban Affairs Coalition. The team had early success in securing $10M from the state for what they called the Fresh Food Financing Initiative. Since then the initiative has raised almost $150M to support thirty-two new or refurbished stores.[20]

A new ShopRite supermarket became the first success when it opened in Philadelphia in September 2004 with the assistance of a $250,000 grant for employee training and development and a $5M renovation loan. The 57,000-square-foot store employs more than 250 people, includes a community meeting room, and sells prepared meals from a local entrepreneur. Nowak estimates that the thirty-one other projects it has supported encompass almost 900,000 square feet and have created or preserved more than 2,600 jobs.[21]

Nowak is succeeding in Pennsylvania because he combines his deep understanding of retail grocery business models and untapped consumer potential with publicly supported capital. He used these resources to take the first risk and thus leverage private investments in these areas. Through a one-time, up-front capital subsidy, FFFI has helped to reduce barriers to entry without losing the market discipline that predicts whether the operation will be able to become self-supporting.[22]

Acquisition Fund

Few efforts that facilitate mainstream markets by underwriting risk operate as well as the Acquisition Fund, a program designed

Finding Risk Capital

Julius Walls of Greyston Bakery wants capital to expand his operations. The last time he expanded, his ownership structure required him to take on debt instead of equity. But he wants partners who will share a role with him, not contributors. Converting to nonprofit status would subvert the message he wants to send to other businesses about the potential of Greyston's employees. Perhaps Walls shows that we need a new legal and investment structure for hybrids like his that produces opportunity for social investors and employees.

Walls' dilemma underscores the difficulty of finding a funder who wants to "capitalize the risk" either at start-up or during expansion for "hybrids" that produce opportunity for social investors and employees. To start up or expand a private company, the founder takes a business model to an investor who evaluates its potential. To start up or expand a social enterprise, the founder contorts his business model to fit the prescribed government or philanthropic rules. Social transformation that derives from understanding and assuming risk will occur when there is greater access to catalytic capital—capital invested with a private approach but with a partial social return.

The acquisition fund and the grocery initiative accomplished their goals by utilizing government grants and guarantees to facilitate market financing. Sometimes civic entrepreneurs can secure a grant more easily than they can attract an investment. Walls advocates for new financing models, legal structures and incentives that will unleash the private capital currently excluded from businesses with a social mission. The following are examples of such efforts:

1. Tax credits. Some tax credit programs can grease the market. An example is the Low-Income Housing and New Markets tax credits, which encourage investment in undercapitalized neighborhoods.

2. CDFIs. Community development financial institutions like The Reinvestment Fund are intermediaries for public

and private dollars to serve the credit needs of marginalized communities.

3. PRIs. Program-related investments from philanthropic foundations are willing to accept lower rates of return because of a shared social mission. PRI investments make it more likely that private capital at market rates of return will follow.

4. L3Cs. Vermont recently created a new legal entity for civic entrepreneurs looking to create a "for-profit with the non-profit soul." The low-profit, limited liability company status makes a wider range of investors available to these for-profit companies with a social mission. By complying with the IRS rules on program-related investments, L3Cs become eligible for philanthropic foundation dollars.[23]

5. CICs. The UK created community interest companies—businesses with a locally grounded social mission. Tax-paying individuals and institutions that invest in CICs via a local community development effort receive a tax deduction of up to 25 percent of the initial investment.[24]

by HUD Secretary Shaun Donovan while he was New York City's housing commissioner. Unprecedented in its size, complexity, and innovative capacity, the fund provides early stage capital to help affordable housing developers acquire private land and buildings. The result: a $230M partnership designed to create or preserve thirty thousand units of affordable housing over ten years.

The fund demonstrates how catalytic change can be ignited when leadership across sectors—government, philanthropists, private financial institutions, and developers—collaborates to underwrite risk for a larger cause. By crafting a unique financial mechanism that allows developers access to bridge loans in a timely way, the fund has broken new ground in quest of much-needed affordable housing.

As commissioner, Donovan first raised the possibility of pooling capital from a number of sources to Bill Frey of Enterprise

Community Partners and Herb Sturz of the Open Society Institute. Through OSI, Sturz had helped launch a credit-enhancement loan program to build homes in South Africa; he believed the concept would be applicable to New York City. Donovan tailored the concept to create the New York City Acquisition Fund with additional help from the Rockefeller Foundation. They brought on the housing finance consulting firm Forsyth Street Advisors, other foundations and nonprofits, commercial bankers, and major CDFIs.[25] The fund pooled $8M from Battery Park City Authority and $32M from various foundations, plus senior lender debt of up to $190M from a fund of fourteen private banks co-managed by Enterprise and Forsyth.

The Fordham Bedford Housing Corporation's acquisition of six fully occupied buildings with 277 units represents a typical Acquisition Fund transaction. With financing from the fund, FBHC ensured that these Bronx homes would be preserved as affordable.[26]

Fundamentally, the Acquisition Fund works because the city guarantees permanent financing, if necessary, for projects that would be unable to secure construction funding from mainstream financial capital markets. Donovan recognized that if the city assumed this market-making risk, the gain to the city's affordable housing supply could be large and the financial risk to the city slight. Too often government officials either try to avoid all risk, which defeats the purpose of their participation, or take so much risk that sustainability becomes difficult. Donovan and the city got this balance just right. Those involved in the fund anticipate that they will "create a new private sector lending market for the benefit of affordable housing and low-income neighborhoods."[27]

Fully Calculating Cascading Return on Investment

The most creative of these market interventions produce multiple layers of benefit—economic and social. Understanding and calculating the benefits helps lay the foundation for government and philanthropic early stage investment. For example, although Philadelphia's Food Trust initially focused on the public health goals of access to fresh fruit and vegetables, since then, the economic impact, which includes new jobs and neighborhood revitalization, appears to be receiving more attention. The organizers report that "every dollar invested in a supermarket results in a $1.45 multiplier effect" along with a boost of about $1,500, on average, to the value of properties in the neighborhood.[28]

Benefits can be categorized in several ways. Investment can renew community hope and trigger additional development in ancillary sites, which translates into enhanced property values. Employment produces not only jobs but additional community spending, further stabilizing the area. As citizens move from consuming tax resources to producing them, government realizes additional property, income, and sales tax dollars and corresponding reductions in welfare expenses. Finally, most important and most difficult to value, is the self-respect and pride that employees like those at Greyston exhibit. Rarely in the business model presented to philanthropists or government does the entrepreneur fully calculate these beneficial by-products.

Some of these benefits can be directly reinvested in the community by the entrepreneur. Bo Menkiti, also a member of our executive sessions, understands the power of sharing rewards. The Menkiti Group, his real estate development and brokerage firm in Washington, D.C., combines deep commercial expertise with an even deeper knowledge of his target neighborhood. Believing that "housing is a fundamental social good," Menkiti describes his effort as a "social purpose for-profit business."[29]

After years in the nonprofit sector, Menkiti relishes the rigor and intense competition of the for-profit marketplace, believing that the added pressure forces his firm to develop in a more sustainable manner and to better serve and better understand its clients. When a firm does not rely on government or philanthropic funding, its survival and growth depend on one thing: acutely responding to consumers' needs in an efficient manner. Menkiti's customer responsiveness in the brokerage business led to a unique understanding of the workforce housing market—the segment involving those who worked in the city but struggled to find homes because their incomes put them between the city's subsidized affordable housing and its luxury housing markets.

In addition to providing high-quality, affordable housing for more than five hundred people, Menkiti and his team have contributed to the restoration of the Northeast Washington, D.C., neighborhood he calls home. He retains some of the profits in the business to create long-term wealth-building opportunities for employees and allocates the remainder to providing educational, economic, and cultural opportunities to youths and residents in the neighborhoods in which they work.

Menkiti seeks to measure the impact of the group's work by the number of vacant homes restored to productive use and the number of first-time home buyers (so far, more than two hundred) supported. But Menkiti speaks carefully in talking about his customers. He does not use the word "helping" because, he says, "We found that the helping was more passively received— someone doing something for you. We talk about supporting people who are doing something for themselves. If an individual or a community does not bring an underlying asset base or value proposition to the table, we will be hard pressed to make an impact with them." Menkiti produces values for the families he represents but also for the neighborhoods where he spends his time and some of his profits. In so doing, he unlocks public value.

Political Risk and Reward

For all but the most entrepreneurial government officials— whether elected, appointed, or civil servants—typically the benefits of hanging one's reputation on a new idea do not outweigh the costs. The consequences of failure include bad press, losing face before one's peers, even losing one's job if the failure is public enough that politicians start looking for a scapegoat. At the same time, maintaining the mediocre costs little in political terms—barring some animation of the public to demand change.

We have seen political strategies that protect risk-taking entrepreneurs. For example D.C. Chancellor Rhee had the backing of Mayor Fenty, an elected official with significant political capital. State Representative Evans, chair of Pennsylvania's House Appropriations Committee, championed taxpayer support for the Fresh Food Financing Initiative. He also provided the political risk capital by insulating Nowak enough that he could run a thoroughly professional process, rather than one in which politics drove decisions.

In the absence of, or as a supplement to, innovative public officials, civic entrepreneurs outside government can open the space for innovation. Entrepreneurial philanthropic foundations like the Skoll Foundation, for example, make grants to support promising ideas and people. Innovative individuals such as Jonah Edelman, Sara Horowitz, and David Lawrence also work to call the public into existence to demand change.

Earlier examples in the book suggest how identifying or publicizing an injustice or some other shortcoming that galvanizes the public will also produce the conditions for change. An engaged public can provide the political capital or will for the benefits of innovation to grow while the risks wane.

Creative public officials mitigate political risk by setting aside venture capital for experimentation, as with the research and development arm of a corporation. The Cabinet Secretary's Office of the Third Sector fills this role in the UK, and the White House Social Innovation Fund fills it in the United States. In cities, a leading developer or philanthropist can also play this role. Shortly after my election as mayor, I asked

Baltimore Mayor Kurt Schmoke if he could arrange a tour of his urban renewal project in Sandtown. When I arrived, to my great delight, legendary developer Jim Rouse was there to personally conduct the tour. Rouse understated his considerable role in the joint effort during the tour, but I still remember his remark when I asked Schmoke how—politically—he could pay this much attention to just one neighborhood. Rouse pointed to himself and suggested that his participation and investment provided the rationale for the mayor.

Strong entrepreneurial leaders shift the cost/benefit equation for the system change gatekeepers by absorbing some of the political risk for those who stand exposed to the public— whether mayor, appointed official, or career civil servant. The story of Blair Taylor and the highly influential Los Angeles Urban League (LAUL) offers an inspiring example of how successful civic entrepreneurs underwrite political risk.

The Urban League commands great respect in Los Angeles, where for almost a century it has championed equality for African-Americans and other minorities, helping them to secure economic self-reliance, parity, and civil rights. Its policy advocacy, educational programs, and employment services have given the Urban League a reputation for being trustworthy and effective. By 2009, LAUL had more than three hundred full-time employees and a $30M budget. It reached as many as one hundred thousand local residents with its programs.

But in 2005 the local United Way, together with the Urban League, published an alarming report, "The State of Black Los Angeles." The report found that in virtually every facet of their lives, African-Americans had fewer opportunities than Angelinos of other ethnicities.[30] The report's bleak picture of deteriorating life for African-Americans became a lightning rod for LAUL. Blair Taylor, who joined LAUL as its president and CEO only months after the release of the report, began to challenge not only public responses in Los Angeles but also the approach of his own organization.

Seeing Opportunity

The first step in turning risk to reward is to see opportunity where others see only trouble—to use the powerful combination of hope, enthusiasm, and analytical acumen to better evaluate potential. Notably, Blair Taylor's background included both civic experience with College Summit as executive vice president and corporate experience as a successful executive at PepsiCo and IBM. He brought his private-sector skills to bear, including a focus on results and the value of strategic relationships.

Taylor maintained that Los Angeles's urban neighborhoods continued to deteriorate because the various social service delivery systems failed to appreciate the "interrelatedness" of struggles in the community. City services operated in silos, with education, employment, safety, health, and housing programs addressing their respective issues independently. Taylor acknowledged that despite a proliferation of efforts—from government, private, and nonprofit sectors—the systems were failing to "effectuate meaningful change on the ground."

Yet Taylor also saw potential. The Urban League was good at what it did—child care, job placement, and other client services—but issues beyond the Urban League's control, such as public safety and health, tended to undermine progress. "The State of Black Los Angeles" gave Taylor both a rationale for action and a path toward progress.

Taylor's position at LAUL provided a trusted platform from which to take on the risk of proposing a bold effort to holistically address the needs of a troubled community. In each of the stories in this chapter, the entrepreneur leading the effort also incurred risk in his or her own organization. In Taylor's case, the risk arose with his willingness to look inward at the Urban League's historical approach. Taylor began the difficult process of convincing supporters that many of the organization's good deeds and efforts had not produced the desired results. His experience offers a lesson on the importance of political or reputational risk taking, particularly for civic entrepreneurs who take the helm of existing nonprofit organizations.

Taking First Risk

Taylor began the change process by using his personal and organizational reputation to make it easier for city, community, school, and other nonprofits to rethink the way they delivered services. In December 2007, after months of working with consultants and talking to the community, LAUL launched "Neighborhoods@Work." It was a $25M, five-year strategic effort designed to concentrate private and government assistance in Park Mesa Heights.[31] Taylor selected the largely African-American seventy-square-block area surrounding Crenshaw Senior High School because the school could serve as an anchor and needed help. LAUL committed to an ambitious plan of action with a clear target—cutting violent crime rates in half. The organization promised to report publicly on its progress. LAUL began by enlisting the help of Police Chief William Bratton. Two years later, the neighborhood had seen a 17 percent reduction in violent crimes and an 80 percent decrease in homicides.[32]

Neighborhoods@Work relies on what Geoff Mulgan of the Young Foundation describes as "new combinations or hybrids of existing elements."[33] At its core, Neighborhoods@Work is a dense set of relationships between private actors and elected public officials and administrators. Another way to think of Taylor is as a systems integrator. He attracts interest and investment from local funders and providers and enables participating government, nonprofit, business, philanthropic, and community partners to see the value in and receive credit for their contributions. Taylor's work furnishes an excellent example of civic realignment as innovation.

In some places the mayor would play this role, although arguably the community benefits when the city is a supporting actor rather than the lead. Taylor can convene meetings as the "mayor" of the Mesa Park area because the Urban League projects credibility up into the power structures of city hall and business and down into the community. Government agencies, in particular the police department, responded to Taylor's proposition. Like Rouse in Baltimore, Taylor provided a rationale for the additional city investment and encouraged community receptivity for the results. Taylor insisted that partners in the effort must subject themselves to an accountability regime that included clear metrics, transparency, and public meetings.

The initiative needed to overcome deep community mistrust stemming from failed attempts in the past, which Taylor described as instances of "very smart people who parachuted into the community, well-intentioned, incredibly resourced, and who failed miserably."[34] The Urban League's involvement helps overcome this mistrust and concern about stability, because its commitment does not depend on a particular public official who is subject to term limits and short political cycles. Because LAUL's staff presence and operations were woven into the community's fabric over decades of work, the organization started with a level of trust that elected officials and even the best-intentioned outsiders could never match.

The interactions of more than a hundred partnerships, together with the engaged commitment of government, corporate, university, and other nonprofit leaders, provide components critical to the success of this undertaking. Like any other kind of complex system, these networks involve joints that become the weakest points. Taylor needed to reduce the risk of failure by strengthening those connections. For example, LAUL agreed to help repair the historically fractious relationship between LAPD and the African-American community. It also agreed to help the LAPD recruit African-Americans.

Every time someone raised the risk of failure as an excuse for not collaborating, Taylor stepped in to assume the risk. "A lot of people told me this was a crazy strategy," he says. "Black people don't get along with the LAPD. You'll never make that work." His response: "Effectively, what we've done is to say OK, point your finger at us. If we can't achieve this in five years, you don't have to go beat up Chief Bratton. You can come right to the door of this community-based organization. Blame us." This inoculation against reputational damage also made it easier for the business community to participate. Taylor says, "Corporations say I'm going to give you two million bucks, because if you're risking the Urban League and you're putting everything you have on the line for this model, then certainly we believe that it's going to work."[35]

Cascading Benefits

At first Taylor's story seemed too collaborative for a book about disruptive change. Yet on closer view, we see an advocate who needed to upset and realign not the organizations but the systems. Strategic partnerships with city leaders like Bratton have been central to the success of the effort. Bratton "got it" early on and redesigned how his officers would operate in Mesa Park. As Taylor remembers, Bratton told him: "I'm going to ask those officers to be true community-based police officers, to really make the effort to learn the community, understand the businesses there, work with your team on designing solutions that are preventative, integrate with the Sheriff's Department that surrounds the area and the school police."[36]

Using Bratton's commitment, Taylor stitched together other community-based organizations and public resources. He persuaded the city attorney to appoint a school prosecutor at Crenshaw High School to address absenteeism and truancy and create a gang intervention plan. The city has redirected millions of dollars' worth of personnel and other resources to the Park Mesa neighborhood. Taylor emphasizes that only with a well-tested, metrics-based model can a community justify this much investment. So he asked the University of Southern California to provide advice about metrics and replication.

Since its inception, the work at Crenshaw Senior High School has grown significantly. Crenshaw was one of the worst-performing schools in the city: It lost its accreditation in 2005; one in three of its teachers turned over every year; and more than half of its students failed to graduate. LAUL asked USC to partner in the school through a new nonprofit corporation, the Greater Crenshaw Educational Partnership. USC brought in leading national educators, who put together a cooperative of community-based organizations, the university, and the school. The partnership in just eighteen months has achieved strong results, evidenced by increased enrollment.[37] Parents saw change and started bringing their children back into the school.

Taylor considers the true test to be not only whether his cooperative succeeds with the pilot in Park Mesa Heights but also whether the model can be replicated across neighborhoods in the Greater Los Angeles region and perhaps in other Urban League cities across the country. It is too early to say whether the initiative will result in lasting change in Park Mesa, much less the rest of Los Angeles. Yet Taylor has fostered an unprece-dented level of dialogue between the superintendent of schools, Bratton, and the CEO of the YMCA for Greater Los Angeles.[38] We also know that he has accomplished a substantial redirec-tion and integration of services and that he made this possible mostly by underwriting the risk—staking his reputation and that of his organization in a manner that encouraged others to join. The LA model shows that civic entrepreneurs need not always come up with new ideas; a trusted party with credibility up and down the power curve can connect best practices and dots in a meaningful way.

Civic alignment strategies like Neighborhoods@Work will succeed where there is sufficient overlapping enlightened self-interest among public and private actors. Even the choice of neighborhood and issue agenda involved a calculation about which parties had a vested interest in a joint venture's suc-cess. In this story, did Taylor perform the role of disruptor or diplomat? Perhaps the answer falls somewhere between: The Urban League executive accomplished disruptive results through the use of diplomacy.

Bringing It All Together: Wraparound Milwaukee

Milwaukee County sits on the shore of Lake Michigan, home to just under one million people, roughly 60 percent of them residing in the city and many of them poor.

In many ways, Milwaukee had a typical mental health system.[39] Various officials—from behavioral health professionals to child welfare case managers to juvenile court judges— determined what services troubled youths needed, often failing to communicate with one another, let alone with the affected families. Limited efficacy often led to unnecessary placements in residential treatment centers, juvenile correctional facilities, and long-term, psychiatric in-patient facilities.[40]

In the mid-1980s, Bruce Kamradt served in child welfare and juvenile court positions before becoming a hospital mental health administrator. His decades of experience inside various parts of the mental health system provided him with keen insights concerning lost value. Kamradt remembers thinking, "If I could, I would pull all the dollars together and bring them into one system, because how we do it now doesn't make any sense." Kamradt's interest had been piqued along the way by insurance programs, and he spent time in the early 1990s trying to understand the risks for complex populations associated with managed care—which could unlock opportunity for integrated and more flexible services if they were driven by need rather than reimbursement formulas.

Finally, the opportunity came to put this idea into place—to take the first risk that would allow him to leverage existing financial resources across agencies within the system by pooling them. The human service systems were running significant deficits each year, with few positive outcomes and considerable fragmentation.

Milwaukee County Executive Tom Ament became concerned as overspending on institutional services for children increased every year. The deficits forced Ament to fund the budget with new unpopular taxes. With frustration at an all-time high among both elected officials and the general public, the space inside local government opened for Kamradt. He next needed to convince the other actors inside the system.

With the Medicaid agency, the county child welfare agency, and the juvenile court all looking to solve their own problems—reducing hospitalization, residential treatment, and the use of correctional facilities—Kamradt's integrated solution made even more sense. Through the local Milwaukee County Behavioral Health Division, Kamradt developed a simple pilot with twenty-five children already in residential treatment with "no immediate discharge plans." His objective was to get the children back home at equal or lower cost. The program worked. Within ninety days, seventeen of the twenty-five children returned home.[41] Within a year the county had sent all the children but one back to their families.[42]

Seeing the pilot's excellent results, the child welfare and juvenile justice departments bought into the idea immediately. The state Department of Mental Health and Social Services, which administers Medicaid, joined soon after to reduce the growing trend toward utilizing psychiatric hospitalization for children.

Within ten years, Wraparound Milwaukee was providing "comprehensive mental health and support services" to more than a thousand youths with severe behavioral health issues—and their families—every year.[43] Of the young people served by Wraparound Milwaukee, the 5 percent with the most serious emotional disturbances typically used as much as 60 percent of all resources.[44] Many of those children were under court control, either through child welfare or juvenile justice.[45]

Most impressive and germane to our discussion is Kamradt's ability to understand, assess, mitigate, and underwrite risk—political, reputational, programmatic, and financial. Kamradt gradually persuaded nearly all the providers, funders, families, and other actors in the county's adolescent mental health system to set aside their concerns and opt into his new model.

Wraparound Milwaukee integrates child services in a fashion that improves results and reduces costs, delinquency, and hospitalizations.[46] The number of youths sent to residential treatment dropped from an average of 375 in 1996 to about 90 in 2008. In 2002, Milwaukee County closed its free-standing inpatient psychiatric hospital for children, which had been one of the largest such facilities in the United States.[47]

Wraparound Milwaukee's annual budget of roughly $40M comes from pooling dollars from three main sources: child welfare, Medicaid, and juvenile courts. Medicaid dollars represent the largest source, at around 45 percent, with almost 90 percent of families served being eligible for Medicaid. Child welfare dollars represent about 25 percent and juvenile justice dollars the other 30 percent. The program generates savings by treating children more comprehensively and thus reducing expensive residential treatment placements.[47] In 2009, the program's average cost per child per month was just over $4000—half the cost of a residential treatment center or juvenile correctional facility and much less than the $1200 per day for a psychiatric inpatient facility.[48]

Wraparound Milwaukee illustrates many of the other principles we present throughout this book. In addition to raising expectations, the program allows choice. Families can choose from more than seventy different services provided by roughly two hundred certified agencies and two thousand individual providers.[49] Wraparound measures and reports outcomes, integrates services, and gains flexibility in return for capitated rates. The county facilitates these results by allowing the program to capture savings no matter where or when they occur. Kamradt successfully repurposed funding, including Medicaid dollars, that was originally designated for institutional care.[50]

Wraparound Milwaukee is the single payer for care. If it overspends because it has incorrectly calculated the capitation and payment, the county retains ultimate liability. On the pro-grammatic side, Kamradt risks not being able to provide youths the services or interventions they need. To date he has handled all these risks and produced substantial value. Wraparound Milwaukee is the first public agency in the country to operate in this manner "totally at risk," as Kamradt describes it. The model succeeds in driving value on multiple levels. Children receive better services. Providers get paid sooner. Both child welfare and juvenile justice offices pay about half what they would pay for a placement in a residential treatment program.[51]

Conclusions

The entrepreneurs profiled above produce value by weav-ing together threads that few others understand. They act as intermediaries and often financial risk-takers, incorporating knowledge of the communities and the people they serve with expertise in a market segment—credit and savings, retail, jobs, housing. Successful transactions occur because these entre-preneurs understand both government and the marketplace, enabling them to propose solutions that accomplish public goals and private purposes.

The more government delivers services in order to treat individuals' deficiencies, the more likely it is that individuals will develop dependencies instead of capturing opportunities. In this chapter we see civic entrepreneurs help individuals succeed in the marketplace by accepting behavioral, financial, or reputa-tional risk. Transformation occurs as these social risk-takers help change residents from passive recipients of government services to productive, tax-paying members of society.

Civic Actions: Chapter 6

Understand and underwrite risk to unlock public value throughout the broader system.

Seeing Opportunity Where Others See Liability

- Mitigate risk by helping clients become better informed or better trained.
- View clients not as passive consumers but as potential producers.
- Open markets to excluded or underserved citizens by recalculating potential rewards and risk.

Taking First Risk

- Use deep knowledge of a community to understand barriers to market.
- Invest financial or political capital to underwrite risk.
- Overcome specific barriers by providing extensive supports yet insisting on quality and strict accountability.

Fully Calculating Cascading Return on Investment

- Share the rewards, whether financial, political, or reputational.
- Recognize when investment success can lead to ancillary benefits.
- Build broad-based goodwill and momentum for further growth and success.

Political Risk and Reward

- Spend reputational or political capital to open the space for innovation and change, assuming full responsibility for its outcome.
- Share the political credit with elected and other public officials.

7

THE FERTILE COMMUNITY

"When we have a city where there are thousands of
kids not getting the education that they need and
deserve, I don't see why we would in any way shut
down more options and new opportunities."

Joel Klein

The John S. and James L. Knight Foundation board members
traveled to Boston in 2007 to examine closely the high-performing group of civic innovators centered there and funded largely
by New Profit Inc. During that visit, Vanessa Kirsch and her colleague Kim Syman proposed a new approach to civic progress.
The pair suggested that, with Knight Foundation's support, New
Profit could drive change across communities by bringing local
civic and political leaders together with the nation's most effective civic entrepreneurs.

New Profit's board had begun thinking about this need as
it watched its portfolio organizations make impressive gains in
growth and in the transformation of lives, but without enough
broad, systemic impact. Kirsch and the board faced the inevitable conclusion that individual organizations lack the resources,
the access, and the reach to substantially transform more of the
social delivery system. Kirsch began to think about designing
local environments in which civic entrepreneurs would be more
likely to achieve the deep impact they sought.

Knight Foundation's Paula Ellis decided to invest in this
concept of bringing to cities the skills, resources, plans, and programs of the most promising and exciting civic entrepreneurs.
In collaboration with the Harvard Executive Session, Kirsch
and Syman further developed the idea, which they called the

Urban Assets Initiative. Predictably, they discovered, as did we, that the work of creating space for civic entrepreneurs was much more difficult than originally envisioned.

Two years later, after a thousand hours of discussions with civic entrepreneurs, public officials, and philanthropists, we can better see the path to community progress. In those two years, conditions changed in good and bad ways. Life for many Americans got much worse as a faltering economy brought them increased losses. Government seemed incapable of responding effectively; foundation giving fell back; and the status quo remained as entrenched as ever. Nonetheless, we also witnessed the resurgence in the number of Americans interested in community service and by the powerful impact of civic leaders and innovators who every day develop solutions that transform lives. These inventers, present in local communities across the nation, continue to discover new ways of solving social problems.

The Obama administration also promises progress on several related fronts: It created a White House Office of Social Innovation, increased resources to support community service, and started a new social innovation fund as a source of growth capital for effective innovations. Can this fund truly overcome some of the challenges inherent in the nature of social sector funding, including political protection of underperforming programs, aversion to risk, and narrow, prescriptive assignments? Most important will be whether this fund—modest in relation to social sector spending overall—can set a higher standard for other federal and state funding, helping government become a catalyst for excellence instead of a bureaucratic stumbling block that protects mediocrity. Will we see more local and state efforts to support civic entrepreneurs similar to those in New York City and in Lieutenant Governor Landrieu's office in Louisiana?

In the end, civic progress has to occur at the community level. Great ideas need room to grow, and for most of the services discussed in this book, no real market exists. Clients do not have choices, and politics insulates well-intentioned underperformers. Yet the successes we profiled show how much can be accomplished when a good idea meets a well-designed and well-executed business plan. The real question, then, is not whether we can produce transformative opportunities but whether we can do it on a scale that benefits far more individuals in need.

The Urban Assets Initiative poses exactly the right question: How might a community mix exciting and successful social innovations with the best of its existing civic capacity to dramatically improve life for its residents? New York City presents us with a model where civic entrepreneurs of all "types"—government, philanthropic, and social—created a fertile enabling environment and then injected a catalyst strong enough to achieve new levels of opportunity.

The Fertile City (and the Entrepreneurial Mayor)

New York City is obviously far from typical; its size, assets, poverty, deep and broad nonprofit sector, wealthy philanthropists, and national foundations all distinguish it. For twenty years, the city has been led by strong individuals willing in quite different ways to take bold risks. Although our study focuses on the past few years and concentrates on social services, the antecedents of many of these approaches can be found in the way that Rudy Giuliani and Commissioner Bill Bratton dramatically improved safety in New York City in the 1990s. Rejecting old approaches, they took a new theory called "broken windows" and combined it with CompStat, a data-driven management accountability approach. These keys—dramatic idea, leadership, data, and accountability—remain at the core of most transformative community change, regardless of the area.

The Bloomberg administration not only built on these efforts but broadened them greatly by celebrating and rewarding civic entrepreneurship, causing it to sprout across government agencies. Game-changing city hall approaches unleash opportunity for social innovation that, in turn, provides hope to struggling residents. New York City's practices illustrate many of the principles suggested in these chapters and provide a useful road map for others.

Strong Public Leadership

In two terms as mayor of New York City, Michael Bloomberg has demonstrated how, with the right attitude and leadership, even the most complex city can challenge dominant thinking and inject social innovation to produce change. Indeed, Bloomberg explicitly makes risk and experimentation political assets in his hiring, funding, rhetoric, and willingness to challenge good deeds that produce few results. We have seen his commitment to social innovation in the previous chapters in his selection and support of Shaun Donovan and Linda Gibbs, both of whom redefined their agencies' very approaches. We see the mayor's game-changing efforts in the creation of the Center of Economic Opportunity which he funded with $200M in public and private venture capital. The CEO fund, designed to leverage new ideas, served as a model for the President's Social Innovation Fund. And we most particularly see this culture of innovative risk taking in Bloomberg's choice of a strong, independent-thinking school chancellor, Joel Klein, whose provocative approaches benefited from the mayor's political blocking and tackling.

New York City operates as an innovation lab for social change because Bloomberg wants it that way. He rewards innovation in his own office, giving his commissioners and other key staff around him the authority to experiment with new ideas. Bloomberg has encouraged them to invite nonprofit, business, and philanthropic organizations as partners in the city's work and to rigorously measure performance and improve practices. He shows us that civic progress achieves greater scale across a community when a strong leader uses the mandate and legitimacy of elected office to overcome parochial interests in order to make room for civic invention.

Nonprofit Leadership That Incubates Local Innovation

Bloomberg invited nonprofits and foundations to play a critical role in transforming city services, and they responded with a broad array of social inventions along with the financial and reputational capital necessary for change. We see this in the leadership of Open Society Institute Director Herb Sturz, whose creative ideas and resources helped further reform in the criminal justice system when he founded the Vera Institute. Sturz also helped to develop the celebrated Acquisition Fund with Shaun Donovan and, most recently, has worked through the Neighborhood Improvement Project to create unique work programs that helped stabilize neighborhoods. Catalytic investments by the Rockefeller Foundation in both the Center for Economic Opportunity and the Acquisition Fund also sparked change.

Discretionary Venture Capital

Bloomberg created a venture fund in the groundbreaking Center for Economic Opportunity (CEO) that leveraged ideas and resources from government agencies and philanthropists alike. CEO helps remove barriers to start-up ideas, rigorously assesses them early in their implementation, and directing resources only to those that work. With CEO, Bloomberg has created not only financial space but also political space for innovation, by backing controversial pilots like the conditional cash transfer program that compensates low-income individuals and students who achieve important goals.

Willingness to Rethink the Mission

Homelessness began to abate only after public innovator and now Deputy Mayor Gibbs radically redefined the Department of

Homeless Services' goal from "serving the homeless" to "ending homelessness." As a result of her actions, service providers were forced to redefine their own missions and be accountable for results. Similarly, only after Housing Commissioner Donovan pushed his department to change its mission from acquiring vacant properties to producing and protecting affordable housing did financial institutions and developers respond. In each of these instances, strong leaders successfully challenged social service actors to refocus effort and repurpose money toward creating public value rather than public activities.

Data-Driven Performance

Most city agencies now use some version of CompStat. For example, John Mattingly, commissioner of the Agency for Children's Services, uses ChildStat to hold officials and nonprofits responsible for performance. He incorporates "stats" into accountability for public managers and contract oversight for nonprofits proffering services to the city. The mayor's personal attention to daily dashboard metrics reinforces this approach by his appointees.

Trusting the Citizen

Although New York City did not concentrate on providing citizens with choices for social services, it did change its approach to require more from clients. The cash transfer program concentrates on individuals taking personal responsibility for their future. People who want housing or welfare benefits can no longer be passive recipients of government services; they must fulfill certain responsibilities.

Civic Entrepreneurs and School Reform

Bloomberg exhibits his entrepreneurial approach to social innovation most vividly in his effort to reform the public schools.

The mayor inherited a school system struggling according to nearly every achievement indicator, with only 50 percent of fourth graders and 30 percent of eighth graders meeting the state's standards in math and reading. Graduation rates hovered at roughly 50 percent, with many high schools posting rates as low as 20 or 30 percent. The achievement gap between white students and African-American and Latino students seemed intractably wide. Parents had virtually no choices if they wanted to send their children to a better school. Books and basic school supplies routinely ran short across the system, and principals had almost no discretion over their own school budgets.[1] No public official in this country faced a school system in which the stakes were higher, the obstacles more dramatic, or the potential improvements so important.

Early on, Bloomberg made education reform a top priority, aggressively seeking approval from the state legislature for direct control over the city schools. The mayor's timing was right, because the public, lawmakers, and other education stakeholders had grown increasingly frustrated by a system fraught with political infighting and cronyism. Bloomberg succeeded in securing control and turned to an unlikely choice to lead the effort: Joel Klein, a business executive and former U.S. deputy attorney general best known for spearheading a high-profile antitrust case against Microsoft. Klein had no educational management experience, but he embraced the challenge with zeal. Beginning in late summer 2002, with the help of a $4M strategic planning grant from the Eli Broad Foundation, he set the table for wholesale reform. The effort was dubbed "Children First" to signal a departure from the "old way" of putting the needs of the adults in the system ahead of those of the children they were there to serve—and to put a face on the changes about to unfold.

Expectedly, Klein faced opposition from strong political interests, including labor, organized parents' groups, and city and state elected officials, as well as from the school system's own bureaucracy. He credits the mayor with giving him the support he needed to get things done. "I knew that the mayor would have my back. I also knew I'd have to make some compromises in the process. I believed from the beginning that it was doable because of the mayor."[2]

We examine not Klein's pedagogy but, rather, his textbook example of government partnering with civic entrepreneurs to help drive change. Klein sought out partnerships with nonprofit, foundation, and private sector supporters to design, test, and implement core innovations across the system. As I saw in my efforts to reform city government in Indianapolis, major change cannot be managed by relying exclusively on either internal or external levers—it takes both. Over time Klein deliberately used both approaches at various points in order to improve educational quality.

Klein's reform efforts provide a template for other jurisdictions and for other social services. He infused the system with catalytic talent from nontraditional areas, partnered with private sector entrepreneurs to widen choice, disrupted traditional school management by developing new routes for advancement, and granted managers the authority and autonomy to innovate.

First, Klein rejected many of the institutional education players who had dominated central decision making and recruited instead advisers predisposed to take risks and innovate, many of whom came from the top levels of fields outside education. From Caroline Kennedy to Jack Welch to former investment bankers and management consultants, Klein surrounded himself with talent and expertise that brought a fresh way of looking at school reform. He sought out education thinkers and practitioners from philanthropies, universities, and nonprofit and for-profit education organizations who had not previously taken leadership roles in the NYC school system. He also turned to national civic entrepreneurs to join him in the effort.

Second, with the help of major foundations, Klein partnered with creative nonprofits to widen school choice by introducing more charter schools. On the first day of school in 2002, only weeks after his arrival, Klein joined the mayor on a visit to two newly created high schools in the Bronx. Both were part of an ongoing school reform called the New Century High School Initiative, funded with $30M in grants from the Gates Foundation, Carnegie, and the Open Society Institute. The core elements of the schools included strong leadership supporting effective instruction; a shared mission; high student expectations; qualified teachers; clear accountability; and a rigorous, standards-based curriculum.[3] During that visit, Bloomberg and Klein, impressed by what they saw, concluded that they needed nonprofit intermediaries as partners in order to develop these new schools.[4]

Klein aggressively pursued these options to open 333 new public schools and more than eighty charter schools between 2002 and 2009. The new schools, most often created by breaking down large high schools into smaller "schools within schools," used Gates, Carnegie, and OSI funding with New Visions for Public Schools as the key school developer. To help develop his school strategy, Klein turned to a handful of experts, including Michele Cahill and Robert Hughes. Klein recruited Cahill from the Carnegie Corporation to help craft the thinking around school restructuring and educational programming innovations. Hughes, a tireless education advocate at New Visions for Public Schools, teamed up with Cahill and the Gates Foundation to help manage the project. New Visions partnered with others to establish where to place the schools, the leadership, and the educational design. New Visions then served as an incubator for community-based partnerships before stepping away to let DOE oversee the schools.

All told, New Visions created ninety-six small schools—a maximum of five hundred students per school—with $70M in outside funding. In creating these schools, New Visions set a core performance metric. Dubbed "80/92," it challenged all schools in the initiative to graduate at least 80 percent of their students and reach 92 percent attendance rates. A New Visions study conducted in year five showed a 78.5 percent on-time graduation rate for the class of 2006, compared with a city-wide rate of 60 percent, and an 85 percent average attendance for the 2005–2006 school year.[5] Since then, New Visions schools have posted graduation percentages in the low- to mid-70th percentile range in 2008.[6]

As time passes, analysts will be better able to judge the overall effectiveness of New York City's major plunge into small schools. Bill Gates, the largest private funder of the strategy both nationally and in New York, offered some clues. Gates put hundreds of millions into the initiatives in districts across the country, highlighted the initiatives as a pillar of his education reform strategy, and punctuated the effort with personal engagement in the work.

It came as a surprise to some when, in November 2008, Gates took a hard look at the foundation's core education initiatives and called much of the small schools work a disappointment. However, to the relief of Bloomberg and Klein, Gates singled them out as a key exception to the general indictment.

By teaming up with intermediaries, the school system gains capacity and social capital from the political relationships and trust it has developed with other institutional players, and from their ability to innovate.[7] Philanthropic contributions proved critical to the ability of the entrepreneurial groups to gain flexibly and independence. When a government-run enterprise such as a school district both operates schools and decides who may charter or operate for the district (buys education), the role confusion tends to create an irreconcilable conflict. This conflict may be less severe with a strong change-minded leader like Klein in place, but over time his decision to move in-house the bulk of the new school creation process may be problematic. As Robert Hughes observes, the now government-coordinated school creation model kept some of the original innovations, but it is by no means an exact replica of the externally run process that preceded it.

Bloomberg and Klein argue that charter schools promote competition and widen parents' choices. When Bloomberg arrived in 2002, New York City had seventeen charter schools serving 3,200 students. In 2003, Klein announced the administration's plan to create fifty new charter schools in five years. To help reach this goal, Bloomberg and Klein created the nonprofit Center for Charter School Excellence, which reflected their belief in the power of merging the resources and talent of public and private sector forces. Klein serves as chair, while foundation, business, civic, and community representatives also sit on the board. "We needed to stimulate interest in charters," Klein says. "We needed to make sure that the policy environment is such that charter operators feel supported, and we also needed to create additional funding sources to support new charter schools."[8]

The center played a role in an important victory for Bloomberg and Klein in 2007, when the state legislature raised the number of allowable new charter schools from one hundred to two hundred statewide and imposed no limits on the number of existing public schools that could be converted to charters—a process that requires an application to the DOE by the school and a majority vote in favor of conversion by the parents of enrolled students.

The growth of charter schools in New York City ultimately rests, of course, on how well they educate. Evidence from one multi-year study led by Stanford economist Caroline Hoxby supports the view that New York's charter schools are outpacing traditional public schools in standardized test scores. The study, released in September 2009, also found that students who attended city charter schools for grades kindergarten through eight performed remarkably well in comparison to their peers in affluent surrounding suburban schools. On average, these students "close about 86 percent of the 'Scarsdale-Harlem achievement gap' in math and 66 percent of the achievement gap in English," according to Hoxby.[9]

We address charter schools here not because they are a panacea but, rather, because the advocacy for and implementation of charter schools illustrates several points important to the open sourcing of social change. For example, advocacy outside the traditional school bureaucracy played a part in the birth of these schools. They also have greater autonomy, more personalization, and more flexibility than traditional public schools. A not-for-profit board of trustees provides the governance. Teachers, exempt from many regulations dictating such things as curriculum development, staffing, and budgeting, can customize their work.

Civic entrepreneurs often insist that charters provide them necessary relief from the union rules that stifle innovation. Randi Weingarten, the former head of the New York City teachers' union and now a national teacher leader, has argued vociferously against this claim. She opened two union-run charter schools in Brooklyn to prove that union contract rules do not hinder school innovation and to demonstrate the importance of teacher collaboration to success.

In assessing charter schools, Weingarten often argues that their original intent, as envisioned by Federation of Teachers leader Albert Shanker (a mentor to Weingarten and an early contributor to the charter school concept), was to allow teachers greater freedom to experiment with innovative teaching approaches in light of their experience and understanding of what works in classrooms, and to give them greater voice in school decision making. Indeed, we see in many areas—education, homelessness, domestic violence, child welfare, and the like—that efforts to increase discretion at the point at which services are delivered may be one of the most important elements of social change.

As contrasted with closed and government-dominated service systems, Klein articulates the value of multiple paths in service offerings:

"So why is it that I—the public schools chancellor—am an unalloyed supporter of charter schools? Frankly, it's simple: educators, families, and children want good schools. Charters are one way to create them. Charters bring in new blood. These are leaders and entrepreneurs who are not otherwise part of the system. They are people with ideas, with creativity, and who are willing to give their all for their students. On that central basis, when we have a city where there are thousands of kids not getting the education that they need and deserve, I don't see why we would in any way shut down more options and new opportunities."[10]

Klein's third strategy is to base his reforms on putting "a great leader in every school." He recognized that rigid internal systems often squeeze out innovators and in response developed an alternative approach to recruiting and training principals shaped in part by General Electric's Crotonville center model and in part by the model created by entrepreneur Jon Schnur. Schnur's New Leaders for New Schools recruits, trains, and places inside public schools high-quality principals who drive change. New Leaders, which won the sought-after Harvard Kennedy School's Innovations in American Government Award in 2009, derives its success from training and supporting talented leaders from outside traditional school administration pipelines. Through the NYC Leadership Academy, principals and aspiring principals attend an intensive boot camp and then mentor and intern with successful experienced principals. In order to create the nonprofit Leadership Academy, Bloomberg and Klein raised more than $80M in private funds. Designed as an alternative vehicle for recruitment, training, and placement of principals, the academy has graduated hundreds of recruits since its inception in 2003, making up approximately 16 percent of New York City's total school leadership. In 2008, the academy shifted to majority public funding.

The Principal Leadership Academy presents an interesting and unresolved question about whether public leaders should work with a successful national entrepreneur like Schnur or copy the model themselves, as New York City schools did.

Twelve Steps to Community Solutions

1. Respect individuals by insisting on higher expectations and good decisions from them.

2. Reach government and philanthropic agreement about the big vision and the definition of public value.

3. Agree on important outcomes and measure them.

4. Require a "sunset" or automatic review of a quarter of existing social programs each year, forcing organizations to justify their contributions. Repurpose money freed up by disbanding unproductive service providers.

5. Solicit and pay attention to the voices of clients in evaluating the importance of services and the effectiveness of their providers.

6. Create philanthropic and governmental venture capital.

7. Give clients a choice about where they get help.

8. Keep government respectful of civil society and help spark more individual acts of service and philanthropy.

9. Seek out, study, and incorporate the best national civic entrepreneurs or their ideas. Use a respected intermediary to accelerate deployment.

10. Create mechanisms that mitigate risk by removing the financial, attitudinal, and behavioral obstacles that prevent the market and its opportunities from working well for marginalized citizens.

11. Offer a dose of competition and transparency through performance funding, creative RFPs, and data accessibility.

12. Support organizations that promise improved performance, civic engagement, and citizen-to-citizen interaction.

The Academy has been the source of considerable debate in New York's education community, with some claiming that the investment has not produced enough top-level principals. *The New York Times* examined the Academy's results and concluded that its graduates "have not done as well as those led by experienced principals or new principals who came through traditional routes."[11] The DOE immediately refuted the paper's conclusion, arguing that the analysis was flawed because, for example, Academy graduates tend to serve in the city's lowest-achieving schools. The first independent analysis of the program, released in August 2009, provides key evidence that New York's "in-house" version is working. The study found that elementary and middle schools led by Academy principals made better English Language Arts gains than schools with new principals who were not Academy graduates, and comparable mathematics gains.[12]

Whatever its track record ultimately, there is no doubt that Klein was able to use the Academy not only as a recruiting and training device but as a way to disrupt the previous entrenched and seniority-driven process of choosing principals.

Fourth, in conjunction with his disruptive leadership focus, Klein shifted greater decision making to principals. As he notes, "Leadership and empowerment to me are interrelated. You want to attract good people, and you want to empower them to do the work."[13] Klein gave principals somewhat more control over teacher selection, marking a major shift from rigid, seniority-based hiring to a more open-market system, in which principals can seek out and hire teachers. He also sought to devolve as much money and programmatic decision making to the schools and principals as the system would allow.

The chancellor provided principals with what in many ways amounted to management partners—teams of people or organizations dedicated to working with them in all key aspects of the schools' educational and operational decision making and implementation. Because these forces could not legally be hired to manage schools, the DOE referred to them as "school support" organizations and aggressively marketed the concept as a way for schools to finally free themselves from the system's bureaucracy and build a tailored approach for achieving results.

This devolution effort brought with it a pilot program in 2004 in which twenty-nine schools earned significant autonomy by promising to meet prescribed academic targets. Klein saw the early signs of progress and increased the program's scale, decentralizing the system to its fifteen hundred principals. As Amy Rosen, an education consultant who worked with Klein and his team on the second restructuring, noted, "By the time this phase of the work had come into play, I think that Joel had come to the conclusion that there was simply no way to manage fifteen hundred schools centrally."[14]

The reorganization removed layers of bureaucracy and converted the role of the central office to schools' accountability enforcer and support system for school-level decision makers. Klein came to view that moving from a single bureaucratic school system to a system of individual schools was essential to success. He kept tight control over accountability, knowledge management, and hiring of principals. Essentially, he "wanted to hold tight a couple of very core things and then let the rest flow to the schools."[15] In addition, the resulting structure made it more likely that principals would form partnerships with neighborhood-based civic groups.

Seven years after Bloomberg and Klein began their reforms, a number of key indicators show strong trends. Four-year graduation rates have risen every year, to an unprecedented high of 60.7 percent in 2008. State standardized test results, released in June 2009, for students in grades three through eight showed significant gains over the preceding three years: 69 percent of students performed at or above grade level in reading, up from 50.7 percent in 2006; and 82 percent did so in math, up from 57 percent in 2006. Looking at these metrics, Klein says, "The thing I am most excited about is this: When I started our schools, in every measure, we were way below the rest of the state. And now, for the first time, in elementary math, our schools are comparable to the rest of the state. They were 25 points behind. Now they're 2 or 3 points behind. This is really a big story, that fundamentally on the same test, at every level, we are basically matching the rest of this state."[16]

Nevertheless, Bloomberg and Klein's moves have brought sharp criticisms from some segments of the education community. Apart from teachers' union president Weingarten, who at times has been conciliatory[17] and at other times has led significant fights against Klein's policy and management methods, perhaps the most vocal critic has been education historian Diane Ravitch. Ravitch not only has criticized Klein's pedagogical choices and heavy attention to standardized testing but also has decried nearly every aspect of his work. In addition, she suggests that his approach is too authoritarian, and complains about the very assets upon which New York predicated change—the congruence of mayoral and chancellor authority.[18] Indeed, this tension between strong leadership for bold change and extended community negotiations is real, and although it can be mitigated by the inclusion of community feedback, it cannot be eliminated.

As New York City's school results continue to unfold, and the inevitable back-and-forth over education practices and policies continues, one thing remains certain: In nearly every facet of the city's educational work, entrepreneurialism is alive and well—and worthy of close review. By deliberately seeking out ways to promote choice and competition, and by engaging in public-private partnerships to provide more and better services to the schools, Bloomberg and Klein have removed barriers to entry, broken out of the old monolithic bureaucracy, and brought about cultural change that reaches beyond the central office and into the city's fifteen hundred schools. The schools have benefited from the talent, energy, and expertise of outside entrepreneurs and results-oriented service providers. In turn, these organizations have provided new opportunities for those outside the system to innovate and implement new initiatives—and to do so in arguably the most complex and challenging school system in the nation.

Entrepreneurial Community Solutions

In the end, perhaps inevitably, I return to what I know best—what happens in the city, where "all politics is local." Let's imagine a community highly engaged across all its sectors in a collective effort to produce social progress. In this city, civic leadership worries about stagnant income mobility, poor education, homelessness, and abuse. Civic and political leaders have high expectations for their citizens, believing that all individuals can thrive with the right set of supports and equal opportunity. How might this community scale transformative change?

The conversation among the best and brightest social entrepreneurs often revolves around scale. These passionate individuals want to contribute as much as they can to as many as they can. To them and the people they might help, the larger the scale the better. Some aim to reach a larger market share within a city with their service, or try to offer more services in the same neighborhood or community. For others, greater impact means expanding the *organization*, either directly or through new branches or affiliates involving local sponsors. For yet others, it means changing policy or furthering a social movement. A young mentor who takes on an additional child to help doubles the scale in a tangible and important way.

Some look at Dorothy Stoneman, former Harlem teacher and civil rights activist, as the ultimate civic entrepreneur. Stoneman took her organization to a large scale with 226 local programs, a special authorizing statute, and specific mention in the 2009 Recovery Act. However, Stoneman's program YouthBuild also serves as a successful model of the system approach advocated in this book. First, YouthBuild has created a dense network of organizations—involving multiple levels of government—that support the development of participating youths. And second, despite substantial government funding, Stoneman insists on retaining a distinctive non-governmental element of success, which she explains as follows: "We say we believe in the power of love. We try to communicate to local staff the ways in which we have to care about young people for it to work. That isn't what government does."[19]

Her description of YouthBuild's success might sound intangible or immeasurable, but Stoneman is an experienced entrepreneur who has learned a number of very useful lessons about growing a social innovation. Stoneman cites as a first step standing ready with evidence of excellent results. Her second step involves mobilizing support from as many corners as possible, including grassroots and national advocacy organizations, public figures, media, and funding decision makers. Stoneman warns entrepreneurs that they face a constant navigation of political considerations and relationships with street-level bureaucrats and political appointees. Interestingly, despite Stoneham's enormous success with federal funding she recommends a degree of financial independence from government funders.[20]

Youth Villages, a mental health service provider for children and youth, also illustrates how a nonprofit can break through entry barriers across states and local communities. For years, hard data on the effectiveness of its approach and its clear cost efficiencies allowed Youth Villages to overcome the natural hesitation of state government decision makers to fund an out-of-state provider. In 2003, the Edna McConnell Clark Foundation gave Youth Villages funding to hire Bridgespan to further develop a growth plan including such components as how to handle the political sphere: securing trusted champions to help make the case; investing in capacity to pursue opportunities; hiring in-state lobbyists; and offering to work under trial contracts to mitigate risk for state officials.[21] This case also sharply illustrates how much social change depends on political decisions.

While encouraging the organic growth of organizations with proven models like YouthBuild and Youth Villages, we focus on community-wide solutions and therefore view the successes that transform a school, a family, or a single child as the building blocks that trigger much broader societal changes. In writing this book, we searched for actions that catalyze system change. We found disruptive interventions and better ways of integrating a delivery network—both of which might be missing ingredients that trigger systemwide reaction. Further, because social services rely on relationships and networks to produce opportunity, looking at innovation solely through an organizational lens limits imagination and, ultimately, results.

Geoff Mulgan's work on the role of networks in innovation shows that continual innovation requires both entrepreneurial start-ups and large organizations: "Innovation thrives best when there are effective alliances between small organizations and entrepreneurs (the "bees" who are mobile, fast, and cross-pollinate) and big organizations (the "trees" with roots, resilience, and size) which can grow ideas to scale."[22] Similarly, NYU's Anthony Shorris offered an insight at a recent online meeting of our Executive Session. "A few charter schools may have some great successes, but unless their lessons are used thoughtfully, they won't help large school system administrators much," he wrote. "We need 'translators' who are open to learning from these efforts (and empowered by their political leadership) but are still skilled enough in large-scale public organization management to move big systems."[23]

I prefer to define the impact that a civic entrepreneur can have even more broadly to include other methods of enhancing opportunities and improving social outcomes for large numbers of people. The Urban Assets Initiative, the White House social innovation efforts, and Bloomberg and Klein's New York City school reforms all pursue scale, achieving it sometimes by policy advocacy and other times by championing a bold new delivery idea. Another important way to change social conditions, which we do not touch on at length but can serve as an effective force multiplier of social innovation, is public awareness efforts.

Better known examples include American Legacy Foundation's "truth" youth anti-smoking campaign and Susan G. Komen for the Cure's pink ribbon campaigns and Race for the Cure events. UNCF's "A Mind Is a Terrible Thing to Waste" is an early example of a campaign that continues today. In an era of social media—when individualized messages reach millions of people instantly through trusted contacts within their own social networks—the opportunities for driving change at scale are even greater. These and other public awareness campaigns can produce good social outcomes by changing behaviors.

As a member of the board of America's Promise Alliance (APA), I have admired the impact of its two remarkable leaders, Alma Powell and Marguerite Kondracke, for several years. But I never thought of the organization as an example of civic entrepreneurship until it took on the high school dropout epidemic. Deftly, APA elevated the national profile of this issue, calling millions to action. It leveraged the participation of its member organizations and strategic partners, including a vast array of youth-serving organizations. Its efforts continue to bring resources, attention, and impatience with the status quo to an agenda, creating the conditions that allow other civic entrepreneurs to expand, coordinate, and further align their good deeds. Powell and Kondracke are civic entrepreneurs whose skills allow them to nominate and draw attention to important areas of social policy facilitate transformative change.

In an effort to combat the nation's dropout crisis, they also showed skill in using policy reports to advance the cause. In 2006, two national thought leaders—John Bridgeland and John DiIulio—released an influential report commissioned by the Gates Foundation entitled *The Silent Epidemic: Perspectives of High School Dropouts*, which helped to catapult the dropout issue to the national stage. The two talked to teenagers themselves to learn why they had dropped out. Students overwhelmingly said that school did not motivate or push them to work hard; nor did it offer relevant coursework. Most were sure they could

have finished school and wanted better teachers, more individualized instruction, and higher expectations—from both teachers and parents.[24] The report's discoveries, including the sad fact
that two thousand public schools were little more than "dropout
factories," grabbed the attention of mainstream media—from a
Time magazine cover story to two episodes on *Oprah*—and in
turn reached the American public.

Alma Powell and Marguerite Kondracke used the attention
given this report to build awareness and trigger action at the
local and national levels, igniting a national campaign called
Grad Nation. From April 2008 to August 2009, America's
Promise hosted more than forty-five summits, each bringing
together up to 350 people from across the community—civic
leaders, business owners, students, and their parents—to focus
attention on high school graduation. As we saw in Detroit, communities are using Grad Nation summits and newly available
data to animate bold change in public education and to spark a
renewed commitment to their youth.

Despite their nationwide or global visions, the remarkable
national civic entrepreneurs we visited face very real local trials.
A mayor's ambition to improve the community in his or her priority areas can create tension with a national entrepreneur's focus
on an innovative offering. And the mayor's preference or commitment to local providers may produce its own set of challenges.

During the first of our Executive Sessions, the talented
mayor of Atlanta, Shirley Franklin, listened as civic entrepreneurs explained the great programs they could import
into Atlanta. Although impressed by their accomplishments,
Franklin volunteered that she understood her city better and
would decide what interventions might be most helpful—and
in what manner. The healthy exchange that followed raised an
important question about how much an entrepreneur with a
proven model can customize it for a local official before it loses
its efficacy. As Greg Dees notes, "Some of the national civic
entrepreneurs feel strongly about the integrity of their approach,

and they have very robust minimal critical specifications. Full-fledged, they want to have control, want a certain culture and approach, and it may rub local folks the wrong way, or they won't be comfortable with it."[25] Indeed, most civic innovations involve more than just copying a set of building blocks. They heavily depend on both leadership and the tacit knowledge of an innovation, not just the explicit knowledge that naturally attracts outsiders or potential adopters.[26]

Yet the possibilities of a marriage are real when the civic entrepreneur engages in dialogue with local community members and adapts his model to accommodate local conditions and partners. At the same time, real progress occurs when mayors and other civic leaders are brave enough to support disruptive change, knowing it will face opposition. Both civic entrepreneurs and local officials must understand that they cannot avoid the political arena if they are to effect real change in social outcomes. At the least, an understanding of these potential tensions and of how each side views the other will go a long way toward achieving a particular social result. Having a powerful civic leader or civic institution who understands both the innovation and the community and establishes a specific vehicle for change helps greatly. Mind Trust in Indianapolis, CEO in New York, Boston's Greenlight Fund, and the White House Social Innovation Fund seek to fill this important role.

Civic entrepreneurs may address these tensions by partnering with a local organization and/or spreading a set of principles or an idea, rather than expanding the organization itself. Jeffrey Bradach, a cofounder of Bridgespan Group, suggests a way entrepreneurs intent on impact can achieve it in more targeted ways. He writes that "the level of inherent complexity is significant" for an innovation, even in organizations that appear to provide a straightforward service. "By understanding its theory of change, an organization may discover that what needs replication is a piece of the program, not the entire program or the organization itself." This form of expansion may allow the organization to better capitalize on existing resources in a community, from networks to established organization infrastructure to local trust.[27]

Now let's look at impact from the vantage of a city where the leaders strive both to change the environment for social progress and to introduce disruptive catalytic providers. This city would challenge assumptions, produce venture funding for new efforts, measure and enforce performance, and change the regulatory environment. A community determined to produce transformative social value would look to innovations that improve outcomes, regardless of whether the interventions involve reforming existing organizations, importing new ones, or devising hybrids. The community would make it easier for old and new players to expand and be creative by ensuring that rules, certifications, and other requirements operate to protect health and safety and not as barriers to entry that protect incumbent providers. In other words, the community would knit together the various threads explored in this book to create the best possible conditions for progress. It would aspire to intentionally position itself as a fertile place for civic progress.

Both the civic entrepreneur and the community would recognize that the missing ingredient for transforming a social service delivery system could be one of a number of things: enhancing the human resource pipeline, improving management, inducing a technical innovation, or providing realignment. Both would also recognize that although innovation and change can be risky endeavors for all involved, each side needs to assume some of the political or financial risk necessary to realize progress.

Catalytic transformation, as we use the term—or ecosystem change, in the words of Greg Dees—relies on the interactions between people in the community, through their social networks, that trigger changes in behavior, norms, or culture. Dees says:

"Changing the ecosystem may be a more powerful way to achieve lasting change than simply growing your organization. . . . Your organization might stimulate others to change their behaviors or stimulate new entrants to come in. They see what you are doing and are attracted by it. They might say we can do it even better. Then you've created an industry . . . you've changed the conditions or the patterns of behavior of the players in the ecosystem."[28]

For better or worse, with government controlling so much of the funding and rule-setting in the areas of civic progress, scale will sooner or later become a political question. Truly dramatic, results-driven change will then require pulling political levers— animating the clients who will benefit from reform, ceding credit to public officials, channeling the frustration of the poorly served, and traditional organizing of both clients and taxpayers. Suzanna Valdez, the talented chief of staff to Mayor Manny Diaz in Miami, points out that in many communities change does not mean simply running over existing authority figures like teachers; it may mean incorporating them in the movement. To Paula Ellis, driving change means getting real community information to (and from) residents in a fashion that connects them emotionally to change. To Michael Lomax it means building indignation while building a broad movement. Whatever the tools and the rhetoric, it is clear that true civic progress requires political success.

Staying Entrepreneurial: Saving Yourself from Success

We add two cautions for civic entrepreneurs. First, they should guard against losing their core values as they become entangled with government and politics. This book advocates for a new relationship between public officials and civic entrepreneurs because government funding, for better or worse, often dominates a service area. How the relationship develops, and on what terms, will determine whether the one-time social disruptor stays part of the solution or becomes part of the problem.

The risks escalate according to the type of participation. A civic entrepreneur engaged in policy advocacy has little trouble keeping clarity of mission and voice when engaged in demanding funding or policy changes that increase opportunity for the working poor. However, when civic entrepreneurs move into contractual or grant relationships with government, they risk losing their voices, flexibility, or fidelity to their business models. Engagement with government by nonprofit organizations hoping to serve more people inevitably will increase tensions with contract managers.

A second word of caution. Performance matters greatly, but because social progress occurs inside a thick system of relationships, responsibility for success or failure is enormously difficult to place. Scientifically rigorous empirical studies can be expensive and take a long time. We argue that although these studies produce important results, they should not be the only means of determining support. Meaningful efforts to capture citizen feedback and measure relevant outputs can be instructive. The cases presented here often relied on early indicators of success that showed meaningful change, even when their innovations had not yet been scientifically validated.

Despite defenders of the status quo and others who insist on waiting long periods for proof of concept, we have seen civic entrepreneurs whose new ideas, passion, and organizational ability swept away hopelessness and replaced it with opportunity. In so doing, they prove that energetic and creative citizens can produce truly important results.

The Future

Families and individuals struggle each day to make ends meet, and institutional programs often fail them. Across the country, there is also a surge in community interest in service and civic engagement, and in entrepreneurs who break new ground by disrupting the status quo and engaging it in a way that makes it work better.

We have seen that civic inventers can produce exhilarating change in people, families, or communities by expecting them to succeed and by viewing their own jobs as clearing away the obstacles. Executive leadership, whether from the president, a governor, a mayor, a foundation president, or a student activist, can create the conditions for change.

Ten years after I left as mayor, I was sitting in an Indianapolis doctor's office, waiting for my appointment. A lady filling out insurance forms behind one of the desks called me over—I assumed to tell me something bad about my insurance. Instead, and much to my delight, she referred to a program I had started as prosecutor two decades before to help struggling mothers with services and child support. She showed me a picture of her daughter, who had just graduated from college, and credited my efforts as a springboard.

Even seemingly modest acts by public and nonprofit officials alike make a difference in families' lives because they operate in a social network that affects both the people assisted and the providers themselves. Civic health requires broader and deeper change and more return on current investments. A leap forward in the quality of life in communities will occur more frequently when government opens the door for catalytic social progress spearheaded by the many leaders profiled in this book and the many more who make change daily in their communities. Together these acts can play a part in turning clients of the state into active, participating, and productive citizens.

Notes

Preface

1. U.S. Census Bureau. "Poverty: 2008 Highlights," www
.census.gov/hhes/www/poverty/poverty08/pov08hi.html
(accessed September 17, 2009).
2. Becky Pettit and Bruce Western. "Mass Imprisonment
and the Life Course: Race and Class Inequality in U.S.
Incarceration." *American Sociological Review*, 2004, 69,
151–169.
3. In 2005, 899,000 children were substantiated or indicated as
abused or neglected, and 506,483 children were in the foster
care system. Child Welfare League of America, www.cwla
.org/advocacy/2008legagenda05.htm.
4. Ron Haskins and Isabel Sawhill. *Creating an Opportunity
Society*. Washington, DC: Brookings Institution Press, 2009,
p. 2.
5. Jane Jacobs. *The Death and Life of Great American Cities*. New
York: Modern Library, 1993. (Originally published 1961)
6. Most recently see David K. Cohen and Susan L. Moffit. *The
Ordeal of Equality: Did Federal Regulation Fix the Schools?*
Cambridge, MA: Harvard University Press, 2009.
7. Teach For America. "2008 TFA Annual Report." Teach For
America, www.teachforamerica.org.
8. CNCS. "Volunteering in America Research Highlights."
Statistics from Sounding from the Listening Post Project, a

national survey of nonprofit organizations done in partnership with CNCS.

9. Stephen Goldsmith. *The 21st Century City: Resurrecting Urban America.* Washington, DC: Regnery Publishing, 1997.

Chapter 1

1. Significant contributors to these two fields who help inform this book include Bill Drayton, Greg Dees, Paul Light, Arthur Brooks, Geoff Mulgan, Beth Anderson, Jeffrey Braddach, Rachel Mosher-Williams, Alex Nicholls, Charles Leadbeater, Jane Wei-Skillern, and Dutch Leonard.

2. Roger L. Martin and Sally Osberg. "Social Entrepreneurship: The Case for Definition." *Stanford Social Innovation Review,* Spring 2007.

3. Mayer N. Zald and Roberta Ash. "Social Movement Organizations: Growth, Decay, and Change." *Social Forces,* March 1966, 44(3), 327–341.

4. See Douglas Henton, John Melville, and Kimberly Walesh, "Civic Entrepreneurs: Economic Professional as Collaborative Leader." *Community Economics Newsletter,* 269 (March 1999), from Center for Community Economic Development; Community, Natural Resource and Economic Development Programs; and University of Wisconsin-Extension, Cooperative Extension Service. Available online at www.aae.wisc.edu/pubs/cenews/docs/ce269.txt (accessed August 31, 2009). Also see Douglas Henton, John Melville, and Kimberly Walesh, *Civic Revolutionaries: Igniting the Passion for Change in America's Communities.* San Francisco: Jossey-Bass, 2004.

5. Center for Advancement of Social Entrepreneurship. "Developing the Field of Social Entrepreneurship," CASE, June 2008.

6. See Robert Michels, *Political Parties: A Sociological Study of the Oligarchical Tendencies of Modern Democracy Transaction*

Publishers, 1959. Original English version published 1915. Available online at http://socserv2.socsci.mcmaster.ca/~econ/ ugcm/3ll3/michels/polipart.pdf. Osterman writes that "enhancing the membership's sense of capacity and agency and building a culture of contestation within the organization that encourages the membership to push the elite who dominate the organization." See Paul Osterman, "Overcoming Oligarchy: Culture and Agency in Social Movement Organizations." *Administrative Science Quarterly*, December 2006, 51, 622–649.

7. William Eggers and author. *Governing by Network: The New Shape of the Public Sector*. Washington, DC: Brookings Institution Press, 2005, p. 8.

8. William Drayton. "The Citizen Sector: Becoming as Entrepreneurial and Competitive as Business." *California Management Review*, 2002, 44(3), 120–132.

9. Greg Dees, interview with author, Miami, Florida, February 27, 2008.

10. See O'Dell and Grayson (1998b), as cited in Robert Behn, "The Adoption of Innovation: The Challenge of Learning to Adapt Tacit Knowledge." In Sandford Borins (Ed.), *Innovations in Government: Research, Recognition and Replication*. Washington, DC: Brookings Institution Press, 2008, p. 153.

11. Kevin Huffman, interview with Tim Glynn Burke, Miami, Florida, February 26, 2008.

12. Ibid.

13. Christopher B. Swanson. "Cities in Crisis: A Special Analytic Report on High School Graduation." Editorial Projects in Education Research Center, prepared with support from America's Promise Alliance and the Bill and Melinda Gates Foundation, April 1, 2008.

14. College Summit. "Results and Metrics." College Summit, www.collegesummit.org/aboutus/results_and_metrics/our_ reach_and_growth (accessed February 23, 2009).

15. Sarah Alvord, David Brown, and Christine Letts. "Social Entrepreneurship and Social Transformation: An Exploratory Study." *The Journal of Applied Behavioral Science*, 40(3), 2004, 260–282.

16. Andrew Wolk. "Advancing Social Entrepreneurship: Recommendations for Policy Makers and Government Agencies." Root Cause/MIT, April 2008.

17. Beth Gazley. "Beyond the Contract: The Scope and Nature of Informal Government–Nonprofit Partnerships." *Public Administration Review*, 68(1), January/February 2008, 141–154.

18. Sungsook Cho and David Gillespie. "A Conceptual Model Exploring the Dynamics of Government–Nonprofit Service Delivery." *Nonprofit and Voluntary Sector Quarterly*, 35(3), September 2006, 493–509.

19. Peter L. Berger and Richard John Neuhaus. *To Empower People: From State to Civil Society*. Washington, DC: American Enterprise Institute, 1996.

20. Leslie Lenkowsky. "The Politics of Doing Good: Philanthropic Leadership for the Twenty-First Century." In William Damon and Susan Verducci (Eds.), *Taking Philanthropy Seriously: Beyond Noble Intentions to Responsible Giving*. Bloomington: Indiana University Press, 2006, p. 60.

21. Isabel Sawhill. "The Behavioral Aspects of Poverty." *Public Interest*, 153, Fall 2003, 79–93.

Chapter 2

1. Bill Milliken, telephone interview with author, July 1, 2009.

2. Communities in Schools. "Communities in Schools at-a-Glance." Communities in Schools, www.cisnet.org (accessed May 22, 2009).

3. Paul Bloom and Gregory Dees. "Cultivate Your Ecosystem." *Stanford Social Innovation Review*, 6(1), 2008, 47–53. The authors also draw from the work of Harvard Business School professor Pankal Ghemawat.

4. Clayton Christensen, Jerome H. Grossman, and Jason Hwang. *The Innovator's Prescription: A Disruptive Solution for Health Care.* New York: McGraw-Hill, 2009, p. x.

5. Chris Pineda. "Mapping Your Community's Faith-Based Assets: An Asset Inventory Tool for Collecting and Using Data on the Faith-Based Community Organizations in Your City." Harvard University Kennedy School of Government, www.innovations.harvard.edu/cache/documents/137/13704.pdf (accessed May 30, 2009).

6. Thanks to Mark Moore for his thoughts on the industrial organization model. Personal communication, Cambridge, Massachusetts, November 28, 2007.

7. Ibid.

8. Herb Sturz, personal communication with author, May 22, 2009.

9. William Schambra. "The View from 1313." Presentation to the Chicago Grantmakers for Effective Organizations, Chicago, Illinois, July 1, 2008, www.hudson.org/files/publications/2008_07_01_Schambra_1313_Strategic_Philanthropy.pdf.

10. Illinois Department of Healthcare and Family Services. Predictive Modeling System Abstract. Available at www.healthtransformation.net/cs/medicaid_best_practices_grant_award (accessed September 17, 2009).

11. Joel Klein, interview with author and Gigi Georges, New York, New York, June 8, 2009.

12. Christopher B. Swanson. "Cities in Crisis: A Special Analytic Report on High School Graduation." April 1, 2008. EPE Research Center, prepared with support from America's Promise Alliance and the Bill and Melinda Gates Foundation.

13. Figures cited from Michael Tenbusch, telephone interview with Tim Glynn Burke, March 25, 2009.

14. Michael Tenbusch, telephone interview with Tim Glynn Burke, March 12, 2009.

15. America's Promise Alliance. "APA Dropout Prevention Summit Update and Highlights." Internal document

received in e-mail correspondence from Charles Hiteshew, February 25, 2009.

16. Mike Tenbusch. "Detroit Dropout Prevention Update: One Year After." United Way of Southeastern Michigan internal document, March 2009. Provided by Charles Hiteshew in an e-mail correspondence to Tim Glynn Burke, March 10, 2009.

17. Charles Hiteshew, telephone interview with Tim Glynn Burke, March 10, 2009.

18. Geoffrey Canada, e-mail message to author, September 16, 2009.

19. Larry Berger, interview with author, New York, New York, February 2, 2009.

20. NYC Department of Education. "School of One: Leveraging Technology to Personalize Learning in 21st Century Schools." Grant proposal, April 8, 2009.

21. Joel Rose, telephone interview with Gigi Georges, June 18, 2009.

22. Michael Fullan. *The New Meaning of Educational Change*. New York: Teachers College Press, 2001.

23. Larry Berger, interview with author, New York, New York, February 2, 2009.

24. Martin Fisher, e-mail message to author, June 25, 2009.

25. Ibid.

26. KickStart. "About KickStart." KickStart, www.kickstart.org/what-we-do/impact/ (accessed November 2, 2009).

27. Monitor. "History and Facts." Monitor, www.monitor.com/AboutUs/WhoWeAre/HistoryandFacts/tabid/116/L/en-US/Default.aspx (accessed December 16, 2008).

28. Tammany Hobbs, telephone interview with Tim Glynn Burke, December 26, 2008.

29. Vanessa Kirsch, telephone interview with author, May 22, 2009.

30. Ibid.

31. New Profit Inc. "Monitor Group: An Unparalleled Partnership." New Profit Inc., www.newprofit.com/comm_sig.asp (accessed December 16, 2008).

32. Aaron Lieberman, telephone interview with Scott Knox and Tim Glynn Burke, May 7, 2009.

33. "To love the little platoon we belong to in society, is the first principle (the germ as it were) of public affections." Edmund Burke, *Reflections on the Revolution in France*, 1790.

34. Corporation for National and Community Service. "Volunteering in America Research Highlights." July 2009, statistics from Sounding from the Listening Post Project, a national survey of nonprofit organizations done in partnership with CNCS.

35. Nathan Dietz, Robert Grimm, Jr., and Kimberly Spring. "Youth Helping America, Leveling the Path to Participation: Volunteering and Civic Engagement Among Youth from Disadvantaged Circumstances." Corporation for National and Community Service, www.nationalservice.gov/pdf/07_0406_disad_youth.pdf (accessed July 13, 2009).

36. John Blomquist, JoAnn Jastrzab, Julie Masker, and Larry Orr. "Youth Corps: Promising Strategies for Young People and Their Communities." Abt Associates Inc., www.abtassoc.com/reports/Youth-Corps.pdf\ (accessed July 13, 2009).

37. Itai Dinour, interview with Gigi Georges, New York, New York, August 6, 2008.

38. Jacob Lew, interview with Gigi Georges, New York, New York, August 12, 2008.

39. Marc Freedman and John S. Gomperts. "Putting Retiring Baby Boomers to Work." *The Chronicle of Philanthropy*, November 24, 2005. http://philanthropy.com/free/articles/v18/i04/04004301.htm (accessed May 22, 2009).

40. Ibid.

41. John Gomperts, e-mail message to author, July 7, 2009. Also see: ExperienceCorps, "Independent Research Shows National Service Program Enlisting Tutors Over Age 55 Produces Big Gains in Student Learning." ExperienceCorps, www.experiencecorps.org/news/releases/nr.cfm?newsID=192 (accessed August 13, 2009).

42. Ibid.

43. Aaron Hurst, interview by author, March 5, 2008.

44. Ibid.

45. See Evan Hochberg, "How to Get an Extra $1-Billion from Business." *Chronicle of Philanthropy*, October 12, 2006, as posted by the Taproot Foundation, www.taprootfoundation.org/about/articles/chron_101206.shtml (accessed August 13, 2009).

46. Aaron Hurst, interview by author, March 5, 2008.

47. Lisa Spinali, telephone interview with Tim Glynn Burke, April 7, 2008.

48. Steve Lohr. "Changing Their Spots, Charities Utilize Some of Capitalism's Virtues." *The New York Times*, December 4, 2008, www.nytimes.com/2008/02/24/business/worldbusiness/24iht-24social.10329242.html (accessed May 28, 2009).

49. In2Books, http://in2books.epals.com/login.aspx?ReturnUrl=/default.aspx (accessed July 15, 2009).

50. Linda B. Gambrell and William H. Teale. "Raising Urban Students' Literacy Achievement by Engaging in Authentic, Challenging Work." *International Reading Association*, 60(8), May 2007, 728–739, as posted at www.epals.com/images/tour/RTarticle.pdf (accessed July 15, 2009).

51. Sunny Antrim. "Donors Choose Facilitates Gifts That Keep Giving." *ABC News 20/20*, December 20, 2007, http://abcnews.go.com/2020/story?id=4028215&page=1 (accessed August 13, 2009).

52. Julie Flaherty, "BLACKBOARD; Because Teachers Don't Always Get What They Want." *The New York Times*, August 5, 2001, Technology section, www.nytimes.com/2001/08/05/education/blackboard-because-teachers-don-t-always-get-what-they-want.html?sec=technology (accessed May 28, 2009).

53. USA Network. "Character Approved: Charles Best 2009 Winner–Giving." USA Network, www.usanetwork.com/characterapproved/honorees/best/index.html (accessed July 15, 2009).

54. Nanci Hellmich. "Prof gives a hand, not a handout." *USAToday*, June 12, 2002, www.usatoday.com/life/2002/2002–06–13-modestneeds.htm (accessed May 28, 2009).

55. Wally Martinson, telephone interview with Tim Glynn Burke, December 15, 2008.

56. Ibid.

57. Krista Sisterhen, written correspondence to author, August 4, 2008.

58. Michael Fullan. *The New Meaning of Educational Change*. New York: Teachers College Press, 2001.

Chapter 3

1. United Ways of Texas. "A Survey of Voter Attitudes on Pre-K Education in Texas." March 2006, as cited in Goldsmith and Meyers.

2. Craig S. Gordon and Gary T. Henry. "Competition in the Sandbox: A Test of the Effects of Preschool Competition on Educational Outcomes." *Journal of Policy Analysis and Management*, 25(1), November, 2005, 97–127, as cited in Goldsmith and Meyers.

3. Melissa Marschall, Mark Schneider, and Paul Teske. *Choosing Schools: Consumer Choice and the Quality of American Schools*. Princeton, NJ: Princeton University Press, 2002, p. 790, as cited in Goldsmith and Meyers.

4. Kevin G. Welner. *Neovouchers: The Emergence of Tuition Tax Credits for Private Schooling*. Lanham, MA: Rowan & Littlefield, 2008, p. 19. Richard Hess, "Making a Market in Education." In *Revolution on the Market*. Washington, DC: Brookings Institution, 2002, p. 52.

5. Mark Casson and Marina Della Giusta. "Entrepreneurship and Social Capital: Analyzing the Impact of Social Networks on Entrepreneurial Activity from a Rational Action Perspective." *International Small Business Journal*, 25(3), 2007, 220–244.

6. Geoff Mulgan. "Cultivating the Other Invisible Hand of Social Entrepreneurship: Comparative Advantage, Public Policy, and Future Research Priorities." In Alex Nicholls (Ed.), *Social Entrepreneurship: New Models of Sustainable Social Change*. New York: Oxford University Press, 2006.

7. Third Sector organizations became significant deliverer of public services (the public sector provides almost 50 percent of sector's earned income, which was £6.6bn GBP in 2004–2005). See Jenny Clark. *UK Voluntary Sector Workforce Almanac 2007*. National Council for Voluntary Organizations and Workforce Hub, October 2007.

8. See www.cabinetoffice.gov.uk/third_sector/about_us.aspx (accessed September 7, 2009).

9. Geoff Mulgan. "Cultivating the Other Invisible Hand of Social Entrepreneurship: Comparative Advantage, Public Policy, and Future Research Priorities." In Alex Nicholls (Ed.), *Social Entrepreneurship: New Models of Sustainable Social Change*. New York: Oxford University Press, 2006, p. 82.

10. Dan Gregory, Cabinet Office, conversation with author, 2009.

11. The White House Office of Faith-Based and Community Initiatives. "Unlevel Playing Field: Barriers to Participation by Faith-Based and Community Organizations in Federal Social Service Programs." White House Office of Faith-Based and Community Initiatives, http://georgewbush-whitehouse.archives.gov/news/releases/2001/08/unlevelfield.html (accessed May 20, 2009).

12. Ibid.

13. The White House Office of Faith-Based and Community Initiatives. "Innovations in Compassion; The Faith-Based and Community Initiative: A Final Report to the Armies of Compassion," December 2008. Bush issued his second executive order (the first established the OFBCI), Executive Order 13279.

14. The White House Office of Faith-Based and Community Initiatives. "Innovations in Compassion; The Faith-Based and Community Initiative: A Final Report to the Armies of Compassion," December 2008.

15. Findings from a Retrospective Survey of Faith-Based and Community Organizations (FBCOs): An Assessment of the Compassion Capital Fund. Cambridge, MA: Abt Associates Inc., April 24, 2007.

16. Geoff Mulgan. "Cultivating the Other Invisible Hand of Social Entrepreneurship: Comparative Advantage, Public Policy, and Future Research Priorities." In Alex Nicholls (Ed.), *Social Entrepreneurship: New Models of Sustainable Social Change*. New York: Oxford University Press, 2006, p. 84.

17. Amy Sullivan. "Obama's Faith-Based Office Gets Down to Work." *Time*, April 9, 2009.

18. Geoff Mulgan. "Cultivating the Other Invisible Hand of Social Entrepreneurship: Comparative Advantage, Public Policy, and Future Research Priorities." In Alex Nicholls (Ed.), *Social Entrepreneurship: New Models of Sustainable Social Change*. New York: Oxford University Press, 2006, p. 81.

19. Kirk A. Dearden et al. "The Power of Positive Deviance." *BMJ*, 329, November 2004, 1177–1179.

20. Ibid.

21. See www.upcsinstitute.org/ (accessed September 7, 2009).

22. Mayor's Office, City of Indianapolis. "Accountability Report on Mayor-Sponsored Charter Schools." Mayor's Office, City of Indianapolis, fall 2007, www.indygov.org/NR/rdonlyres/52B0BAF8-E7F5-4135-9460-3750BACEC174/0/AccountabilityReportUSE.pdf.

23. Christopher B. Swanson. "Cities in Crisis: A Special Analytic Report on High School Graduation." Editorial Projects in Education Research Center. Prepared with support from America's Promise Alliance and the Bill and Melinda

Gates Foundation, April 1, 2008, www.americaspromise.org/~/media/Files/Our%20Work/Dropout%20Prevention/Cities%20in%20Crisis/Cities_In_Crisis_Report_2008.ashx (accessed August 12, 2009).

24. Annie E. Casey Foundation. "Closing the Achievement Gap: Co-Investment." Annie E. Casey Foundation, 2008, www.aecf.org/~/media/PublicationFiles/6Coinvestment_r10.pdf (accessed July 23, 2009).

25. Frederick M. Hess and Bryan C. Hassel. "Fueling Educational Entrepreneurship: Addressing the Human Capital Challenge," www.hks.harvard.edu/pepg/PDF/Papers/Hess-Hassel_Human_Capital_Policy_PEPG07–06.pdf. Discussion paper presented at an American Enterprise Institute, Washington, D.C., October 2006 (accessed July 23, 2009).

26. The Mind Trust. "History." The Mind Trust, www.themindtrust.org/about/mission.aspx (accessed July 23, 2009).

27. The Associated Press. "Man Looks to Take Learning-Through-Music Nationwide." USA Today, April 30, 2008. www.usatoday.com/news/education/2008–04–30-teacher-music_N.htm (accessed July 23, 2009).

28. David Harris. Application to the Innovations in American Government Awards Program: Charter Schools Initiative, City of Indianapolis, September 14, 2005.

29. Byron R. Johnson and William Wubbenhorst. "Ohio Compassion Capital Program: A Case Study." Baylor Institute for Studies of Religion, February 2008, http://216.157.17.136/pdf/case_ohiocompassion.pdf (accessed May 19, 2009).

30. Krista Sisterhen, telephone interview with Tim Glynn Burke, October 24, 2008.

31. The Roundtable on Religion and Social Welfare Policy. "An Interview with Krista Sisterhen of the Ohio Governor's Office of Faith-Based and Community Initiatives," May 9, 2005, www.socialpolicyandreligion.org/interviews/interview_upd.cfm?id=89&pageMode=general (accessed May 19, 2009).

32. Krista Sisterhen, telephone interview with Tim Glynn Burke, October 24, 2008.

33. Roundtable on Religion and Social Welfare Policy. "An Interview with Krista Sisterhen of the Ohio Governor's Office of Faith-Based and Community Initiatives." The Roundtable on Religion and Social Welfare Policy, May 9, 2005, www .socialpolicyandreligion.org/interviews/interview_upd.cfm?id =89&pageMode=general (accessed May 19, 2009).

34. Ibid.

35. Krista Sisterhen, telephone interview with Tim Glynn Burke, October 24, 2008.

36. Wally Martinson, telephone interview with Tim Glynn Burke, December 15, 2008.

37. Roundtable on Religion and Social Welfare Policy. "An Interview with John DiIulio." Roundtable on Religion and Social Welfare Policy, November 6, 2007, www.religionand-socialpolicy.org/interviews/interview_upd.cfm?id=155&pag eMode=general (accessed May 20, 2009).

38. Krista Sisterhen, telephone interview with Tim Glynn Burke, October 24, 2008.

39. Anne Farris and Claire Hughes. "States Peer Over Borders for Best Practices." The Roundtable on Religion and Social Welfare Policy, December 19, 2006. www.religionandsocial-policy.org/newsletters/article.cfm?id=5748 (accessed May 19, 2009).

40. The White House. "Transforming Government: A Level Playing Field and New Partners." The White House, February, 2008, http://georgewbush-whitehouse.archives. gov/government/fbci/fs_trans-govt.html (accessed July 22, 2009).

41. The White House Office of Faith-Based and Community Initiatives. Innovations in Compassion; The Faith-Based and Community Initiative: A Final Report to the Armies of Compassion," December 2008.

42. David Gragan. "The Public Contracting Process in Support of Entrepreneurial Solutions." Working paper prepared as pre-reading for the Harvard Kennedy School Executive Session on Transforming Cities Through Civic Entrepreneurship, Cambridge, Massachusetts, January 15, 2009.

43. Ibid.

44. Jason Whetsell. Comments at the Executive Session on Transforming Cities Through Civic Entrepreneurship, Cambridge, Massachusetts, January 16, 2009.

45. Sunset Advisory Commission. "Guide to the Texas Sunset Process," July 2008.

46. Collin Levy. "Schoolhouse Rock: D.C. Education Chief Says School Choice Shouldn't Be Reserved for the Rich." *The Wall Street Journal*, December 22, 2007.

47. Adrian Fenty. "Lessons of Driving Education Reform in D.C." Panel discussion at Gathering of Leaders, Miami, Florida, February 25, 2009.

48. Michelle Rhee. "Lessons of Driving Education Reform in D.C." Panel discussion at Gathering of Leaders, Miami, Florida, February 25, 2009.

49. Michelle Rhee, interview with Gigi Georges and author, Miami, Florida, February 25, 2009.

50. Ibid.

51. Ibid.

52. Ibid.

53. Ibid.

54. Michelle Rhee. "Lessons of Driving Education Reform in D.C." Panel discussion at Gathering of Leaders, Miami, Florida, February 25, 2009.

55. Michelle Rhee, interview with Gigi Georges and author, Miami, Florida, February 25, 2009.

56. Ibid.

57. Kaya Henderson, interview with Gigi Georges, September 10, 2008.

58. Michelle Rhee, interview with Gigi Georges and author, Miami, Florida, February 25, 2009.
59. Ibid.
60. Adrian Fenty. "Lessons of Driving Education Reform in D.C." Panel discussion at Gathering of Leaders, Miami, Florida, February 25, 2009.

Chapter 4

1. From the full text of the Serve America Act, Public Law 111–113, available from the Government Printing Office website at http://frwebgate.access.gpo.gov/cgi-bin/getdoc .cgi?dbname=111_cong_public_laws&docid=f:publ013.111 (accessed July 29, 2009).
2. The Center on Philanthropy at Indiana University. "Key Findings: Center on Philanthropy Panel Study, 2005 Wave." The Center on Philanthropy at Indiana University, 2008, www.philanthropy.iupui.edu/Research/Key%20Findings%20 January%202008.pdf (accessed September 8, 2009).
3. The Center on Philanthropy at Indiana University. "Giving USA 2008." Indianapolis: Giving USA Foundation, 2008, as cited by Independent Sector, Facts and Figures About Charitable Organizations, November 7, 2008; Sharon Bond. "U.S. Charitable Giving Estimated to Be $306.39 billion in 2007." Giving USA Foundation, 2008, www.aafrc.org/press_ releases/releases/20080622.htm (accessed July 6, 2009).
4. Amy Blackwood, Thomas H. Pollak, and Kennard T. Wing. The Nonprofit Almanac 2008. Washington, DC: Urban Institute Press, 2008.
5. Murray S, Weitzman et al. The New Nonprofit Almanac and Desk Reference, 2002. Washington, DC: Independent Sector, 2002: 106, 108, 112, 113, as cited by Independent Sector, Facts and Figures About Charitable Organizations, November 7, 2008.

6. Jim Collins. "Good to Great and the Social Sector." Keynote Address at Gathering of Leaders, Mohonk, New York, February 2005.

7. William Drayton. "The Citizen Sector: Becoming as Entrepreneurial and Competitive as Business." *California Management Review*, 44, 3, Spring 2002, 120–132.

8. See Paul J. DiMaggio and Walter W. Powell. "The Iron Cage Revisited: Institutional Isomorphism and Collective Rationality in Organizational Fields." *American Sociological Review*, 48(2), April 1983, 147–160.

9. Steve Visser. "Shelter's Lack of Results Is Its Undoing." *The Atlanta Journal-Constitution*. April 19, 2009.

10. Susan Rosegrant. "Linda Gibbs and the Department of Homeless Services: Overhauling New York City's Approach to Shelter." Harvard Kennedy School Case # 1873.0. August 16, 2007.

11. Ibid.

12. Harvard Kennedy School ASH Institute for Democratic Governance and Innovation, IAG Profile [2006 Finalist]. "Homebase Homelessness Prevention Services," www.innovations.harvard.edu/awards.html?id=52611 (accessed April 27, 2009).

13. Susan Rosegrant. "Linda Gibbs and the Department of Homeless Services: Overhauling New York City's Approach to Shelter." Harvard Kennedy School Case Program, Case # 1873.0, August 16, 2007.

14. Sara Zuiderveen. Homebase Innovations in American Government Award Program Second Round Application, 2006.

15. Ibid.

16. Harvard Kennedy School ASH Institute for Democratic Governance and Innovation, IAG Profile [2006 Finalist]. "Homebase Homelessness Prevention Services," www.innovations.harvard.edu/awards.html?id=52611 (accessed April 27, 2009).

17. Homebase. IAG Second Round Application.

18. Much of this case originally published by Kelly Ward and author, "The Active Partnership of Others: Social Entrepreneurs and Cross-Sector Efforts for Change (Two Case Studies)," developed as pre-reading for a Gathering of Leaders, New Profit Inc., February 2006.

19. Judge Payne, telephone interview with Kelly Ward and author, December 27, 2005.

20. In 2004, Lomax became president and CEO of the United Negro College Fund (UNCF) after an impressive career in both academia and government. He was a professor and public official in Atlanta and Fulton County for twenty years, serving under Maynard Jackson, Atlanta's first African-American mayor, and then as the first African-American chairman of the Fulton County Board of Commissioners.

21. Michael Lomax. "Energizing a Movement: Reflections from a Civil Rights Activist." Keynote address, Gathering of Leaders, Miami, Florida, February 28, 2008.

22. Michael Lomax. Comments at Harvard Kennedy School Executive Session on Transforming Cities Through Civic Entrepreneurship, Cambridge, Massachusetts, January 14, 2009.

23. Ibid.

24. Michael Lomax, interview with Tim Glynn Burke, Cambridge, Massachusetts, July 14, 2009.

25. Christopher B. Swanson. "Cities in Crisis." EPE Research Center, April 1, 2008.

26. Michael Lomax. Comments at Harvard Kennedy School Executive Session on Transforming Cities Through Civic Entrepreneurship, Cambridge, Massachusetts, January 14, 2009.

27. Ibid.

28. Michael Lomax, interview with Tim Glynn Burke, Cambridge, Massachusetts, July 14, 2009.

29. Michael Lomax. Comments at Harvard Kennedy School Executive Session on Transforming Cities Through Civic

Entrepreneurship, Cambridge, Massachusetts, January 14, 2009.

30. UNCF. "Impact 2008 UNCF Annual Report." UNCF.

31. Live United. "History." Live United, www.liveunited.org/about/history.cfm (accessed April 29, 2009).

32. Brian Gallagher, interview with author, Alexandria, Virginia, April 15, 2009.

33. New Profit Inc. "2007–08 Annual Report." New Profit Inc., http://newprofit.com/learn_pub.asp.

34. Vanessa Kirsch, telephone interview with author, May 22, 2009.

35. Robert Ferguson and Michael Wolfe. "New Money, New Demands: The Arrival of the Venture Philanthropist." *Museum News,* January/February 2001, www.aam-us.org/pubs/mn/MN_JF01_NewMoneyNewDemands.cfm (accessed August 12, 2009).

36. Mark Kramer. "Catalytic Philanthropy." *Stanford Social Innovation Review,* Fall 2009.

37. Vanessa Kirsch, telephone interview with author, May 22, 2009.

38. New Profit Inc. "Our Model of Venture Philanthropy." New Profit Inc., http://newprofit.com/about_model.asp (accessed July 27, 2009).

39. Vanessa Kirsch, telephone interview with author, May 22, 2009.

40. Live United. "Our Leaders." United Way, www.liveunited.org/about/leadershipteam.cfm (accessed April 29, 2009).

41. Brian Gallagher, interview with author, Alexandria, Virginia, April 15, 2009.

42. See recently Lisbeth B. Schorr, "Innovative Reforms Require Innovative Scorekeeping." *Education Week,* August 26, 2009. Also see Lisbeth B. Schorr, "To Judge What Will Best Help Society's Neediest, Let's Use a Broad Array of Evaluation Techniques." *The Chronicle of Philanthropy,* August 20, 2009. Schorr's books include *Common Purpose: Strengthening*

Families and Neighborhoods to Rebuild America and *Within Our Reach: Breaking the Cycle of Disadvantage*.

43. Operational Services Division. "Multi-Year Contracting for Human and Social Services." Operational Services Division, www.mass.gov/Aosd/docs/pos/multiyear.doc (accessed June 30, 2009).

44. Brian Gallagher, interview with author, Alexandria, Virginia, April 15, 2009.

45. Center for College Affordability and Productivity Staff. "America's Best Colleges: Methodology," www.forbes.com/2009/08/02/best-colleges-methodology-opinions-ccap.html (accessed September 5, 2009).

46. Moore, Mark. "Accounting for Change." Washington, DC: Council for Excellence in Government, 1993.

47. Lisbeth B. Schorr. "To Judge What Will Best Help Society's Neediest, Let's Use a Broad Array of Evaluation Techniques." *The Chronicle of Philanthropy*, August 20, 2009.

48. Sara Zuiderveen. Homebase Innovations in American Government Award Program Second Round Application, 2006.

49. D. Stuart Conger. "Social Inventions." *Canada: The Innovation Journal*, 2002 (originally published in 1970).

50. Brian Gallagher, interview with author, Alexandria, Virginia, April 15, 2009.

51. Michael Lomax. "Energizing a Movement: Reflections from a Civil Rights Activist." Keynote address, Gathering of Leaders, Miami, Florida, February 28, 2008.

Chapter 5

1. Robert Putnam, e-mail correspondence with author, 2006, originally published in Meyers and author's, "Pre-K: Shaping the System That Shapes Children." *Civic Bulletin*, 42, Manhattan Institute for Policy Research, August 2006.

2. Joseph A. Schumpeter. *Business Cycles: A Theoretical, Historical, and Statistical Analysis of the Capitalist Process.* New York: McGraw-Hill, 1939, pp. 94–95.

3. Ted Gaebler and David Osborne. *Reinventing Government: How the Entrepreneurial Spirit Is Transforming the Public Sector.* Reading, MA: Addison-Wesley, 1992.

4. See John Dewey, *The Public and Its Problems.* Athens, OH: Swallow Press, 1954.

5. Herbert Blumer. "Social Movements." In Barry McLoughlin (Ed.), *Studies in Social Movements.* New York: The Free Press, 1969, as cited in Stuart Conger, "Social Inventions." *Canada: The Innovation Journal,* 2002 (originally published in 1970), p. 27.

6. Michael Lomax, interview with Tim Glynn Burke, Cambridge, Massachusetts, July 14, 2009.

7. Iris Chen, comments at an online meeting of the Executive Session for Transforming Cities through Civic Entrepreneurship, September 24–26, 2009, www.newtalk. org.

8. Our intent here is to show how certain entrepreneurs have benefited by mobilizing citizens, but not to make a definitive statement on social movements. We defer to social movement experts like my Harvard colleague Marshall Ganz. For more information, see Ganz's website on social movements: www.hks.harvard.edu/organizing/index.htm.

9. Sara Horowitz. Comments at an online meeting of the Executive Session on Transforming Cities Through Civic Entrepreneurship, July 2, 2009.

10. Ibid.

11. Suzanna Valdez. Comments at an online meeting of the Executive Session on Transforming Cities Through Civic Entrepreneurship, July 2, 2009.

12. Sara Horowitz. Comments at an online meeting of the Executive Session on Transforming Cities Through Civic Entrepreneurship, July 2, 2009.

13. Jonah Edelman, interview with author, Miami, Florida, February 27, 2008.

14. Vanessa Kirsch, telephone interview with author, May 22, 2009.

15. Jonah Edelman, interview with author, Miami, Florida, February 27, 2008.

16. David Lawrence, interview with author, Miami, Florida, February 24, 2009.

17 Paula Ellis. Comments during conference call of the Executive Session on Transforming Cities Through Civic Entrepreneurship, August 21, 2008.

18. Knight Foundation. "New Knight Initiative Seeks to Address Local Information Needs Engaging Community Foundations." Knight Foundation, www.knightfoundation.org/news/press_room/knight_press_releases/detail.dot?id=331122 (accessed August 12, 2009).

19. Alberto Ibargüen. Speech delivered "to a group of journalism educators, business, nonprofit and media leaders at the Boston Foundation on Thursday, June 10, 2008, www.knightfoundation.org/news/press_room/knight_press_releases/detail.dot?id=330912 (accessed April 20, 2009).

20. Social Innovation Camp. "And the Winning Ideas Are... ." Social Innovation Camp, www.sicamp.org/?p=299 (accessed August 13, 2009).

21. Ben Hecht. "Wholesaling Social Change: Philanthropy's Strategic Inflection Point." *Nonprofit and Voluntary Sector Quarterly,* 37(1), March 2008.

22. See Steven Clift, Participation 3.0 Draft 1.4, September 5, 2009, www.e-democracy.org/ (accessed September 5, 2009).

23. Paula Ellis, personal communication with author, September 9, 2009.

24. National Center for the Study of Privatization in Education. "Frequently Asked Questions: Educational Vouchers, 2003." http://ncspe.org/readrel.php?set=pub&cat=83 (accessed September 17, 2009).

25. Jeffrey R. Henig. *Rethinking School Choice: Limits of the Market Metaphor.* Princeton, NJ: Princeton University Press, 1995.

26. This narrative on the Bradley Foundation relies on the good work of John J. Miller in *Strategic Investment in Ideas: How Two Foundations Reshaped America*, from The Philanthropy Roundtable, Washington, D.C., 2003.

27. William Schambra, telephone interview with Tim Glynn Burke, July 6, 2009.

28. John J. Miller. *Strategic Investment in Ideas: How Two Foundations Reshaped America.* Washington, DC: The Philanthropy Roundtable, 2003.

29. Ibid.

30. William Schambra, telephone interview with Tim Glynn Burke, July 6, 2009.

31. John J. Miller. *Strategic Investment in Ideas: How Two Foundations Reshaped America.* Washington, DC: The Philanthropy Roundtable, 2003.

32. William Schambra, telephone interview with Tim Glynn Burke, July 6, 2009.

33. Mitch Roob, personal conversation with author, October 30, 2009.

34. J. B. Schramm, interview with author, Washington, D.C., May 14, 2009.

35. Ibid.

36. George L. Kelling and James Q. Wilson. "Broken Windows." *Atlantic Monthly*, March 1982.

37. Isabel V. Sawhill. "The Behavioral Aspects of Poverty." In *Public Interest.* Washington, DC: Brookings Institution, 2003, p. 153.

38. Maurice Miller, interview with Mark Moore, Cambridge, Massachusetts, April 22, 2009.

39. Diane Cardwell. "Bloomberg Details City's Antipoverty Experiment." *The New York Times*, March 29, 2007.

40. Linda Gibbs, comments at an online meeting of the Executive Session for Transforming Cities through Civic Entrepreneurship, September 24–26, 2009, www.newtalk .org.

Chapter 6

1. Suzanne Boas. Comments at The Executive Session on Transforming Cities Through Civic Entrepreneurship, Cambridge, Massachusetts, January 15, 2009.
2. CFED. "Assets and Opportunity Scorecard." CFED, www. cfed.org/focus.m?parentid=&siteid=504&id=505 (accessed July 17, 2009).
3. Julius Walls. Comments at The Executive Session on Transforming Cities Through Civic Entrepreneurship, Cambridge, Massachusetts, April 25, 2008.
4. Greyston Bakery. "Greyston Bakery." Greyston Bakery, www. greystonbakery.com/index.php (accessed June 9, 2009).
5. Ibid.
6. Julius Walls. Comments at The Executive Session on Transforming Cities Through Civic Entrepreneurship, Cambridge, Massachusetts, April 25, 2008.
7. Ibid.
8. Ibid.
9. Ibid.
10. Ibid.
11. Ibid.
12. Ibid.
13. Ibid.
14. Jeff Faulkner, e-mail correspondence with author, September 14, 2009.
15. Julius Walls. Comments at The Executive Session on Transforming Cities Through Civic Entrepreneurship, Cambridge, Massachusetts, April 25, 2008.

16. R.W. Cotterill and A.W. Franklin. "The Urban Grocery Store Gap: Food Marketing Policy Issue Paper No. 8." Storrs, CT: Food Marketing Policy Center, University of Connecticut, 1995, as cited in Tracey Giang et al., "Closing the Grocery Gap in Underserved Communities: The Creation of the Pennsylvania Fresh Food Financing Initiative." *Journal of Public Health Management Practice*, 14(3), 2008, 272–279.

17. David Adler and Lynne Ruby. Fresh Food Financing Initiative Second Round Application to the Innovations in American Government Award Program, 2008.

18. Ibid.

19. Tracey Giang et al. "Closing the Grocery Gap in Underserved Communities: The Creation of the Pennsylvania Fresh Food Financing Initiative." *Journal of Public Health Management Practice*, 14(3), 2008, 272–279.

20. David Adler and Lynne Ruby. Fresh Food Financing Initiative Second Round Application to the Innovations in American Government Award Program, 2008.

21. Ibid.

22. Ibid.

23. Robert M. Lang, Jr. "Americans for Community Development Overview." The Mary Elizabeth and Gordon B. Mannweiler Foundation Inc., www.americansforcommunitydevelopment.org/supportingdownloads/ACDOverview.pdf (accessed June 15, 2009).

24. Linklaters. "Legal, Regulatory, and Tax Barriers: A Comparative Study. Recommendations for Governments, Policymakers, and Social Entrepreneurs in Brazil, Germany, India, Poland, The United Kingdom, and the United States." London: Linklaters, 2006.

25. NYC Acquisition Fund Application, 2009 Harvard Kennedy School Ash Institute Innovations Awards.

26. Ibid.

27. Elizabeth Greenstein. NYC Acquisition Fund Second Round Application to the Innovations in American Government Award Program, 2009.

28. David Adler and Lynne Ruby. Fresh Food Financing Initiative Second Round Application to the Innovations in American Government Award Program, 2008.

29. Bo Menkiti. Comments at The Executive Session on Transforming Cities Through Civic Entrepreneurship, Cambridge, Massachusetts, April 25, 2008.

30. Marge Nichols. "State of Black Los Angeles." United Way of Greater Los Angeles and Los Angeles Urban League, July 2005, www.unitedwayla.org/getinformed/rr/socialreports/Pages/StateofBlackLosAngeles.aspx (accessed August 13, 2009).

31. John L. Mitchell. "Urban League Targets Aid to South L.A. Neighborhood." *Los Angeles Times*, December 7, 2007.

32. Christine Sabathia. "Los Angeles Urban League Unveils Neighborhood Revitalization Plan." *Los Angeles Sentinel*, December 13, 2007.

33. Geoff Mulgan et al. "Social Innovation: What It Is, Why It Matters and How It Can Be Accelerated." Working paper for Skoll Center for Social Entrepreneurship, 2007.

34. Blair Taylor. Comments at The Executive Session on Transforming Cities Through Civic Entrepreneurship, Cambridge, Massachusetts, January 15, 2009.

35. Blair Taylor, interviewed by Tim Glynn Burke, Miami, Florida, February 27, 2008.

36. Blair Taylor, interviewed by author, Los Angeles, May 29, 2009.

37. Ibid.

38. Blair Taylor, interviewed by Tim Glynn Burke, Miami, Florida, February 27, 2008.

39. Michael F. Hogan. "President's New Freedom Commission on Mental Health, Achieving the Promise: Transforming Mental Health Care in America, Final Report," July 2003.

40. Bruce Kamradt. Wraparound Milwaukee Second Round Application to the Innovations in American Government Award Program, 2009.

41. Bruce Kamradt, interview with Tim Glynn Burke, Cambridge, Massachusetts, May 27, 2009.

42. Bruce Kamradt. Wraparound Milwaukee Second Round Application to the Innovations in American Government Award Program, 2009.

43. Milwaukee County Behavioral Health Division. "Wraparound Milwaukee 2005 Annual Report." Milwaukee County Behavioral Health Division, www.milwaukeecounty. org/ImageLibrary/User/jmaher/Wraparound_Milw_2005_ Annual_Report.pdf (accessed August 13, 2009).

44. Bruce Kamradt, interview with Tim Glynn Burke, Cambridge, Massachusetts, May 27, 2009.

45. Michael F. Hogan. "President's New Freedom Commission on Mental Health, Achieving the Promise: Transforming Mental Health Care in America, Final Report," July 2003.

46. Ibid.

47. Bruce Kamradt. Wraparound Milwaukee Second Round Application to the Innovations in American Government Award Program, 2009.

48. Bruce Kamradt, interview with Tim Glynn Burke, Cambridge, Massachusetts, May 27, 2009.

49. Bruce Kamradt, e-mail correspondence with author, September 14, 2009.

50. Pamela Erdman. "Wraparound Milwaukee Quality Assurance/Improvement Semi-Annual Report: July 1–December 31, 2007." Milwaukee County Behavioral Health Division, www.milwaukeecounty.org/ImageLibrary/ User/trandall/QA/SEMIANNUALQAREPORT20072ndH ALF.doc (accessed August 13, 2009).

51. Michael F. Hogan. "President's New Freedom Commission on Mental Health, Achieving the Promise: Transforming Mental Health Care in America, Final Report," July 2003.

Chapter 7

1. NYC Department of Education. Presentation at the Manhattan Institute, New York, New York, March 25, 2008.

2. Joel Klein, interview with author and Gigi Georges, New York, New York, June 8, 2009.

3. Additional characteristics included active roles for students in all aspects of school life, assessment of student work and a culture of continuous improvement, caring and respectful relationships between teachers and students with every student known well by an adult, and demonstration of the capacity to address the needs of English language learners and students with special needs. Michele Cahill, "Design Characteristics of Effective Schools" (internal document provided to Gigi Georges, October 2008).

4. New Visions for Public Schools. "Reforming High Schools: Lessons from the New Century High Schools Initiative 2001–2006." New Visions for Public Schools, 2007.

5. Ibid.

6. Data compiled by New Visions for Public Schools from New York City Department of Education website, provided by Robert Hughes via e-mail to Gigi Georges, July 6, 2009.

7. Garth Harries, interview with Gigi Georges, New York, New York, August 21, 2008.

8. Joel Klein. "Remarks to the New York Charter School Association's Conference." Progressive Policy Institute, www.ppionline.org/ppi_ci.cfm?contentid=252665&knlgAreaID=110&subsecid=134 (accessed July 27, 2009).

9. Caroline M. Hoxby, Sonali Murarka, and Jenny Kang " The New York City Charter Schools Evaluation Project: How New York City's Charter Schools Affect Achievement," National Bureau of Economic Research, www.nber.org/~schools/charterschoolseval/how_NYC_charter_schools_affect_achievement_sept2009.pdf (accessed September 23, 2009).

10. Joel Klein. "Remarks to the New York Charter School Association's Conference." Progressive Policy Institute, www.ppionline.org/ppi_ci.cfm?contentid=252665&knlgAreaID=110&subsecid=134 (accessed July 27, 2009).

11. Elissa Goottman and Robert Gebeloff. "Controlling Interests: Principals Younger and Freer, but Raise Doubts in the Schools." *The New York Times*, May 25, 2009, www.nytimes.com/2009/05/26/nyregion/26principals.html (accessed July 27, 2009).

12. Sean P. Corcoran, Amy Ellen Schwartz, and Meryle Weinstein. "The New York City Aspiring Principals Program: A School-Level Evaluation." New York University Institute of Education and Social Policy, http://steinhardt.nyu.edu/scmsAdmin/uploads/003/852/APP.pdf (accessed September 13, 2009).

13. Joel Klein, interview with author and Gigi Georges, New York, New York, June 8, 2009.

14. Amy Rosen, interview with Gigi Georges, Miami, Florida, February 26, 2009.

15. Joel Klein, interview with author and Gigi Georges, New York, New York, June 8, 2009.

16. Ibid.

17. Weingarten has been a partner with Klein in some groundbreaking initiatives, including schoolwide performance pay for teachers.

18. Diane Ravitch. Testimony at hearings of New York State Assembly Committee on Education, New York University, February 6, 2009.

19. Dorothy Stoneman, telephone interview with author, September 9, 2009.

20. Ibid.

21. Allen Grossman, Catherine Ross, and William Foster. Youth Villages. Harvard Business School Case # N2-309-007. November 6, 2008.

22. Geoff Mulgan et al. "Social Innovation: What It Is, Why It Matters and How It Can Be Accelerated." Working paper for Skoll Center for Social Entrepreneurship, 2007.

23. Anthony Shorris, comments at an online meeting of the Executive Session for Transforming Cities through Civic

Entrepreneurship, September 24–26, 2009, www.newtalk .org.

24. John M. Bridgeland, John J. DiIulio, Jr., and Karen Burke Morison. "The Silent Epidemic: Perspectives of High School Dropouts." Report by Civic Enterprises in association with Peter D. Hart Research Associates, Washington, D.C., March 2006.

25. Greg Dees, interview with author, Miami, Florida, February 27, 2008.

26. For an interesting exploration of the difference between tacit and explicit knowledge in replicating innovation, see my colleague Robert Behn's, "The Adoption of Innovation: The Challenge of Learning to Adapt Tacit Knowledge." In Sanford Borins (Ed.), *Innovations in Government: Research, Recognition and Replication*. Washington, DC: Brookings Institution Press, 2008. Also see Bill Eggers and the author's *Governing by Network: The New Shape of the Public Sector*. Washington, DC: Brookings Institution Press, 2004.

27. Jeffrey Bradach. "Going to Scale: The Challenge of Replicating Social Programs." *Stanford Social Innovation Review*, 2003.

28. Greg Dees. Comments at the Executive Session on Transforming Cities Through Civic Entrepreneurship, Cambridge, Massachusetts, January 14, 2009.

References

Alvord, Sara H., David Brown, and Christine W. Letts. "Social Entrepreneurship and Social Transformation: An Exploratory Study." *The Journal of Applied Behavioral Science*, 40(3), 2004, 260–282.

America's Promise Alliance. "APA Dropout Prevention Summit Update and Highlights." Internal document received in e-mail correspondence from Charles Hiteshew, February 25, 2009.

Annie E. Casey Foundation. "Closing the Achievement Gap: Co-Investment." Annie E. Casey Foundation, 2008, www.aecf.org/~/media/PublicationFiles/6Coinvestment_r10.pdf (accessed July 23, 2009).

Antrim, Sunny. "Donors Choose Facilitates Gifts That Keep Giving." *ABC News 20/20*, December 20, 2007, http://abcnews.go.com/2020/story?id=4028215&page=1 (accessed August 13, 2009).

Associated Press (The). "Man Looks to Take Learning-Through-Music Nationwide." *USA Today*, April 30, 2008, www.usatoday.com/news/education/2008-04-30-teacher-music_N.htm (accessed July 23, 2009).

Behn, Robert. "The Adoption of Innovation: The Challenge of Learning to Adapt Tacit Knowledge." From Sandford Borins (Ed.), *Innovations in Government: Research, Recognition and Replication*. Washington, DC: Brookings Institution Press, 2008, p. 153.

Berger, Peter L., and Richard John Neuhaus. *To Empower People: From State to Civil Society*. Washington, DC: American Enterprise Institute, 1996.

Blackwood, Amy, Thomas H. Pollak, and Kennard T. Wing. *The Nonprofit Almanac 2008*. Washington, DC: Urban Institute Press, 2008.

Blomquist, John, JoAnn Jastrzab, Julie Masker, and Larry Orr. "Youth Corps: Promising Strategies for Young People and Their Communities." Abt Associates Inc., www.abtassoc.com/reports/Youth-Corps.pdf (accessed July 13, 2009).

Bloom, Paul, and Gregory Dees. "Cultivate Your Ecosystem." *Stanford Social Innovation Review*, 6(1), 2008, 47–53.

Blumer, Herbert. "Social Movements." In Barry McLouglin (Ed.), *Studies in Social Movement*. New York: The Free Press, 1969.

Bond, Sharon. "U.S. Charitable Giving Estimated to Be $306.39 billion in 2007." Giving USA Foundation, 2008, www.aafrc.org/press_releases/releases/20080622.htm (accessed July 6, 2009).

Bradach, Jeffrey. "Going to Scale: The Challenge of Replicating Social Programs." *Stanford Social Innovation Review*, 2003.

Bridgeland, John M., John J. DiIulio, Jr., and Karen Burke Morison. "The Silent Epidemic: Perspectives of High School Dropouts." Report by Civic Enterprises in association with Peter D. Hart Research Associates, Washington, DC, March 2006.

Burke, Edmund. *Reflections on the Revolution in France*, 1790.

Cardwell, Diane. "Bloomberg Details City's Antipoverty Experiment." *The New York Times*, March 29, 2007.

Casson, Mark, and Marina Della Giusta. "Entrepreneurship and Social Capital: Analyzing the Impact of Social Networks on Entrepreneurial Activity from a Rational Action Perspective." *International Small Business Journal*, 25(3), 2007, 220–244.

Center for Advancement of Social Entrepreneurship. "Developing the Field of Social Entrepreneurship." CASE, June 2008.

Center for College Affordability and Productivity Staff. "America's Best Colleges: Methodology," www.forbes.com/2009/08/02/best-colleges-methodology-opinions-ccap.html (accessed September 5, 2009).

Center on Philanthropy at Indiana University (The). "Key Findings: Center on Philanthropy Panel Study, 2005 Wave." The Center on Philanthropy at Indiana University, 2008, www.philanthropy.iupui.edu/Research/Key%20Findings%20January%202008.pdf (accessed September 8, 2009).

Center on Philanthropy at Indiana University (The). *Giving USA 2008*. Indianapolis: Giving USA Foundation, 2008.

Cho, Sungsook, and David Gillespie. "A Conceptual Model Exploring the Dynamics of Government–Nonprofit Service Delivery." *Nonprofit and Voluntary Sector Quarterly*, 35(3), September 2006, 493–509.

Christensen, Clayton, Jerome H. Grossman, and Jason Hwang. *The Innovator's Prescription: A Disruptive Solution for Health Care*. New York: McGraw-Hill, 2009. p. x

Clark, Jenny. *UK Voluntary Sector Workforce Almanac 2007*. London: National Council for Voluntary Organizations and Workforce Hub, October 2007.

Cohen, David K., and Susan L. Moffit. *The Ordeal of Equality: Did Federal Regulation Fix the Schools?* Cambridge, MA: Harvard University Press, 2009.

Conger, D. Stuart. "Social Inventions." *Canada: The Innovation Journal* (2002, originally published in 1970).

Corcoran, Sean P., Amy Ellen Schwartz, and Meryle Weinstein. "The New York City Aspiring Principals Program: A School-Level Evaluation." New York University Institute of Education and Social Policy, http://steinhardt.nyu.edu/scmsAdmin/uploads/003/852/APP.pdf (accessed September 13, 2009).

Corporation for National and Community Service. "Volunteering in America Research Highlights." July 2009 statistics from Sounding from the Listening Post Project, a national survey of nonprofit organizations done in partnership with CNCS.

Cotterill, Ronald W., and Andrew W. Franklin. "The Urban Grocery Store Gap: Food Marketing Policy Issue Paper No. 8." Storrs, CT: Food Marketing Policy Center, University of Connecticut, p. 199.

Dearden, Kirk A. et al. "The Power of Positive Deviance." BMJ, 329, November 2004, 1177–1179.

Dewey, John. The Public and Its Problems. Athens, OH: Swallow Press, 1954.

Dietz, Nathan, Robert Grimm, Jr., and Kimberly Spring. "Youth Helping America, Leveling the Path to Participation: Volunteering and Civic Engagement among Youth from Disadvantaged Circumstances." Corporation for National and Community Service, www.nationalservice.gov/pdf/07_0406_disad_youth.pdf (accessed July 13, 2009).

DiMaggio, Paul J., and Walter W. Powell. "The Iron Cage Revisited: Institutional Isomorphism and Collective Rationality in Organizational Fields." American Sociological Review, 48(2), April 1983, 147–160.

Drayton, William, "The Citizen Sector: Becoming as Entrepreneurial and Competitive as Business." California Management Review, 44(3), 2002, 120–132.

Erdman, Pamela. "Wraparound Milwaukee Quality Assurance/Improvement Semi-Annual Report: July 1–December 31, 2007." Milwaukee County Behavioral Health Division, www.milwaukeecounty.org/ImageLibrary/User/trandall/QA/SEMIANNUALQAREPORT2007 2ndHALF.doc (accessed August 13, 2009).

Farris, Anne, and Claire Hughes, "States Peer Over Borders for Best Practices" The Roundtable on Religion and Social Welfare Policy, December 19, 2006

Ferguson, Robert, and Michael Wolfe. "New Money, New Demands: The Arrival of the Venture Philanthropist." Museum News, January/February 2001, www.aam-us.org/pubs/mn/MN_JF01_NewMoney NewDemands.cfm (accessed August 12, 2009).

Findings from a Retrospective Survey of Faith-Based and Community Organizations (FBCOs): An Assessment of the Compassion Capital Fund. Cambridge, MA: Abt Associates Inc., April 24, 2007.

Flaherty, Julie. "Because Teachers Don't Always Get What They Want." The New York Times, August 5, 2001, Technology section, www.nytimes

.com/2001/08/05/education/blackboard-because-teachers-don-t-always-get-what-they-want.html?sec=technology (accessed May 28, 2009).

Freedman, Marc, and John S. Gomperts. "Putting Retiring Baby Boomers to Work." *The Chronicle of Philanthropy*, November 24, 2005. http://philanthropy.com/free/articles/v18/i04/04004301.htm (accessed May 22, 2009).

Fullan, Michael. *The New Meaning of Educational Change*. New York: Teachers College Press, 2001.

Gaebler, Ted, and David Osborne. *Reinventing Government: How the Entrepreneurial Spirit Is Transforming the Public Sector*. Reading, MA: Addison-Wesley, 1992.

Gambrell, Linda B., and William H. Teale. "Raising Urban Students' Literacy Achievement by Engaging in Authentic, Challenging Work." *International Reading Association*, 60(8), May 2007, 728–739, as posted at www.epals.com/images/tour/RTarticle.pdf (accessed July 15, 2009).

Gazley, Beth. "Beyond the Contract: The Scope and Nature of Informal Government–Nonprofit Partnerships." *Public Administration Review*, 68(1), January/February, 2008, 141–154.

Giang, Tracey et al. "Closing the Grocery Gap in Underserved Communities: The Creation of the Pennsylvania Fresh Food Financing Initiative." *Journal of Public Health Management Practice*, 14(3), 2008, 272–279.

Goldsmith, Stephen. *The 21st Century City: Resurrecting Urban America*. Washington, DC: Regnery Publishing, 1997.

Goldsmith, Stephen, and Bill Eggers. *Governing by Network: The New Shape of the Public Sector*. Washington, DC: Brookings Institution Press, 2004.

Goottman, Elissa, and Robert Gebeloff. "Controlling Interests: Principals Younger and Freer, but Raise Doubts in the Schools." *The New York Times*, May 25, 2009.

Gordon, Craig S., and Gary T. Henry. "Competition in the Sandbox: A Test of the Effects of Preschool Competition on Educational Outcomes." *Journal of Policy Analysis and Management*, 25(1), November, 2005, 97–127, as cited in Goldsmith and Meyers.

Gragan, David. "The Public Contracting Process in Support of Entrepreneurial Solutions." Working paper prepared as pre-reading for the Harvard Kennedy School Executive Session on Transforming Cities Through Civic Entrepreneurship, Cambridge, Massachusetts, January 15, 2009.

Haskins, Ron, and Isabel Sawhill. *Creating an Opportunity Society*. Washington, DC: Brookings Institution Press, 2009, p. 2.

Hecht, Ben. "Wholesaling Social Change: Philanthropy's Strategic Inflection Point." *Nonprofit and Voluntary Sector Quarterly*, 37(1), March 2008.

Hellmich, Nanci. "Prof Gives a Hand, Not a Handout." *USAToday*, June 12, 2002, www.usatoday.com/life/2002/2002–06–13-modestneeds.htm (accessed May 28, 2009).

Henig, Jeffrey R. *Rethinking School Choice: Limits of the Market Metaphor.* Princeton, NJ: Princeton University Press, 1995.

Henton, Douglas, John Melville, and Kimberly Walesh. "Civic Entrepreneurs: Economic Professional as Collaborative Leader." *Community Economics Newsletter*, No. 269, March 1999. From Center for Community Economic Development; Community, Natural Resource and Economic Development Programs, and University of Wisconsin-Extension, Cooperative Extension Service. Available online at www .aae.wisc.edu/pubs/cenews/docs/ce269.txt (accessed August 31, 2009).

Henton, Douglas, John Melville, and Kimberly Walesh. *Civic Revolutionaries: Igniting the Passion for Change in America's Communities.* San Francisco, CA: Jossey-Bass, 2004.

Hess, Frederick M., and Bryan C. Hassel. "Fueling Educational Entrepreneurship: Addressing the Human Capital Challenge." www .hks.harvard.edu/pepg/PDF/Papers/Hess-Hassel_Human_Capital_ Policy_PEPG07–06.pdf. Discussion paper presented at an American Enterprise Institute, Washington, D.C., October 2006 (accessed July 23, 2009).

Hess, Richard. "Making a Market in Education." In *Revolution on the Market*, Washington, DC: Brookings Institution, 2002.

Hochberg, Evan. "How to Get an Extra $1-Billion from Business." *Chronicle of Philanthropy*, October 12, 2006, as posted by the Taproot Foundation, www.taprootfoundation.org/about/articles/chron_101206 .shtml (accessed August 13, 2009).

Hogan, Michael F. "President's New Freedom Commission on Mental Health, Achieving the Promise: Transforming Mental Health Care in America, Final Report," July 2003.

Hoxby, Caroline M., and Sonali Murarka. "New York City Charter Schools Overall Report/New York City Charter Schools Evaluation Project." National Bureau of Economic Research, www.nber.org/~schools/ charterschoolseval (accessed July 21, 2009).

Illinois Department of Healthcare and Family Services. Predictive Modeling System Abstract. Online at www.healthtransformation.net/cs/med-icaid_best_practices_grant_award (accessed September 17, 2009).

Independent Sector. "Facts and Figures About Charitable Organizations," November 7, 2008.

Jacobs, Jane. *The Death and Life of Great American Cities.* New York: Modern Library, 1993. (Originally published 1961).

Johnson, Byron R., and William Wubbenhorst. "Ohio Compassion Capital Program: A Case Study." Baylor Institute for Studies of Religion, February 2008, http://216.157.17.136/pdf/case_ohiocompassion.pdf (accessed May 19, 2009).

Kelling, George L., and James Q. Wilson. "Broken Windows." *Atlantic Monthly*, March 1982.

Kramer, Mark. "Catalytic Philanthropy." *Stanford Social Innovation Review*, Fall 2009.

Lenkowsky, Leslie. "The Politics of Doing Good: Philanthropic Leadership for the Twenty-First Century." In William Damon and Susan Verducci (Eds.), *Taking Philanthropy Seriously: Beyond Noble Intentions to Responsible Giving.* Bloomington: Indiana University Press, 2006.

Levy, Collin. "Schoolhouse Rock: D.C. Education Chief Says School Choice Shouldn't Be Reserved for the Rich." *The Wall Street Journal*, December 22, 2007.

Linklaters. "Legal, Regulatory and Tax Barriers: A Comparative Study. Recommendations for Governments, Policymakers and Social Entrepreneurs in Brazil, Germany, India, Poland, The United Kingdom, and the United States." London, England: Linklaters, 2006.

Lohr, Steve. "Changing Their Spots, Charities Utilize Some of Capitalism's Virtues." *The New York Times*, December 4, 2008, www.nytimes .com/2008/02/24/business/worldbusiness/24iht-24social.10329242. html (accessed May 28, 2009).

Marschall, Melissa, Mark Schneider, and Paul Teske. *Choosing Schools: Consumer Choice and the Quality of American Schools.* Princeton, NJ: Princeton University Press, 2002, p. 790, as cited in Goldsmith and Meyers.

Martin, Roger L., and Sally Osberg. "Social Entrepreneurship: The Case for Definition." *Stanford Social Innovation Review*, Spring 2007.

Mayor's Office, City of Indianapolis. "Accountability Report on Mayor-Sponsored Charter Schools." Mayor's Office, City of Indianapolis, Fall 2007, www.indygov.org/NR/rdonlyres/52B0BAF8-E7F5–4135–9460–3750BACEC174/0/AccountabilityReportUSE.pdf.

Michels, Robert. *Political Parties: A Sociological Study of the Oligarchical Tendencies of Modern Democracy Transaction Publishers*, 1959. Original English version published 1915 [available online at http://socserv2.socsci.mcmaster.ca/~econ/ugcm/3ll3/michels/polipart .pdf].

Miller, John J. *Strategic Investment in Ideas: How Two Foundations Reshaped America.* Washington, DC: The Philanthropy Roundtable, 2003.

Milwaukee County Behavioral Health Division. "Wraparound Milwaukee: 2005 Annual Report." Milwaukee County Behavioral Health Division,

www.milwaukeecounty.org/ImageLibrary/User/jmaher/Wraparound_
Milw_2005_Annual_Report.pdf (accessed August 13, 2009).

Mitchell, John L. "Urban League Targets Aid to South L.A. Neighborhood."
Los Angeles Times, December 7, 2007.

Moore, Mark. *Accounting for Change*. Washington, DC: Council for
Excellence in Government, 1993.

Mulgan, Geoff et al. "Social Innovation: What It Is, Why It Matters and
How It Can Be Accelerated" (working paper for Skoll Center for
Social Entrepreneurship, 2007).

Mulgan, Geoff. "Cultivating the Other Invisible Hand of Social
Entrepreneurship: Comparative Advantage, Public Policy, and Future
Research Priorities." In Alex Nicholls (Ed.), *Social Entrepreneurship:
New Models of Sustainable Social Change*. New York: Oxford University
Press, 2006.

New Profit Inc. "2007–08 Annual Report." New Profit Inc., http://newprofit.
com/learn_pub.asp.

New Visions for Public Schools. "Reforming High Schools: Lessons from the
New Century High Schools Initiative 2001–2006." New Visions for
Public Schools, 2007.

Nichols, Marge. "State of Black Los Angeles." United Way of Greater Los
Angeles and Los Angeles Urban League, July 2005, www.unitedwayla.
org/getinformed/rr/socialreports/Pages/StateofBlackLosAngeles.aspx
(accessed August 13, 2009).

NYC Department of Education. "School of One: Leveraging Technology
to Personalize Learning in 21st Century Schools." Grant Proposal,
April 8, 2009.

Operational Services Division. "Multi-Year Contracting for Human and
Social Services." Operational Services Division, www.mass.gov/
Aosd/docs/pos/multiyear.doc (accessed June 30, 2009).

Osterman, Paul. "Overcoming Oligarchy: Culture and Agency in Social
Movement Organizations." *Administrative Science Quarterly*, 51,
December 2006, 622–649.

Pettit, Becky, and Bruce Western. 2004. "Mass Imprisonment and the Life
Course: Race and Class Inequality in U.S. Incarceration." *American
Sociological Review*, 69, 151–169.

Pineda, Chris. "Mapping Your Community's Faith-Based Assets: An Asset
Inventory Tool for Collecting and Using Data on the Faith-Based
Community Organizations in Your City." Harvard University
Kennedy School of Government, www.innovations.harvard.edu/
cache/documents/137/13704.pdf (accessed May 30, 2009).

Rosegrant, Susan. "Linda Gibbs and the Department of Homeless Services:
Overhauling New York City's Approach to Shelter." Harvard
Kennedy School Case Program, Case # 1873.0, August 16, 2007.

Roundtable on Religion and Social Welfare Policy (The). "An Interview with Krista Sisterhen of the Ohio Governor's Office of Faith-Based and Community Initiatives." May 9, 2005, www.socialpolicyandreligion.org/interviews/interview_upd.cfm?id=89&pageMode=general (accessed May 19, 2009).

Roundtable on Religion and Social Welfare Policy. "An Interview with John DiIulio." Roundtable on Religion and Social Welfare Policy, November 6, 2007, www.religionandsocialpolicy.org/interviews/interview_upd.cfm?id=155&pageMode=general (accessed May 20, 2009).

Sabathia, Christine, "Los Angeles Urban League Unveils Neighborhood Revitalization Plan." *Los Angeles Sentinel*, December 13, 2007.

Sawhill, Isabel V. "The Behavioral Aspects of Poverty." In *Public Interest*. Washington, DC: Brookings Institution, 2003.

Schorr, Lisbeth B. "Innovative Reforms Require Innovative Scorekeeping." *Education Week*, August 26, 2009.

Schorr, Lisbeth B. "To Judge What Will Best Help Society's Neediest, Let's Use a Broad Array of Evaluation Techniques." *The Chronicle of Philanthropy*, August 20, 2009.

Schumpeter, Joseph A. *Business Cycles: A Theoretical, Historical, and Statistical Analysis of the Capitalist Process*. New York: McGraw-Hill, 1939.

Serve America Act, Public Law 111–13. Available from the Government Printing Office website at http://frwebgate.access.gpo.gov/cgi-bin/getdoc.cgi?dbname=111_cong_public_laws&docid=f:publ013.111 (accessed July 29, 2009).

Sullivan, Amy. "Obama's Faith-Based Office Gets Down to Work." *Time*, April 9, 2009.

Sunset Advisory Commission. "Guide to the Texas Sunset Process," July 2008.

Swanson, Christopher B. "Cities in Crisis: A Special Analytic Report on High School Graduation." Editorial Projects in Education Research Center. Prepared with support from America's Promise Alliance and the Bill and Melinda Gates Foundation, April 1, 2008,

Teach For America. "2008 TFA Annual Report." Teach For America, www.teachforamerica.org.

U.S. Census Bureau. Poverty: 2008 Highlights. www.census.gov/hhes/www/poverty/poverty08/pov08hi.html (accessed September 17, 2009).

UNCF. "Impact 2008 UNCF Annual Report." UNCF.

United Ways of Texas. "A Survey of Voter Attitudes on Pre-K Education in Texas." March 2006, as cited in Goldsmith and Meyers.

USA Network. "Character Approved: Charles Best 2009 Winner–Giving." USA Network.

Visser, Steve. "Shelter's Lack of Results Is Its Undoing." *The Atlanta Journal-Constitution*, April 19, 2009.

Weitzman, Murray S. et al. *The New Nonprofit Almanac and Desk Reference, 2002.* Washington, DC: Independent Sector, 2002.

Welner, Kevin G. *Neovouchers: The Emergence of Tuition Tax Credits for Private Schooling.* Lanham, MD: Rowan & Littlefield, 2008.

White House (The). "Transforming Government: A Level Playing Field and New Partners." The White House, February 2008, http://georgewbush-whitehouse.archives.gov/government/fbci/fs_trans-govt.html (accessed July 22, 2009).

White House Office of Faith-Based and Community Initiatives (The). "Unlevel Playing Field: Barriers to Participation by Faith-Based and Community Organizations in Federal Social Service Programs." White House Office of Faith-Based and Community Initiatives, http://georgewbush-whitehouse.archives.gov/news/releases/2001/08/unlevelfield.html (accessed May 20, 2009).

White House Office of Faith-Based and Community Initiatives (The). "Innovations in Compassion; The Faith-Based and Community Initiative: A Final Report to the Armies of Compassion." December 2008.

Wolk, Andrew. "Advancing Social Entrepreneurship: Recommendations for Policy Makers and Government Agencies." Root Cause/MIT, April 2008.

Zald, Mayer N., and Roberta Ash. "Social Movement Organizations: Growth, Decay and Change." *Social Forces*, 44(3), March 1966, 327–341.

Index

preneurship, and, 17–20; mobilizing a community for, 114–116. *See also* Civic progress; Community solutions

Social change catalyst: choosing the right, 36–58; identifying the missing, 30–36, 62; technology as, 41–49

Social delivery system: five principles for measuring accountability of, 121–124; identifying missing ingredient for transforming, 220; organization resistance to changing, 165–166; social media feedback on, 124, 149–152

Social entrepreneurship: barriers to "scaling up" by, 6–12; definitions of, 4; lack of financial support of, 4–5; personality characteristics of, 10. *See also* Civic entrepreneurship

Social entrepreneurship barriers: curse of professionalism, 9–10, 135–139, 160; irrational capital markets, 6–8; poor metrics and causal confusion, 8, 102; preference to local providers, 10–12; vertical solutions for horizontal problems, 8–9

Social innovation: barriers to, 6–12; choosing the right catalyst for, 36–58; civic entrepreneurship as solution to, 12–17, 24–25; creating space for, 118–119; discovering the missing ingredient for, 30–63; examining fertile communities for, 197–221; links between entrepreneurship, social change, and, 17–20; Nehemiah Foundation's unique approach to, 58–61, 87; opening space for, 73–79; tacit knowledge basis for, 10–11; tension between accountability and, 121–125. *See also* Catalyzing Social Change

Social Innovation Fund, 74

Social innovation methods: civic discovery as, 30–31, 35; personal discovery as, 32–33, 35; predictive discovery as, 33–34, 36; system discovery as, 31–32, 35

Social Inventions (Conger), 126

Social Investment Taskforce (UK), 75

Social media: accountability feedback through, 124; leveraging for change through feedback of, 149–152

Social movements: animating face of change for, 144–147; civic entrepreneur role in building, 139–142, 147–149, 214–221; gaining trust and commitment for, 143–144, 166; process of growing, 147–149; stages and leadership style of, 140; tapping into shared identity for, 142–143, 166; three voices of, 142–147, 167. *See also* Citizen engagement

Social problem-solving: Nehemiah Foundation's unique approach to, 60–61; networking approach to, 9, 92, 93,

112–113, 114; predictive modeling systems for, 34; twelve steps to community solutions and, 210

Social problems: disruptive innovation model applied to, 29–30; homelessness, 107–109, 115–116, 201–202; increasingly complex and interlocking nature of, 9; new decision making required for, 9–10. *See also* Community solutions

Social service professionalism: cure of, 135–139; as social entrepreneur barrier, 9–10; top-down intervention typical of, 160

Social service systems: entrenchment problem of, 138–139; growth stunting problem of, 137–138; misdirection problem of, 137; professionalism component of, 9–10, 135–139, 160

Spinali, Lisa, 55, 56

Stand for Children, 144–146

Starnes, Debi, 106

"The State of Black Los Angeles" report (2005), 186

Stitt, Skip, 133

Stoneman, Dorothy, 214

Sturz, Herb, 32–33, 182, 201

Sullivan, Mercer, 137

Sunset clauses, 90

Sunset Commission (Texas), 90

Syman, Kim, 197–198

System discovery, 31–32, 35

T

Tacit knowledge: as basis for innovations, 10; value of overlapping, 10–11

Taproot Foundation, 54

Taylor, Blair, 28, 74, 169, 186, 187–190, 191

Taylor, Keith, 32, 58

Teach Baton Rouge, 92

Teach For America (TFA): failure experience in Detroit, 11–12; networking relationship with, 92, 93, 112–113; New Profit membership of, 119; political and education leadership development by, 146–147; Political Leadership Initiative of, 147; public value of, 16, 95, 111; social movement role played by, 141; The Mind Trust's recruitment of, 84; UNCF relationship with, 114

Teaching Fellows program (TNTP), 96

Technological glue, 41–45, 63

Technology: catalytic, 41–45, 63; civic management of, 45–49, 63; educational, 42; innovator's)use of, 41